ANDY'S NATURE

ASPERGER'S, OBESITY AND THE SUPERNATURAL

Andrew Tait

Grosvenor House
Publishing Limited

This book is published by
Grosvenor House Publishing Ltd
Link House
140 The Broadway, Tolworth, Surrey, KT6 7HT.
www.grosvenorhousepublishing.co.uk

A CIP record for this book
is available from the British Library

ISBN 978-1-80381-642-5

Most names outside the public eye have been changed.

For Mam and Dad.

Okay, What's All This About?

Hello, welcome to my book, and thank you for reading its opening sentence.

This book is my account of growing up with difficulties perplexing, unfashionable and, contrary to what some people seemed to suspect, due to subtler conditions than my supposed laziness or selfishness.

This book is also about phenomena which I believe to be supernatural. Aged seventeen, I began to see broadcast and recorded faces in such a way which persuaded me, undoubtedly, of their relation, independently of genetic transition, to each other. I later termed this tendency transgenic kinship.

Aged about twenty, I began, occasionally, to see stars and aeroplanes behave unaccountably; for example, what appeared to be a star, in a clear sky, seemed, before my eyes, to disappear and reappear.

I realise that what I claim may sound like self-deluding fantasy. But, if you're interested, whether in observation of a delusion or the possibility of a glimpse beyond the realm of matter – or even the perspective of a fat kid with Asperger's – feel free to come in and have a look.

1987

Going Home

I was born at ten past three in the morning, on Saturday the 18th of July 1987, at Ashington Hospital, Northumberland. Shortly afterwards, my father, known to his sons as Dad, drove my mother, known to her sons as Mam, and me, Andrew Tait, back home to Rothbury.

The large village, or small town, was, that weekend, host to both the annual Music Festival, and heavy rain.

The Living Room

Into the living room's gloom, the tall windows cast soft daylight. Outside, above the sloping roadside green, towering trees shaded a row of housing.

I sat in a small, plastic bath. My brother James, not quite six, having been instructed by our mother's younger sister Jess in the art of swearing, offered impudent commentary.

In the armchair behind me, Mam supervised my bath. On a friend's borrowed video camera, Dad captured the scene.

I, intrigued by the blue sponge in my hands, decided to find out what it tasted like.

1988

Who?

I can't really remember much about this year.

A memory which may have been constructed later involves the square, glass-screened box in the living room's right hand corner.

The telly shows a distant scene. In clear daylight, across urban streets, glides a smooth, white, bulky metallic dome, with projecting mechanical limbs.

From a low angle shot, a small, wavy-haired man, his eyes filled with dangerous secrets, glares at the creature.

In years to come, a name would rouse memory of this man. A genius, a time traveller, an alien, an explorer of the terrible and wondrous – whether for good or ill not yet clear.

The name was *Doctor Who*.

1989

Rothbury

I liked going outside.

Across the paved valley floor, amidst roads and forested green, rows of housing met in three streets of shops.

Above a tree-shaded graveyard loomed the squared, clock-faced tower of All Saints Church.

Behind our terraced house lay the village park. Its grass, by the tranquil River Coquet, reached a forested riverside path. Across the river, fields sloped for miles towards the pine-shaded, boulder-crowned Simonside hills, home of the legendary Dwarves.

The park had a towering slide, a climbing frame, see-saw, spring-mounted horse and two sets of swings. In windswept air, beneath a hot blue sky, the colours of this place shone with soothing brilliance. Frequently host to the merry yells of children and the easy mumbling of adults, the park was a place of purest peace.

Along our terrace pavement, my older brother James, now aged eight, rode a gaudily coloured skateboard. He'd been schooled in this mode of transport by fifteen-year-old Ted, whose accent merged Canada with Northumberland. In awed fascination, I watched the two boys roll along the pavement.

Right of the terrace, a broad, flat green held the twenty-four-foot Armstrong Cross. From the slam of a car door to a casually calling human voice, the open air soothed to distance any sound.

In Dad's red Fiesta, past sheep-grazed fields, we rode up the Cemetery Bank, around the farming estate of Whitton and onto a small road between two fields.

Rightward stood Sharpe's Folly, a crenellated tower.

Leftward, a field overlooked the horizon-spanning, heather-swathed Bilberry hills, whose rightward crest of pines bridged

Cragside, a moor host to thousands of trees, mainly pine, planted by Victorian engineer Lord William Armstrong and wife Lady Margaret Armstrong.

On the valley floor lay the village of Rothbury.

Climbing the Wall

At the front of the house, above the living room, Mam, Dad, newborn John and I slept in the largest bedroom. One evening, with Dad and me in bed, Mam sat on the edge of the double bed, feeding Johnny. Through the open door, light from the upstairs landing partially illuminated the darkened room.

Right of the door, Mam looked at the wall – and saw what she immediately took to be me.

The first thing she noticed, and was therefore perplexed by, was that this being, who resembled my two-year-old self, appeared to be crawling up the wall.

It definitely looked like me. However, it wore a flowing white gown. Around the small body shone a faint, golden aura. The being turned his face to Mam and smiled.

"What's Andy doing walking up the wall?" Mam bewilderedly asked.

Dad, however, was half-asleep.

Barrowburn

In the Fiesta, Dad took us further afield. Sixteen miles into the Upper Coquet Valley, beneath the Cheviot hills, lay Barrowburn.

Having been worked by my father's family since the 1860s, the farm had been purchased in 1941 by the Ministry of Defence, from whom Dad now rented it. Its farmhouse, a 1961 two-storey replacement for a bungalow, was equipped with old furniture. In the event of heavy snow, Dad would spend the night.

Travel here meant a half-hour car ride past rugged fields and smooth hills. Often to the merry sounds of Mam's Jason Donovan tape, I thrilled to the speed.

Past the farmhouse, a concrete path reached a yard where stood several ancient stone farm buildings. Before the outermost wandered several hens, whose unpredictable motion had me staunchly nervous.

Sometimes, on the red quad bike, or the four wheeler as he called it, Dad drove me around the fields. The vehicle's raspy engine, with lurching speed, ploughed us through blustering wind.

Before its handlebars lay a rectangular plastic box. One day, I had a ride in here. Corrie, one of Dad's Border Collie sheepdogs, decided to join me. Although an amiable creature, sudden proximity to his powerful body gave me quite a fright.

1990

Home and Away

On mine and Johnny's respective beds, Mam sat and eased our passage to sleep with songs. Throughout the days, at my every request, she readily embraced me.

On the sofa, Dad read me Enid Blyton's *Noddy* books and respective prose adaptations of *Thomas the Tank Engine*, *Postman Pat*, *Fireman Sam* and *Ghostbusters II*.

Everything my older brother James said and did, with his sobriety, reflectiveness and eloquence, inspired me. By his example, I sought to get into the habit of calling my mother "Mam" rather than "Mammy."

On some days, to prepare me for the eventual shock of having to start school, Mam took me to playschool. Amidst bright yellow walls and a crowded wood-tiled floor, Mam, with reassurance of her imminent return, explained that she would have to leave me here for a while.

Enforced separation from my mother, for even a few hours, devastated me. On the several occasions of my confinement to this place, I sobbed almost constantly.

For much of the time, kindly, Standard-English-accented Mrs Fennell had us all sit on the floor and sing.

"Let's try that again," she said, after one such concert.

"Yes, let's try that again," I blubbered, in search of anything that might conceivably soothe me.

Up at the Pinfold

Sometimes, Dad drove John and me across the village and up a steep bank which led to a bungalow district termed the Pinfold. Up a set of broad concrete steps, Granda Tait welcomed us to his small house.

Born in 1922 to a farming estate near Ashington, Granda Tait had taken employment thirty miles north at Barrowburn, and by Nana Tait, who died in 1989, had two children.

His face, while stern, was peaceably open. A steely voice, accented with Broad Northumbrian, drew its vowels across a soft, throaty r-roll. Denied a place in the army by his farming duties, Granda Tait had met the outbreak of the Second World War by joining the Upper Coquetdale Home Guard.

Granda Tait enjoyed Dandelion and Burdock and ice cream, ideally combined in a mug, a recipe I myself came to savour. Affectionate without sentiment, he had much time for cartoons, many of which he taped, to watch with Dad, John and me. Favourites included *Bangers and Mash* and *Popeye and Son*.

Next Door

To John and me, Mam announced that we were all going to see Granda. I understood the title of Granda to refer to two people. I asked if we were going to see Granda Tait.

"No," said Mam, "we have to go and see Granda Widdrington."

Through the heavy front door, we stepped onto the doorstep, and to our right mounted a joint doorstep, which bridged another front door.

Through the following hallway, we approached the kitchen. Right of the table, in a bare armchair, sat my mother's father, Granda Widdrington. His weathered face regarded me with impudent delight.

"Hello, Tiger Dick!" he said.

One of nineteen siblings, Granda Widdrington had been born, in 1938, to an impoverished Longhorsley farmer and a Scottish mother reputedly cousin to television inventor John Logie Baird. In 1959, during his National Service stint in the army, Granda Widdrington had married Nana Widdrington, to have four children.

Born in 1938 in Rothbury, Nana Widdrington had instilled in my older brother James a love of the piano, having taught him to play Henry Mancini's theme from *The Thorn Birds*.

Granda Widdrington was prone to severe anxiety. He warned fiercely against things that were "highly dangerous," such as fire, electric wires and Aunty Jess's driving. He lamented the degenerate brutality that stalked the world.

"Terrible people, son," he'd said to James. "Terrible people in the world w' live today."

In his own infancy, James had returned from next door with the awed summation: "There's a lot of *bad people* in the world, isn't there?"

From next door, Granda Widdrington was a frequent, unannounced visitor.

"This," he said of my brothers and me, "is wor second crop."

His eldest son, Uncle Ross, worked with him in the building trade. Ross, easy-going and jovial, was raptly cautious in regard to electronics and dog faeces. He addressed James and me with civil candour – making sure we knew not to "fool on" with electric sockets and such like.

Granda Widdrington's youngest son, Uncle Gordon, a pianist and self-taught guitarist with a degree in architecture, had left for Sydney, Australia, to marry.

Mam and Gordon's younger sister, Aunty Jess, worked for the police in Ashington – although would sometimes return to raid the cupboards for sugary snacks, or "ket."

Telly

In the living room's front rightward corner, atop a chest of draws, perched on a video recorder, was the telly.

Mam and James followed *Neighbours* and *Home and Away*; sun-drenched sets and Australian accents had a soothing consistency.

A video of James's held several episodes of Britt Allcroft's adaptation of the Rev W Awdry's *Thomas the Tank Engine*. In intricate, open-aired sets, to a droll, jaunty score, Ringo Starr's dreamy drawl voiced brightly coloured train-engines.

On *Postman Pat*, amidst model buildings and greenery, Ken Barrie's North-West-accented narration voiced a nurturing community of stop-motion puppets. *Fireman Sam*'s mellow eponymous hero, with affectionately drawn neighbours and colleagues, voiced in the Welsh affectations of John Alderton, offered a warm-hearted blend of comedy and action. Both shows, with richly joyous songs and score, wove realism in a veil of whimsy.

One evening, as John and I sat in the bath, Dad mimicked the high-pitched, agitated tones of *Fireman Sam*'s shopkeeper, Dilys Price. This jovial parody of a cherished fantasy somehow embarrassed me.

"Don't say that," I managed to articulate.

James's VHS copy of Cosgrove Hall's 1989 hand-drawn cartoon adaptation of Roald Dahl's *The BFG* opened with orphan Sophie's (voiced by Amanda Root) late night glimpse of a black-cloaked, hooded giant, who reached a hand into the dormitory to snatch her.

In his cave, the Big Friendly Giant's removal of his cloak soothed the fearful atmosphere. David Jason's West Country impression voiced both a childlike excitability and ancient wisdom.

From Sophie's moonlit village to the starlit void of Dream Country, the film, with tenderly awed electronic score and songs, offered fear, tenderness and pure wonder.

Ghosts, I understood, were what people turned into when they died.

James's Channel-4-recorded tape of Clive Donner's deliciously scored 1984 version of *A Christmas Carol*, or *Scrooge*, as we always called it, featured a memorable ghost in the form of Frank Finlay's Jacob Marley. In the darkness of his front yard, Scrooge (George C Scott) sees his lion-faced door knocker shine the blue-glowing, deathly staring face of his seven-years-dead partner. This blend of matter with spirit so awed me that I persuaded Mam to buy for our front door a similar knocker.

James also owned a VHS copy of *Ghostbusters* (1984). Towards the start, the New York City Library is explored by three men, detachedly dry Dr Peter Venkman (Bill Murray), affectionately enthusiastic Dr Ray Stantz (Dan Aykroyd) and calmly intense Dr Egon Spengler (Harold Ramis). On the basement floor they find the transparent, purple-glowing shade of elderly librarian Eleanor Twitty (Ruth Oliver). Her sudden transformation into a flaming, skull-faced fiend was scary, but not quite overwhelmingly so.

Later joined by drily practical Winston Zeddemore (Ernie Hudson), the Ghostbusters, in beige jumpsuits, with back-born Proton Packs, hand-held Particle Throwers and rectangular ghost traps, face ravenous green blob Slimer and Sumerian god Gozer (Slavitza Jovan, voiced by Paddi Edwards), who eventually manifests as the gargantuan Stay Puft Marshmallow Man. Persecution of politely reserved Dana (Sigourney Weaver) by bear-sized, demonically horned Terror Dog Zuul (voiced by Ivan Reitman) lends genuine menace.

The tangible marvel of gadgetry, the primal thrill of the ether, and the blend thereof in the world of bills, business, alcohol and romance, set to a jauntily eerie score, offered an exciting glimpse into the mystery of adulthood. The mere sight of the *Ghostbusters* logo, set to Ray Parker Junior's theme song, roused in me a unique glee.

Shortly after Christmas, from SPAR, Mam and Dad rented *Ghostbusters II*. On a tranquil daylit street, the pram housing Dana's baby son Oscar (played respectively by Will and Hank Deutschendorf) is suddenly psychokinetically wheeled across the pavement and into heavy traffic. The scene sets the film's tone; the ghostly threats, while serious in the first film, now terrorise a mother and baby.

Peter, Ray and Egon, on the spot where the pram suddenly stopped, drill through the road and uncover an old air shaft. On a winch, Ray is lured into its darkened depths, to dangle, eventually, through a hole in the roof of an underground subway tunnel, through whose track flows a ponderous river of glutinous, glowing pink slime. The image roused in me a fearful, fascinated awe.

1991

One's Plenty

On two years' acquaintance with it, I'd cultivated a zest for solid food. Having wolfed down my own, I eyed Johnny's uneaten Yorkshire pudding and sausages. Of my enthusiasm to ensure they weren't wasted, Mam grew wary.

Whereas Mam and Johnny could hardly ever bring themselves to finish a meal, I, on finishing mine, always remained hungry. A dull, expectant sinking in my stomach and a residual dragging sensation in my throat stoked an impassioned desire for reunion with taste and texture.

At a speed similar to that of Granda Tait, I ate with fervour. I needed food's regenerative nurture immediately and thoroughly.

At mid-morning, Mam, whose willowy thinness now held a post-natal paunch, often enjoyed a small snack, termed a "ten o'clock." This typically entailed a bag of crisps, poured onto the table and shared with Nana Widdrington.

James, Johnny and I might each have a bag of Wotsits. While no one else seemed to desire a second bag, I saw little point in having only one. While the flavoured corn fingers supposedly weren't very fattening, Mam eventually forbade sequels.

"One's plenty," she said.

My insatiable desire for extra food was starting to take noticeable effect.

"That laddie," Granda Widdrington warned Mam, "is ganna fall off his legs."

Splash

Sometimes, an excitingly long car ride brought us to Cramlington Swimming Baths, a cavern of sleek, bright tiles, in which lay a vast body of warm water.

While Dad and James were off having a swim, I stood in the shallow end with Mam, who held onto Johnny. Across the pool, children yelled, jumped and splashed.

With wanton raucousness, these unknown people cavorted before me. Had they no decorum, no sense of personal space?

"Boys and girls," I called sternly, "don't you dare splash!"

Mam nervously soothed my ire.

A boy slightly older than me happened to pass through our vicinity.

"Who are you?" I sternly acknowledged the newcomer.

Back home, I proudly told Nana of the encounter.

"'What's your name,'" she corrected gently.

"What a Load of Crap"

Dad bought a Sky Box. This black plastic device supplied the telly with satellite-aired channels. With Dad's guidance, I learned to use the Sky Box's small remote control, or the Gadget, as such devices were termed in our house. Following my usual breakfast of Oxo sandwiches in a blue plastic bowl, I adjourned to the living room.

"Press 'five' on the telly and 'three' and 'two' on the Gadget," Dad reminded me, before heading off to Barrowburn.

Joined eventually by Johnny, I watched the Children's Channel. One of my favourite of its offerings was *The Little Green Man*. In bright, gentle animation, with the narrating voice of Jon Pertwee, it wove a tale of interstellar friendship. Having arrived in a flashing conical spaceship, the Little Green Man and sentient miniature sun Zoom Zoom befriend young Skeets, with whom they explore the planet Earth.

For some reason, when James echoed their names, or the lyrics of the catchy theme tune, I would feel embarrassed. In their medium of expressive colour and emotive sound, these figures were a conspicuous addition to the room – an extravagance, in whom my indulgence felt decadent.

On some mornings, when John and I sat on the living room floor, engrossed in the telly, we'd hear the heavy crash of the front door, followed shortly by the click of the living room door and its slow slide across the carpet. Granda Widdrington drifted into the room and regarded us with amused delight.

"Here's Granda come to see y'," he announced.

He noted the sounds and images which streamed from the television screen and speakers. A playful smirk lit his face.

"What a load o' *crap*," he said.

I felt some indignation.

One day, either John or I expressed discomfort at his authoritative inspection.

"You mustn't like Granda anymore," he said with a gentle hint of sorrowful reproach.

One or both of us hastened to assure him otherwise, but he was already drifting towards the door.

"Granda knows where he's not wanted... Granda'll go..."

Granda Widdrington learned of my fear of sitting on toilets. These eccentrically fashioned chairs, with a hole leading to goodness knew where, were scarily mysterious. Might I not fall down the hole and into the irretrievable unknown?

I'd briefly seen the next-door toilet. Its seat was an eerie shade of black.

On a visit to next door with Mam, my need of the toilet became apparent. While the toilet back home daunted me, the one here was downright frightening.

Granda Widdrington held me aloft against his chest and tried to force me out of the room. In panicked desperation, I wailed and struggled. After a fearsome minute or so, he relented.

Slime

The Sky Box's provision of the Movie Channel allowed a repeat viewing of *Ghostbusters II*.

The film was announced with a black screen's display of the British Board of Film Classification's yellow PG certificate.

Re-encounter with the River of Slime renewed my fearful fascination. Did the experimental subway track usually have a river of water, which had been replaced by the slime? Did all roads, then, have rivers flowing beneath them?

In the recreation room of the Ghostbusters' headquarters, Ray (Dan Aykroyd) and Egon (Harold Ramis) show Peter (Billy Murray) and Winston (Ernie Hudson) the psycho-reactive properties of the pink Mood Slime: on shouted insults, a dish of the stuff froths and grows. When ladled into a toaster, and introduced to Jackie Wilson's "Higher and Higher," the slime rouses the toaster to dance across the Ghostbusters' pool table.

The scene offered a glimpse into the mystery of adulthood – the recreation room, with its domestic furnishings and heavy equipment, recalled Uncle Ross's bedroom next door. The Ghostbusters' intense discussion of Mood Slime presented the burdens of manhood in a context of intrigue.

The scene where the slime comes out of the bath tap and amasses into a growling blob which reaches for baby Oscar (respectively played by Will and Hank Deutschendorf) was intensely scary, yet fascinating, the fun kind of scary. The idea that a tap could suddenly spout pink goo was mind-blowing.

By ghost-summoning pink slime, parental concern and a score rich in fear and care, *Ghostbusters II* staged the Ghostbusters with an edge of tenderness and vulnerability.

Rothbury County First School

I proudly anticipated starting school. Going to school was what James did – to do so myself would be to share in his mysterious career. I recalled attending playschool last year, and the fright and loneliness of being taken away from my family and left in a roomful of strangers. In my youthful zest, I now trusted that this time might somehow be different.

On the first day of my five years at Rothbury County First School, Mam led me along pavements, across the road, past the Queen's Head pub and up a steep bank.

A broad, single-storey greystone building with high windows and a bluish grey roof, Rothbury County First School, beneath the Bilberry hills, from across a concrete yard, overlooked the village.

As with the rest of the inside, the long bare walls of the Reception classroom were a bracing shade of yellow. Around the wood-tiled floor were plastic-topped tables, with small plastic chairs. The room was crowded with people my age. Within a minute of our arrival in this lurid scene, Mam reminded me that she'd have to leave me here until noon.

Realisation that I was to be forcibly parted from my mother and confined to a place alien to everything I knew overwhelmed me with despairing sorrow. I sobbed and beseeched her not to leave me. Reluctantly, and with much reassurance, she eventually did.

At a central table, small, dark-haired, County-Durham-accented Mrs Hunter supplied reassurance to a tearful few. Enfolded in the dutiful arms of a stranger, I eventually managed to contain my distress.

Over the next week, Mam and I parted similarly.

"Pete Venkman doesn't cry when he has to leave his Proton Pack," she coaxed.

My time here gradually became more tolerable. Between occasional handwriting tasks, I hovered indecisively around the classroom. Some tables held such recreational items as crayons, plasticine and Lego.

I felt little, if any, inclination to interact with other students. At first, I was too busy being sad. At having been torn away from home, no one else seemed quite as bothered.

By this point, my torso had swollen to a cumbersome bulk of loose flesh.

"You're fat," a classmate told me.

Mrs Hunter shared charge of the Reception class with Mrs Tendall, a stout, towering woman with short dark curly hair. Her deep, Standard-English-accented voice was mild but strict.

To the far end of the classroom, I was frequently summoned to glue a colourful array of paper shapes onto a blank sheet. The intended arrangement was called a Sticky Picture.

I wasn't very good at making Sticky Pictures. On Mrs Tendall's instruction, I, to one of the paper shapes, applied a plastic glue spreader. I couldn't seem to grasp that one and only one side of the shape should be smeared with glue.

"*An*-drew!" said Mrs Tendall sharply, when I tried to obey her in this task. Her loud, urgent voice issued a lamentation which I uncomprehendingly recalled as something along the lines of "a bir-bir, bir, bir, bir!"

I came to regard the term Sticky Picture with a creeping dread.

One morning, when Nana brought me to school, my gaze fell on a black-haired, heavily freckled boy. His expression put me in mind of gormless roughness. His name was Keith Dobson. Whether I ever addressed him in such a way as to provoke dislike, I can't remember, but over the coming years, he would have no shortage of fat jibes for me.

Scrumptious

At noon, on the ring of a hand-held bell from the central hallway, we formed a line, filed out of the main building, across the yard and into a small stone building, which housed the Dinner Hall. Across its bare floor stood rows of metal-legged, plastic-topped rectangular tables. Through high windows, daylight dimly lit the grey walls.

Once everyone was seated, their loud, discordant babble would continue for a minute or so. I felt no desire to add to it. These strangers held no comfort for me.

On our first visit here, a Dinner Nanny called for quiet.

"We say a prayer," she announced, "before you eat."

"For what we are about to receive, may the Lord make us truly thankful. Amen," was the prayer.

Each noon, after about a minute, a Dinner Nanny would call for attention.

"For dinner today, it's either – er, *quietly* – for dinner today, it's either..." – there followed today's choices – "and for pudding, it's..." – there followed today's choices – "...hands together, eyes closed."

After prayer, we rose from our benches to form a line. By the serving counter, a table held stacked green plates and a box of cutlery. One could choose certain foods, but others were compulsory.

While I could force myself to gnaw at balls of mashed potato, aversion to peas and carrots overwhelmed me. A smooth, orange block implied a moist, stiff crunch. A mound of tiny spheres implied a stiff chewiness. Their vivid green evoked the vile notion of mucus.

Mrs Tendall occasionally strode between tables. She noticed my reluctance to eat certain things. I dreaded her smiling commands to "*try* it!"

One day, she watched me swig Ribena from the detachable cup of the plastic flask I'd brought in my bag.

"No, eat something first – *then* we have a drink," she instructed.

On more sinister occasions, she gestured to the fearfully avoided mound of peas which remained on my plate.

"Look at that," she urged, "*scrumptious!*"

One day, she took a more direct approach to this not eating peas business. She picked up my spoon, plunged it into the mound of peas, gathered a load, wielded the spoon into a preparatory position and commanded me to open my mouth.

Afraid not to, I obeyed.

The peas were pushed into me. Horrified, I forced myself to swallow the small, firm spheres.

I've disliked the word "scrumptious" ever since.

Wall

At half past ten, and on leaving the Dinner Hall, we were sent onto the concrete front yard. Here, the children would run, talk, shout and play games. Sometimes, a car would roll onto the yard.

"Get to the wall!" called Mrs Tendall.

The children dashed across the yard, to stand either at the school building's wall, or by the yard's rightward wall.

I devised a way to avoid the panic of running for my life. I spent whole break periods standing by the rightward wall.

Other children began to notice.

One afternoon, half a dozen or so of them gathered in a semicircle to watch this fat, anxious recluse. One of them took up a chant.

"An-drew's a nincompoop! An-drew's a nincompoop!"

Several others joined in.

While their leers and inane raucousness were mildly intrusive, I was largely just glad to be safe.

Mrs Tendall arrived, dismissed peripheral onlookers and scolded the singers.

"Sorry, Andrew," several of them mumbled and dispersed.

Sometime later, Mrs Tendall announced the recent installation of traffic cones around the yard's inner entrance, so there would be no more need for "get to the wall."

Shortly after dinner, Reception children were taken home. On release from the Dinner Hall, I would cross the yard to the short leftward wall, atop which a tall frame of meshed wire screened a downward-sloping field. Around the fence coiled a few small, bunched loops of wire. I twiddled these and imagined that I was operating the controls of some fantastically advanced computer. I had an idea that this process somehow arranged the arrival of Mam, who would then come to take me to freedom.

Society

Within a few weeks, Reception children had to stay at school for the full six and a quarter hours. No longer fearful of vehicle collision, I now spent break times meandering across the yard. I enjoyed the freedom of my mind to wander, often in adventures shared with an imaginary version of myself and various fictional characters.

One or two older boys and girls would approach me casually and proffer a black, fist-sized rubber spider, whose dangling legs bristled with rubber fur. Horrified, I retreated to the school wall, under the reassuring watch of one or two Dinner Nannies.

Some of my peers approached me with the scornful address of "Fatty." On my angry approach, they ran, laughing in triumphant knowledge of my inability to keep up.

The fractured, brown-stained frame of my two front teeth, shattered by a fall from the table two years ago, earned me the nickname of Rotten Teeth.

"I don't like girls," I announced one day.

"A lot of people don't like girls," said Mam understandingly, albeit with a hint of resignation, as if my outlook wasn't quite as wholesome as it might be.

I had no real contempt for girls. What I really resented was school, with its enforced separation of me from home, its horde of alienating strangers and rituals – just what was Mrs Hunter's obsession with sitting us all on the floor and making us sing? It was embarrassing.

With their finely dainty faces, long hair and gay attire, girls seemed to have a tender respectability, and so served as my chosen scapegoat for the system that had turned my life upside down.

Walking with Mam through a supermarket, we neared a girl of about three with a dummy in her mouth. At the refinement of her dainty features and fine curly hair, I felt a tiny sense of intrusion. As we passed, I curled my forefinger against my thumb and launched it against the sleeve of her coat.

"You," I explained gently, "get the Bick Flick."

Rather than a sign of contempt, I meant it as a social designation. Embarrassed, Mam urged me away.

Our small back yard, enclosed by a stone wall and black metal gate, bridged a downward sloping lawn, shared by the rest of the terrace, and by a vertically opposite row of houses. That directly behind ours housed the Sintons, Rodd and Jan with daughters Vera, a year older than me, and Eve, same age as John. During the merrily rambling interactions of the four of us, my supposed aversion to girls was nowhere in sight.

Toilet

At home, I didn't mind standing before a toilet, as long as someone accompanied me. Between us, John and I kept a custom of escorting each other to the bathroom. John soon lost any need for such moral support; I, not so easily. At school, it wasn't available.

Even at home, I remained daunted by prolonged direct contact with the toilet seat. While no longer overwhelmed with fear at the prospect, I still preferred the comfortable simplicity of postponing it for as long as possible.

I ate too much, I was too heavy, and my fears, to which others of my age were desensitised, resulted in barbarous defilement of my clothes. I realised I must be getting something wrong.

Video

One of James's Virgin VHS releases of Belvision's *Hergé's Adventures of Tintin* opened with a promotional reel of other titles, including a few seconds of DIC's 1985 series *Care Bears*, a cartoon adaptation of a range of greetings cards by Those Characters From Cleveland. In a brightly coloured cartoon realm, small, pink and blue anthropomorphised bears walked about on a cloud.

On the Children's Channel, I watched a few minutes of another cartoon. Similarly soft and bright, it entailed a teddy bear, who, on rubbing noses with his young girl owner, came to life. I knew this wasn't *Care Bears*, but called it that, for simplicity's sake.

In concession to my desperation for reunion with the cartoon, Mam and Dad, at Bridge Street's short-lived video shop, bought me the only available *Care Bears* video. Of the *Tempo Kids' Club* range, it included two ten-minute episodes, *The Magic Lamp* and *The Caring Crystals*.

On sight of the cardboard video case, whose cover was quite distinct from what I'd watched today, I felt some dismayed vexation. This was the only one they could get, explained Mam. I conceded the point and resolved to see what I could make of the new video.

The cartoon was delicious. In richly detailed backgrounds, to a gently euphoric score and jubilant theme song, softly expressive characters were drawn with both humour and affection.

Before a storm-cloud-mounted castle, hooded sorcerer No Heart, whose face encompasses hooded darkness, bushy eyebrows and glowing red eyes, with the silken, thunderous voice of Chris Wiggins, conjures, from a vaporous abyss, pink Bubbles of Uncaring.

Purple-haired, similarly bushy-eyebrowed niece Shreeky, with the softly lilting voice of Terri Hawkes, excitedly watches No Heart fling dwarfish troll Beastly, voiced with a guttural cackle by John Stocker, into the abyss. In one of the rising Bubbles floats Beastly, now with feral tusks and a crazed glare. Despite her aspirations to evil, Shreeky gets a fright.

In the hint of dark fantasy, semi-spectral No Heart, aptly named Beastly and feral yet slightly vulnerable Shreeky, I found myself engrossed.

Grumpy Bear, with the frustrated yet earnest voice of Bob Dermer, ventures alone into a mine, in search of the Caring Crystals. With his blue colouring, love of rain, stubbornness and petulance, I delightedly empathised with Grumpy.

With *The Care Bears Family*, I became irretrievably obsessed.

"Load o' bloody crap!" said Granda Widdrington, on exposure.

As Christmas neared, I longed to own a plush effigy of Grumpy. For some reason, the thought of referring to the character by name embarrassed me. The cartoon, with its sumptuous colours, jovial expressionism, fanciful imagery and buoyant voices, had an exotic exuberance, my engrossment in which, I somehow felt, was an imposition on my elders. I could only bring myself to refer to Grumpy as "the Blue One With the Rain On Its Belly."

1992

Bed

At bedtime, Mam sitting on John's or my bed and singing provided a sense of reassurance which helped me to fall asleep. However, this effect was noticeably lessening. After twenty minutes of songs, while John had fallen asleep, I remained awake. For long afterwards, either Mam or Dad would remain in the room, in aid of my elusive relaxation.

I came to regard the approach of ten o'clock with sorrowful dread. As I lay in the semi-darkness, the world around me was climbing further into the savagery of night, a time when even adults had to go to sleep. My inability to escape into sleep frightened me.

I desperately tried to relax, but it was no good. Forlornly, I wondered why I alone inflicted this on my parents – why could John fall asleep, but not me?

One night, when it was Dad's turn to stay in the bedroom, I asked what time it was.

"Ten o'clock," said Dad.

While sobs didn't quite come, my distress was such that I almost managed to force them.

Mam eventually resorted to lying beside me on the bed. This worked, but only after many minutes.

Greedy

My face now had a slight extra breadth. My torso, as mightily as ever, bulged in a hefty flow. When sitting down, I could comfortably cover my hands with my stomach flab. Such exertion as walking uphill or running strained my lungs and legs more quickly than those of James, John or my classmates.

Dad, at my age, while nowhere near my size, had been slightly overweight, but, without any laborious dieting, had eventually slimmed. It was vaguely hoped that I would follow suit.

Around seven, supper for John and me often consisted of two small grilled Co-op pizzas each. John seldom finished his. On finishing mine, a faint dragging sensation in my chest stoked an urgent desire for more food. I was allowed a packet of crisps, but that was *it*, mind.

With my torso as large as ever, my parents decided to wean me onto more modest fare – a sandwich and a packet of crisps. Meanwhile, Mam guarded against any urge I might have to eat in between meals.

The Rothbury Practice waiting room, as well as magazines, had several children's books. *Greedy Graham* (I forget precisely which year I read it) depicts a young boy who, despite his elders' warnings, fecklessly indulges his appetite. A stomach ache (or some such; I can't seem to find the book online) eventually enlightens him to the error of his ways – until, in comedic subversion, he commandeers an entire chocolate cake.

The cartoon illustrations of an overweight boy offer an image of childhood innocence, comically distorted by bulbous excess flesh. Greedy Graham bloats his young frame to ungainliness – all because of his disinclination to stop being greedy. If only he could reign in his childish excesses, he'd be normal.

Why did I still feel hungry on finishing a meal? Did I alone have this residual hunger? Or did everyone have it, albeit usually with maturity enough to restrain it?

Why did I lack such resolve?

Why was I frightened of toilets and hens?

I had no answer.

Blood

In the Dinner Hall, I joined the queue to return my tray and utensils. In line, I stood ahead of Mark Cowens. Mark was one of those who sometimes made fun of me, although his jibes were impudent rather than scornful.

In line, he now stepped ahead of me, to stand level with the counter.

"Andrew, Andrew!" He grinned, as if at some secret joke. I looked blankly at him.

"Bonk me on the head!" he urged and turned to face the counter.

In acceptance of this offer of a taste of free vengeance, I contracted my hand into a loose fist and brought it lightly onto the top of his head.

The next few seconds were a confused blur. Towards the counter, Mark fell forward. He straightened and began to wail in severe distress. Most of the inside of his gaping mouth was layered with some dark red substance. I idly wondered if he'd snuck some of the strawberry jam to be served with today's pudding.

Several Dinner Nannies led away poor Mark.

I collected a bowl of semolina and returned to my table. Shock and remorse lay on me like a wet blanket. In my prideful desire for revenge, I'd reduced Mark to a bloodily despairing mess. The burden of what I'd done horrified me.

As it turned out, Mark had slipped on the floor and, on the counter, split his lip open, a wound later treated with stitches.

At home, with my shock having numbed, my family rallied around me. James urged me to tell the teachers that my parents had said "well done," although Mam advised against this.

It would be a few years before I fully logically accepted that Mark's mishap had been an accident of his own manoeuvre.

Sharks

Mam and Dad had both seen *Jaws* (1975), which, in a few nights' time, would air on BBC One. It was about a shark, the kind of large fish as seen on *Tintin*, which *Jaws*, famously misleadingly, portrayed with a partiality to human flesh. Intrigued by the idea of a fish bigger than a person, I asked Mam and Dad to tape and let me watch it. With some reservation, they agreed.

"You don't see the shark for a long, long time," warned Dad.

On sunlit Amity Harbour, my curiosity feasted on the erroneously slain tiger shark. In its sleekness, peaceful gaze and might, I delighted.

24

Arrival of John Williams' legendarily ominous theme would announce the eponymous jaws to be on the scene.

"Don't look," said Mam.

Before the seaborne *Orca*, with an explosive splash, the enormous head of the Great White surges above the water. The sea's production of something so wondrously strange yet gloriously powerful amazed me. When the poor shark got blown up at the end, I was rather indignant.

In the media, any hint of a shark now delighted me. The *Care Bears Family* episode *Hearts at Sea*, with lush pastels and soft expressionism, embraced the Great White.

How wondrous that a fish, placid denizen of the deep, could be so big and powerful. Fish, I understood, were preyed on by birds. For their dainty grace and ravaging of my exotic brethren, I acquired a brief, irrational contempt.

"Bords is the most beautiful things in nature," Granda Widdrington gently chided.

"They've got to eat something," said Mam.

Cats also ate fish, which inspired a similar, although slighter contempt – I knew they really couldn't help it. Since dogs were supposed to chase cats, I reasoned, dogs were "heroes to fish." Even though direct contact with the mightily bounding animals still scared me, my admiration of man's best friend was renewed.

From Bridge Street's ill-fated video shop, Mam bought a copy of *Jaws: The Revenge* (1987). Not yet familiar with the recent certification of the British Board of Film Classification, Mam didn't realise the video's "15" certificate officially deemed it unsuitable for those of us beneath that age. Near the film's start, the nighttime dismemberment of Sean Brody (Mitchell Anderson) rather took us aback.

Nana protested mine and John's watching the film.

"You have to be fifteen!" she said.

Mam bought me the rather more age-appropriate *Sharks: The Death Machine* (1980). Later, a televised shark documentary hosted by Ron and Valerie Taylor heartened me with appreciative talk of sharks, and introduced the horrifyingly cruel practice of cutting off shark fins and throwing back the carcasses to die.

In British waters, bigger sharks, apparently, were comparatively scarce. However, an hour down the road, Tynemouth Sealife Centre had several smaller sharks, a species known as dogfish.

Past several brightly lit fish tanks of local aquatic exotica loomed an underwater glass tunnel. Through the overhead depths glided what were clearly sharks, albeit about a foot in length. I savoured their serene, eerie beauty.

With the chance of souvenirs in the gift shop, followed by sandwiches in the car, and a visit to the nearby beach, the Sealife Centre became a favourite outing.

For my fifth birthday, I excitedly unwrapped Shark Chase, a board game whose fish-shaped counters were designed for evasion of a plastic shark with a battery-operated chomping jaw.

Penguins

One day, Dad proposed a trip to Edinburgh Zoo. After a two-hour car ride across the border, Mam, Dad, James, John and I wandered a broad walkway.

We passed a fenced concrete yard. Mam and Dad noted the penguins. In glaring sunshine, I squinted through the fence and caught a distant view of several tall, waddling birds.

They were being fed, my parents observed. Sure enough, a man with a bucket now approached the penguins.

What were they being fed?

Well, fish, of course.

This revelation gripped me with a burning, humiliated resentment. Sharks were fish. Of the mysterious beauty of fish, I felt proudly protective. Even though I myself enjoyed eating fish, I was galled by the notion of birds and cats doing so. In their dainty, lauded grace, presumption of these creatures to prey on my spiritual kith felt an outrageous intrusion.

Helpless with anger, I faced the distant penguins and loudly pronounced my disgust. In forlorn embarrassment, Mam and Dad steered us all away.

Perhaps in regret of my misplaced ire, I would later find myself poignantly moved by the vulnerable image of the penguin.

Selfish

From September, while my class still occupied the Reception classroom, we were now in Year One and shared the classroom with the newly arrived Reception children. Mrs Hunter taught both classes.

One afternoon, as home time neared, Receptions and Year Ones alike sat on the wooden floor. While parents occasionally entered to take home their children, Mrs Hunter, at a table, lifted home-brought items from the Blue Tray for owners to claim.

While Mam stood in the corner in wait for me, I saw a raised item to look familiar – a six-inch soft plastic dolphin.

For my last birthday, I'd received an identical item.

Logically, I knew I hadn't brought it into school.

In the hand of Mrs Hunter, the item's familiarity, and my sense of territorialism, somehow overruled logic to persuade me that unforeseen circumstances must have conspired to tip the dolphin into my bag, remove it and put it in the Blue Tray.

With only a vague sense that I shouldn't, I raised my hand and declared myself its owner.

To "return" it to me, Mrs Hunter seemed hesitant. Closer to her table, someone else also seemed to have claimed it. Mam concernedly stepped in to persuade me to renounce my false claim. As we left, Mam noted Lindsey Logan to have been crying.

While Mam didn't berate me, I realised myself to have done something particularly wrong – in my territorialism, I'd made a younger child cry. In grudging shame, I became conscious of the brutality to which my introverted self-assertion might lead.

Nativity

As Christmas neared, the teachers had us all singing even more than usual. In addition to the morning assembly concert, lesson time was devoted to sitting us on the floor and singing Christmas songs.

Mrs Hunter addressed the pertinence of Christmas to Jesus. The archangel Gabriel's announcement of Mary's conception by God of Jesus, Mary and Joseph's eventual shelter in the cattle shed, and respectively star-inspired and angelically guided visit by the Wise Men and shepherds to the baby Jesus, were observed with such songs as "Little Donkey."

Of my enforced participation in reverential sing-songs, I grew weary. Christmas was supposed to be about getting stuff and watching Scrooge warned of the error of his miserly ways by the ghost of Jacob Marley. At Mrs Hunter's earnest observance of the Nativity, I rebelled.

Mam and James gently urged me against such impiety.

While our parents passively acknowledged the creed into which we were all christened, James, with his usual sobriety, pondered its cosmic implications.

I was ultimately persuaded against my rebellion. Even if academic observance thereof was tedious, the figure of Jesus embodied a cosmic sacredness – and if James adhered to this, then so, there was no point denying, should I.

Mega Drive

On Christmas morning, one of James's presents was a sleek, black, plastic Mega Drive. Dad connected it to the telly.

On-screen, above a bright blue ocean, in a red, banner-adorned ring, a blue, pointy-eared creature, with a reassuring smirk, wagged a white-gloved finger.

Via a wire-attached, boomerang-shaped "joypad," James manoeuvred, around an on-screen background, a smaller embodiment of the blue creature. This, James explained, was Sonic the Hedgehog, protagonist of something called a computer game, sort of like a video, but one you could partially control – like James's old Commodore 64.

I watched James pilot Sonic across a digital painting of a colourful rural landscape. On contact with spikes, or one of the villainous robots that roamed the land, Sonic would leap into the air, spread his limbs and fall to the bottom of the screen and out of sight. This meant he had been "killed," and had to start again.

"There's a shark," said James, of one of the robotic piranhas who constantly leapt above a small wooden bridge. Despite my stirrings of instinctive disdain for this grand endeavour, I began to succumb to its colourful splendour.

James gave me a go with the joypad, whereupon I deliberately ran Sonic into one of the robots.

"Did you want to kill Sonic?" asked James.

My answer was non-committal.

1993

Sonic

In James's bedroom, the Mega Drive was placed, beside the small portable telly, atop an ancient school desk which had somehow fallen into James's possession. At an incautious pull of the joypad wire, the Mega Drive fell onto the floor, where, James decided, it would be safer.

The largest bedroom, once shared by Mam, Dad, John and me, was now James's. Light blue walls framed a hairy brown carpet, on whose middle stood a snooker table – James raptly followed BBC2-aired snooker games. Even if I maintained these to be boring, I appreciated their sober intensity – I even wished I had it within me to enjoy them myself. To me, anything that inspired James had an alluring eminence.

As the year began, I watched James guide Sonic through the Zones of Mobius. Before long, everything about the game delighted me. With the strong blues of sea and sky, the deep green of vegetation and the rich brown of earth, the Green Hill Zone gleamed a sleek, digital lustre. Masato Nakamura's score, a euphoria of electronic chimes and flutes, stoked a sense of excited curiosity. Through the Zones swarmed Badniks, robotic animals, each of which, when smashed, released one of Sonic's animal pals.

And then, there was Sonic himself. About a centimetre high, the dark blue figure, with his large, tilted eyes, sweeping dorsal spines and red shoes, had a reserved merriment. How could a hedgehog be blue? Or have a circular head? Such incongruity had its own eccentric mystique. At the press of the joypad's "right" button, Sonic ran, until his small blue legs became a circular blur. At the press of one of three round buttons, he became a blue ball and leapt through the air.

A fearsome change of score announced the arrival of a small, ovoid flying machine, from whose belly dangled a wrecking ball.

The craft was piloted by a bald man with a huge brown moustache and spherical torso – the sinister Dr Robotnik.

"What's that thing he's in?" I asked.

"One of his latest inventions, probably," said James.

Before Robotnik "killed" Sonic, Sonic had to "kill" him – which meant leaping eight times into the flying Egg-O-Matic, until it bloomed several small explosions, whereupon a scowling Robotnik would fly away in wait for revenge.

Under my guidance, Sonic kept getting fatally whacked by the wrecking ball.

"Better give me a go," said James, "before he kills the daylights out of you."

Sonic the Hedgehog, dauntless explorer and conqueror of evil robots, was, to me, a joy. On weekends, with sunshine streaming through the landing window, exciting possibilities lay not only in the chance of something interesting on telly, but in helping Sonic reach a new Zone. James generously kept giving me goes, and my prowess improved.

The Mega Drive had also come with *Sonic the Hedgehog 2*, in which Sonic was accompanied by Miles "Tails" Prower, a small, doe-eyed, two-tailed fox, who aided Sonic's quest by mimicking the player's movements.

"Tails," decided John, "is mah favourite boy."

One of James's Sega magazines announced the release of a Sonic comic. Giddy with anticipation, I awaited this new perspective of Sonic's world. On Saturday the 29th of May, around noon, Mam returned from the shops and produced, from a grey paper carrier bag, a magazine. On a white cover, ablaze with multicoloured titles, Sonic, with a dynamic smirk, bounded forth.

In the sunlit kitchen, while I looked at the pictures, James read aloud the dialogue.

"Who said that?" I kept asking.

"Him," said James, pointing.

Not quite attuned to the concept of speech bubbles, I wondered how James knew.

Each fortnight, I cherished a further such glimpse of this world: the Zones' fanciful vibrancy, and the characters' quirky whimsy, shone in bright inks. Helped by the rather more prudent Tails, Sonic fought with jovial egotism.

One of James's Sega magazines had a page of merchandise available for purchase. In superimposed thumbnail lay a plush Sonic figurine, labelled "Sonic the Hedgehog Cuddly Toy: £12.99." Mam and Dad agreed to order me one.

Fourteen inches high, with a large, spherical head and dangly limbs, its sleek fibres offered a solid approximation of the beloved image. I cherished it.

At nine on Sunday morning, Channel 4 aired the first episode of *Adventures of Sonic the Hedgehog*. A jolly orchestral theme tune oversaw whimsically warped backgrounds, over which Sonic, with madcappery in the style of *Tom and Jerry* or *Road Runner*, foiled Dr Robotnik (voiced by Long John Baldry) and Badniks Scratch (voiced by Phillip Hayes) and Grounder (voiced by Gary Chalk).

Sonic (voiced by Jaleel White) spoke with a good-naturedly cocky North American drawl. Beneath his self-aggrandisement, love of speed and chilli dogs lay a deep protectiveness of Tails (voiced by Christopher Welch). While certainly not without merit, the cartoon's sparse backgrounds and madcap lightheartedness, for me, rather missed the games' scenic lustre and high-stakes thrill. Nevertheless, because it involved Sonic, I watched with religious devotion.

Friend

In the second term of Year One, the new Reception children had become more familiar. While solitude remained my general preference, I fell into fond acquaintance Jason Brown. Someone who held me in open esteem, with whom to converse in mutual good humour was a pleasant surprise.

"I like you this much!" I said, vertically spreading my arms to their limit.

"I like you *this* much!" he retorted, mimicking the gesture.

Around this time, Mam told me of a cassette tape, once owned by James, of a dramatisation of Roald Dahl's *The BFG*.

At my entreaty, she tirelessly mined the draws and finally unearthed a red cassette tape: Roald Dahl's *The BFG*, dramatised by Edward Kelsey.

With its gently spooky incidental music and minimal cast, I rapturously savoured yet another adaptation of the beloved story. To hear aloud nearly every line of dialogue offered a similar thrill to that of the film, but with the intrigue of their printed roots.

To something called "the pictures," Dad and James went to see *Jurassic Park*. Directed by Steven Spielberg, who'd made *E.T.* and *Jaws*, its depiction of dinosaurs was said to be astounding. The next day, James recalled "a *really* realistic triceratops," and how, when eaten by the T-Rex, a man had "his body parts flicked across the screen."

Since the film was only a PG, Dad was eventually persuaded to take John and me to see it. We rode up the steep bank of the Pinfold to pick up Granda Tait and then undertook the hour-long drive to Gateshead, where stood the Metrocentre.

Going to the pictures, explained Granda Tait, was like watching the telly, only really, really big.

In the dark hall of the auditorium, we, having bought from SPAR a supply of toffee-flavour popcorn, sat on plush, reddish purple seats. I gazed at the vast screen. Set to the heartfelt awe of John Williams' score, jungle-heavy Islar Nublar's survival contest with mightily animate dinosaurs re-introduced me to the miracle of captured sounds and images.

For my sixth birthday, I received, from Soulsby's toyshop, a bright yellow cassette personal stereo – now, like James, I could listen to recorded sound in the privacy of headphones!

That afternoon, I proudly welcomed Jason over for cherryade and cake.

While he and John inspected my presents, I sat in an armchair and, on my new Walkman, listened to *The BFG*. Around me, John and Jason, in their exploration, conversed loudly. Their happy yelps frequently diluted the recorded dialogue in which I was engrossed. I crossly demanded quiet. While I loved to talk to Jason at school, running around and shouting held no interest for me.

Mam and Dad noticed my grumpy protestations. With no ire, they conveyed their despondence – instead of welcoming my friend, I'd angrily dismissed him in favour of reclusive spectatorship.

Ashamed and saddened by my parents' sorrow, I pondered the boundaries I'd breached. My obsession with a recorded story had trounced any capacity I might have had to make my friend feel welcome. Not only did I eat too much and lack the will to overcome such petty fears as solitary toilet visits, but my introversion had now gendered heartless indifference to my friend.

What an Idle Boy

In September, my class finally moved out of the shared Reception classroom and into the first of the classrooms which rowed the hallway's far wall. Year Two's teacher was Mrs Scott. A sweep of urchin-short black hair topped a thin face, often pinched in understatement, with her Standard English voice lowered to a playfully sarcastic drone.

Schoolwork now involved frequent use of photocopied sheets. Before distributing these, Mrs Scott told the class which photocopied ink box required what arrangement of numbers or words.

Within seconds of the start of her explanation, Mrs Scott's talk of addition, punctuation and arrangement thereof quickly slipped my grasp. Within seconds, I forgot the meaning of each instruction and failed to grasp its relation to its successors. In seconds, the briefing was a barely intelligible drone.

After staring bewilderedly at the worksheet for some time, I approached Mrs Scott's desk.

"Mrs Scott," I said, in the First School drone of deferential ascent, "wha' d' y' have to *dooo?*"

Mrs Scott had just told us all what to do. Hadn't I listened?

My incessant demands for repeated explanation galled and wearied her. With solemn sternness, she urged me to *listen*. While not shouted, her urgency steadied me with cautious fear. For some reason, try as I might, I seemed unable to force myself to listen. Instead of risking further admonishment, I cultivated the habit of keeping my perplexity to myself.

James, as he sometimes somewhat sternly reminded me, had been able to tie his shoelaces at the age of three, and to tell the time at the age of five. At well over the age of five, I could do neither.

One day, as my work rate sorely lagged, Mrs Scott placed before me a stack of worksheets, each of which had been respectively completed by my classmates, as well as one for me. She told me to concentrate on this task for now.

I thought she wanted me to fill in everyone else's already completed worksheets. Although baffled, I set about adding to each already graphite-inscribed space the required combination of letters. As I worked, I vaguely supposed it to be unlikely that the teacher would want me to graffiti everyone else's work. This reservation was overwhelmed by a decisive aspiration to obedience.

Mrs Scott returned, and, at my vandalisation of my classmates' work, was aghast.

"What an *idle* boy!" she said.

While the word evoked a stern-faced totem pole as worshipped by obscure islanders in *Tintin*, I understood it to refer to laziness. Was that where my inhibitions lay? In a grossly selfish lack of motivation?

Vengeance

Keith Dobson continued to supply me with impudence and scorn. Arnold Ainsley and Mark Cowens sometimes lent a hand, but Keith was my arch-enemy, and I his.

At mid-morning break and lunchtime, I continued to wander the yard in fanciful contemplation, often to meet observations of my weight.

I, urged by Mam, James and Granda Widdrington, replied in ready defiance.

"Just give them a bit o' *that*, son," urged Granda, miming a punch.

However, punching wasn't an option.

"Eeeh, you're not *alloooowed* to say *thaaat*," a classmate might intone, at the utterance of the mildest of rude words. "I'm *telluuuun'*."

At my taunters, I launched scornful dismissals, heated utilisation of the word "stupid," or perhaps, even, a light shove.

My defiant self-assertion gendered a rather bloated sense of my entitlement thereto. One warm afternoon, in the queue for re-entry at the end of break time, several boys repeatedly mentioned Keith. It got a bit repetitive. While not today, Keith had taunted me many times before. I took this as licence to remove my fleece jacket and swing its edge into Keith's face. Moments later, once I'd turned, the zipper of Keith's own fleece jacket whacked me smartly from behind.

One afternoon, at home time, in the cloakroom, I, for some reason, felt a surge of annoyance towards Jennifer Bolam. She generally came across as neat, well-behaved and quiet. An aloofly unforthcoming passing remark may have persuaded me of her share in the guilt of my persecutors; in truth, I can't quite remember.

In any case, while her friends took their coats and bags, Jennifer sat on a bench. I brought over my purple light fleece jacket, swung it above her head and brought it down.

While Jennifer continued to sit, her friends hastened to her aid. Of my assault, they told a grim Mrs Scott, who in turn told my mother. It was agreed that I must apologise to my victim.

Next day, as commanded, I approached Jennifer, and to her virtuous gaze said sorry. She airily accepted.

"Did you say sorry to Jennifer?" asked Mrs Scott.

"Yes."

"Did she forgive you?"

"Yes."

On my playground taunters, I might just as easily seek justice from one of the on-duty Dinner Nannies.

To Mrs Telford, a weathered, short-haired woman with a loud, brusque voice, I reported a jibe from a Year One girl.

"No, she didn't," said Mrs Telford with a rare smile. She claimed to have witnessed the exchange – or, as she claimed, lack thereof.

In the hubbub between classroom instruction, Mrs Scott, to my satisfaction, might award Keith's jibes a solemn rebuke.

One rainy mid-morning break, the class gathered on the hallway's wooden floor to watch a video – Disney's *The Adventures of Ichabod and Mr Toad* (1949). At a few brusque jibes from Keith, I replied in kind.

Mrs Scott sent the two of us to stand by the wall – my retorts seemed to be as much of a problem as Keith's instigations.

An occasionally absent Mrs Scott was briefly replaced by supply teacher Miss Lome. To my retaliations to my taunters, Miss Lome took particular exception.

Retaliation was wrong, she said.

"*Do-you*-agree-*with-me*?"

My gall at this wasn't quite strong enough to overcome my fear of the consequences of failing to murmur "yes."

"I think she'll be very religious, Miss Lome," said James.

"What does 'religious' mean?" I asked.

"She believes in God a lot."

I had some grasp of Jesus's instruction to meet scorn with a turning of the other cheek. While such submissiveness seemed almost unfathomable to me, I held a sliver of regard for the cosmic virtue of its prescription. I supposed there was indeed something unwholesome about my constant petulance towards my taunters. I, in my bloated torso, with my inordinate timidity, sluggish inattentiveness and reticent reclusiveness, seemed to be a hotbed of disharmony.

Toilets

At home, I finally found myself able to brave the solitude of the bathroom without asking John to tag along for moral support. School, however, was a different story. At break and lunchtimes, when my peers bustled in and out, I could happily use the facilities. However, should my bladder weigh during lesson time, straying from the bustle of the classroom down the dim hallway and into a distant, silent room proved too much for me.

One dragging afternoon, my bladder began to weigh uncomfortably. Amidst the babble of my peers, with as little grasp as usual of today's task, I kept resisting my duty to visit the toilets – I just couldn't bring myself to face the overwhelming mystery of their distance, darkness and silence.

It soon became hilariously obvious to my peers that I'd demeaned myself in a way no longer quite socially acceptable. I tried to seem as if I were as amused by the mishap as everyone else.

At Mam's explanation of my fear of solitary toilet visits, Mrs Scott arranged for several other boys to accompany me there. On arrival, my cohorts fell into drawls of impudence.

"Perhaps it's scarier to go to the toilet *with* other people?" Mrs Scott advised me.

Cowardly

At Barrowburn, Maid, one of Dad's Border Collies, had pups. Behind the small wooden door of the old stone pig house, on a hay-layered floor, crept several tiny, softly rounded Border Collies, their yapping squeals a marvel. Unafraid of their placid mother, I delightedly watched.

While Dad found most of them homes, he decided to keep and train one, whom he named Willy Whiskers. As Willy grew, I afforded him the fretful caution with which I usually met Dad's dogs.

Dad acquired another dog, a small Border Terrier, Squeak, who lived with Willy in the pig house. Little Squeak had a particular fondness for jumping up at people. While I admired dogs, the threat of abrupt bodily contact with such vibrant animals continued to keep me at a fearful distance. I realised this to be irrational; the most a Barrowburn dog was likely to do was jump up or roll onto its back in hope for belly rubs.

At bedtime, Dad, to John and me, read stories from Enid Blyton anthology *The Sneezing Dog* (1993). In "Boo! Boo! Boo!", eight-year-old Harry stays on Uncle Jim and Aunt Nell's farm and is scared of hens and dogs. When a goose strays into the garden, Harry hides under a bush.

Uncle Jim scorns Harry as cowardly.

Instructively exposed to livestock, Harry learns he's just being silly, and all is well.

Blyton seems to define cowardice as a wilful concession to fear, honed by Harry's inexperience and self-regard. Uncle Jim's disgust seems not only to be at the feebleness of a young boy's fear, but at its selfishness, its insipid self-indulgence.

My parents, patient with my inordinate timidity, supposed I would eventually grow out of it.

On the school yard, shortly after little Austin was seen with a heavily bloodied face, Mrs Hunter announced the boy's nose to have been "bust open" by a football. Henceforth, whenever a football came anywhere near me, I fled – these heavy, leaping, lightning-fast missiles now overwhelmed me with instinctive fear.

At the river, while my brothers had no problem crossing the village stepping stones, I could hardly bring myself to step onto the first.

Why should I alone be so scared? So fat? So inattentive? So greedy?

In Enid Blyton short story "Lazy Lenny," eponymous anti-hero Lenny, on a seaside holiday with cousins Karen, Rachel and George, declines to help build sandcastles.

Some hard digging, says George, would ease Lenny's weight.

Was I just lazy? Too lazy to restrain my appetite, too lazy to pay attention, too lazy to conquer petty fears? The term seemed to befit my cumbersome torso – were I hardened by deprivation and discipline as one of Granda Widdrington's generation, the bulge to which I'd bloated my flesh would supposedly recede, and I'd be normal.

On the school playground, as I distantly beheld my bounding schoolmates, I enviously wondered what it must be like to have a torso proportional to the rest of my body.

"Let's not beat about the bush," said Mam, "you eat too much."

"Get ya sel' away for a walk," urged Granda Widdrington.

Telly II

From Sky channel Nickelodeon, I sought frequent inspiration.

Doug's gently surreal animation, with heartfelt optimism, staged the naturalistic trials of its eponymous eleven-and-a-half-year-old.

Japanese-Australian co-production *Ultraman: Towards the Future* merged space exploration, giant rubber monsters and emotional realism.

Appetite for such delights roused hostility to James's occasional requests to watch the snooker, or for the telly to be switched off that he might practise the piano. Gentle correction from Mam and Dad steered me grudgingly to reason.

Visiting from next door, Granda Widdrington, on sight of whatever John and I were watching on the telly, continued to give a playful sneer. Telly, he seemed to feel, was an extravagance, a flow of obtrusive sound and absurd images with which his more robust generation had done well without. No finer pursuit, he hinted, could be found than in James's mastery of the piano. The wall above the piano now held several framed certificates awarded to James by the Associated Board of the Royal School of Music, signed by piano teacher Miss Hammond.

"Grand thing, music," said Granda solemnly.

I appreciated, of course, James's craft – anything that inspired James had an edge of worldly refinement.

Spookiness

The cooling air held an autumnal richness. In shop displays arrived the insignia of Halloween. Pumpkins, witches' hats, lurid plastic masks and paper ghosts – a cosy hint of the eerily wondrous, the unique deliciousness of spookiness.

On Nickelodeon, an advert reel included previews of a new show. A narrating voice, playfully hushed, announced tales of the supernatural. A live-action montage included scenes of a nightly forest, through which drifted a figure draped in a white veil, a distant shot of a nightly cemetery, through which walked a figure in a hooded, inwardly lit white sheet, and a car, which passed seamlessly through a tall metal gate.

These images had me instantly enraptured – I simply must watch this. The new show was called *Are You Afraid of the Dark?* and would be aired Saturday and Sunday at 6.30 pm.

It introduced the nightly woodland campfire of the teenage Midnight Society, each of whom, each episode, introduced their respective tale, which unfolded in separately filmed scenes. Vibrant young faces, worldly in their seniority and North American accents, underwent such awed chills as a haunted cemetery, a vengeful spectral clown and a cupboard whose interior manifested various scary phantasms.

With its youthful warmth, lush scenery and sense of unadulterated wonder, *Are You Afraid of the Dark?* engrossed and delighted me. While John found Zeebo the Clown a bit much, I didn't quite start to feel overwhelmed until the arrival of the silhouetted inter-dimensional apparitions.

Mam, reminded of *Tales of the Unexpected*, seemed also to enjoy this new show.

One night, James, on BBC One, watched a fairly new film whose broadcast he recorded – James Cameron's *Terminator 2: Judgement Day* (1991).

With the metal skeletons, time travel and Arnold Schwarzenegger's stoic, cybernetic hero, John and I became fascinated. Robert Patrick's shape-shifting T-1000, although terrifying, rarely killed with on-screen bloodshed.

"Don't look!" warned Mam, of certain scenes.

While she had some reservations about letting John and me watch it, the advertised toy figurines, she reasoned, were aimed at ages three and up.

Even so, Nana and Granda sternly warned her, and us, against such inappropriate material.

Beneath the windowsill, from deep in the bookcase, Mam unearthed two paperbacks: Nigel Blundell and Robert Boar's *The World's Greatest Mysteries* (1980) and Nigel Blundell's *The World's Greatest Ghosts* (1984). Both had once belonged to Uncle Gordon.

James eagerly delved into both and shared accounts with John and me. I was awed and mildly chilled by reports of unaccountable knockings, faces on a floor and a skull said to sweat blood in anticipation of war. However, *The World's Greatest Mysteries* was, at some point, lost. I worried, with surprising intensity, that should Gordon return to these shores, a reckoning might be due.

Christmas Music

For the Year Four Christmas play, held in the Dinner Hall, the rest of the school were required to sit on chairs before the stage and sing. I was sick of being made to sing – it was tiring and embarrassing. Since I knew Mam to be in the audience before us, I, for once, dared to defy school orders.

During a collective rendition of "Little Donkey," Mrs Scott glared at me.

"*Sing!*" she whispered crossly.

I proudly kept my mouth shut.

Top of the Pops showed a new music video. In a bright blue sky, amidst abstract CGI shapes, floated two men in gaudy jumpsuits and helmets, one visored. Lilting, synthesised chimes and beats wove a melody of tender exultancy.

The foremost of the two men, his high, soft voice both pensive and joyous, sang the melody. On arrival of the chorus, the screen turned to a crowd composed of numerous duplicates of his visored associate. Through his mouths, a deep choir roared the song's title: "Go West."

The images, and the song they enthroned, filled me with delight.

Aunty Jess, fond of this band, introduced them to me as the Pet Shop Boys and readily agreed to get me for Christmas the *Very* album.

1994

Very Pet Shop Boys

On weekend runs to Barrowburn, I required *Very* to be installed in the Subaru cassette player. In songs of vexation, mourning, yearning and surrender, the high, soft voice of Neil Tennant led a symphony of electronic chimes. The music lifted my imagination through a multicoloured infinity. *Terminator 2* and *Sonic the Hedgehog* fed fancies of a leather-jacketed, sunglasses-clad cartoon version of myself shotgun blasting a robotic seagull who wanted to eat a shark and beating up a computer game version of Keith Dobson.

"What's this song about?" I would often ask.

"Falling out," Mam supposed.

She treated me to the revelation that the two Pet Shop Boys lived in Newcastle – they were our regional kith. This was a misapprehension; only singer Neil was originally from the North East, specifically the Tyneside coastal town of North Shields.

Mention of Neil's sexual orientation introduced me to the concept that some men fancied other men rather than women.

Dad, eventually, apologetically insisted on leaving *Very* off for a while.

I felt a grudging shame – that which to my imagination gloried was a pest.

"You get a better variety of songs on the radio," said James.

Dad eventually allowed the tape back on.

At school, Mrs Scott had the class draw pictures to depict our respectively favoured pursuits. I drew myself in an armchair beneath Mam's hi-fi.

Swelling with pride, I showed the picture to Mrs Scott and explained it to show myself listening to the music of the Pet Shop Boys.

Mrs Scott fixed me with a look of solemn shock.

"*Really?*" she breathed.

43

Bedtime Stories

On Saturday and Sunday, 6:30 pm saw new episodes of *Are You Afraid of the Dark?* The spooky intrigue of the first season now reached such frights as a silent movie vampire stepping down from the cinema screen, a lonely old woman revealed, in her sudden rage, to be a ghost, and grimy, deathly-faced Water Demons.

Adolescent heroes underwent such mind-blowing ordeals as an attic door which transferred entrants to a nearby dollhouse. Sincere tenderness emerged in such themes as a misunderstood werewolf, a spectral firefighter and the gradual reunion of an unwittingly deceased young couple. I really could ramble on for pages about the delight this show inspired in me, but we have to get on.

"I'll tell y' why you cannot get to sleep," said Granda Widdrington. "It's 'cause you're watching shite like this!"

The fellowship and wonder I found in recorded sounds and images, at a stern word from Granda Widdrington, were rendered an obtrusive extravagance.

Bedtime remained difficult. Dad now stayed in mine and John's bedroom to read us a story. He might often read us an old Roald Dahl favourite, or a short story from one of James's old Enid Blyton anthologies.

At a school book fair, I acquired Martin Adams' Virgin-published novel *Sonic the Hedgehog in Castle Robotnik*. With my reading skills at a minimum, I initially experienced the book through Dad's readings. One dark, stormy night, Sonic and Tails, with their animal pals, watch a vampire film. Following walrus Joe Sushi's suddenly vampiric tendencies, Sonic and Tails find Dr Robotnik to have been cloning their friends in the likeness of horror film icons.

The prose wove a Green Hill Zone peopled with peace-loving anthropomorphised animals. Amiably egotistical and highly moral, Sonic cherished home, friends, extreme speed and copious amounts of fast food. With a boastful computer game hero and semi-ironic use of such terms as "radical," the prose was drily, jovially modern. As quickly as possible, I obtained the three

44

prequels: *Sonic the Hedgehog and the Silicon Warriors*, *Sonic the Hedgehog in the Fourth Dimension* and *Sonic the Hedgehog in Robotnik's Laboratory*.

Enid Blyton's short stories saw uncooperative children taught the error of their ways by pixies – a genteel idyll in which the righteous were strict and certain. These short stories were cosy, sometimes aspired to genuine compassion and had a playful sense of whimsy. Feeling slightly chided by their properness, I preferred Sonic.

Dad, who preferred to read us Enid Blyton's *Noddy*, laughingly bemoaned Sonic to be boring.

Sonic the Comic and several Ladybird-published illustrated storybooks had introduced Sonic and Tails' pal Sally Acorn, a femininely large-eyed, red bow-adorned squirrel. The Virgin-published novels cast her as a kindly if somewhat strict mother-figure to the rest of the Green Hill Zone. Her feminine properness and innocence began to evoke a sense of my intrusion on such refinement. The pretty name roused an embarrassed sense of tenderness.

Following his reading to us, Dad, with an aviation magazine, lay on the floor, halfway through the bedroom doorway, until I showed signs of falling asleep. I seldom did so until well after ten.

Stress

One bright weekend noon, Mam worked alone at the kitchen sink. Without much conviction, I decided it might be comical to jump into the room and shout "raa!" A thrill of opportunity overruled doubts of such comedy's inspiration or tact.

I jumped into the room.

"Raa," I said, quite loudly.

Mam gave a yell of shock.

I'd never heard her raise her voice to a shout. I withdrew onto the stairs and blubbered.

"Andy, come here," Mam called softly from the kitchen.

In self-righteous reticence which I ultimately knew to be pathetic, I refused her consolation. She left me to compose myself.

At my foolish startling of my mother, and at my refusal of her comfort, I felt a dull, enormous sadness. Refusal of my mother was to shun a joy so deep as for my existence to depend upon it. For my brutal petulance, I would always hold myself in contempt.

One night, in preparation for an early sheep gathering, Dad spent the night at Barrowburn. Well after eleven, I remained awake. Mam invited me to come into her and Dad's double bed. With several of my plush toys, I took up residence on Dad's side of the bed.

Saved from the dread of lateness by the reassuring presence of my mother, I soon fell asleep.

This arrangement prevailed over the next few nights, until it was common practice – when Mam and Dad went to bed, Dad would swap places with me.

Soon enough, my stubborn inability to fall asleep returned. One night, hours passed with no sign of sleep.

"Let's just go and make breakfast," said Mam. I eventually fell asleep at half past one.

Between such restless nights, Mam frustratedly bemoaned our unusual arrangement and its disruption of her own sleep.

"You can't be doing this when you're *fifteen*!" she stressed.

While Dad had a loud voice, apt for calling sheepdog commands across hills and fields, he almost never raised it in anger.

One weekend afternoon in the Barrowburn front room, John and I watched an episode of CITV's *Wizadora*. Absent-minded scarecrow Tatty Bogle (Steven Ryde), at one point, instead of saying "okay" said "kay-oh."

That night, with John and me in bed, Dad, as usual, came in to read us a story. He confided to me that he wasn't feeling very well and so asked me to restrain my levity.

"Kay-oh," I said, unsure of what he meant, but eager to please.

He succumbed to brief annoyance.

"See, you're doing it again!"

At the brief ire, I realised my disquiet, which lingered for a few days, to be inordinate.

Pack a Lunch With Healthy Appeal

At some point, I cultivated a fascination with the inner workings of the human body.

In Alnwick, as a post-dentist treat, Dad got me Kathryn Senior and David Salariya's *The X Ray Picture Book of Your Body* (1993). From the highly detailed illustrations and accessible if technical wording, I enjoyed a clear grasp of the digestion process.

The book featured a chapter on reproduction.

Mam, keen to divert my attention to less graphic fare, got me a postal subscription to *How My Body Works*, a monthly series of A4-sized, cartoon-illustrated hardbacks. With their simpler, semi-narrative descriptions, these were good fun. However, once I'd built up a sizeable collection, there arrived an ominously titled instalment: *A Good Diet*.

Antagonist Toxicus, for an illustrated lesson in healthy eating, is recast from a blue bacterium to a paunchy man. High above his feckless maw, he holds a huge bun stuffed with sausages. The narration, as I recall, compares him to a balloon. Exhausted by such tasks as running upstairs, Toxicus is told by the bearded Professor to eat right.

To a cartoon bad guy, the book assigns the vice of overeating. His carelessness, in its supposed dangers, imbues disgust with moral authority. Such reproval dwelt a numb, weary despondence.

Elsewhere in the book, an illustration of a plate filled with red meat and pastries sat by one filled with vegetation. Above the former, a cartoon boy frowned and raised a prohibitive hand; above the latter, a cartoon girl smiled and made the thumb and forefinger "okay" sign.

Not only did I succumb to what the book warned against; I failed to achieve what it prescribed – save for cherries, berries, currants, sweetcorn, occasional cauliflower, and, at a pinch, broccoli, I still couldn't force myself to eat fruit and vegetables. I positively enjoyed fruit in juice form, but, at the thought of biting into anything so smoothly firm, was overwhelmed by disgust.

Certain things that seemed to come naturally to others had, for me, proven difficult. I'd been overwhelmed with fright by solitary bathroom visits, getting hit in the face with a ball, crossing stepping stones and being jumped up at by one of Dad's friendly dogs. Residual wariness of toilets stayed my usage thereof to procrastination. I took an outrageously long time to fall asleep. I couldn't seem to force myself to grasp teachers' instructions. On finishing a meal, I couldn't seem to force myself to stop being hungry. I wondered: why should any of this be?

In such texts as *A Good Diet*, in teachers' frustration with my unwillingness to listen, and in Granda Widdrington's urges for me to get away from That Bloody Telly and go for walks recurred a hinted implication – laziness.

I found a slight balm in the eating habits of Granda Tait, who, at Barrowburn, I occasionally saw eat. Towards his mouth he wrenched forkfuls and chomped with unabashed haste. While nowhere near my proportions, his stomach had a pronounced paunch. And yet he, older than Granda Widdrington, had also lived through wartime rationing. I voiced my worry that my overeating might be a sin. Granda Tait reassured me that God wanted us to savour His gift of food.

My school days underwent a slight modification – once a month, at home time, Mam and I were required to report to a cloakroom. A curly-haired middle-aged woman watched me stand on a set of bathroom scales. She supplied Mam with instruction leaflets on how to get me to lose weight.

Pack a Lunch With Healthy Appeal was illustrated by a cartoon of several children who joyously bounded beneath a floating row of such fare – including vegetables. Well, that was out of the question – I just couldn't face the things.

However, my overall tastes didn't seem particularly unhealthy. My least wholesome preference was crisps, and I could just as well, if not more so, enjoy such low-fat corn snack equivalents as Skips, Wotsits and Thingies. I was never all that fussed about chocolate and sweets – I enjoyed but didn't crave them frequently.

One of the leaflets suggested using a smaller plate, so as to make my portions seem bigger. This sounded quite promising – for assured satisfaction, I needed to be persuaded of excess.

So – smaller portions, no eating between meals and less fatty stuff.

It didn't work.

Unfriendly

Dad often took John and me down to the park. This laundered fringe of lush wilderness now held a complex of brightly painted, open-walled wooden towers.

One bright, warm evening, several unknown children around my age occupied the rubber tiles on which the towers stood.

With two of them, a girl and a boy, John exchanged greetings.

Intrigued, I enquiringly addressed the newcomers.

The boy uncertainly replied.

I improvised further discourse.

The girl replied with what I took to be aloof indignation.

I replied with defensive indignation, as was my habit – at the contempt of my schoolmates, I was always ready to lash out in return.

Dad, in forlorn disapproval, took us home.

In the brightly sunlit kitchen, Dad, to Mam, recounted the confrontation.

In recollection of the affection I'd readily shown in infancy to other children, Mam bemusedly lamented my latter tendency to unwarranted aggression.

Hectic

I occasionally found myself sharing a classroom table with Ellen Miller. Her social circle tended to consist of one or two like-minded girls, mainly Cora Moore, with whose fluffy, pig-shaped pencil case, Piggy, they held a fond acquaintance. With amiable placidity, Ellen received my ramblings on Sonic and sharks, but was adamant of the fallacy of ghosts.

My own pencil case, a red and yellow rubber tube, was elaborately fashioned in the likeness of a cartoon shark, whose rubber teeth framed a zipper-gated mouth for pencil storage. By Ellen's example of adding affectionate "y"s to eponymously named belongings, I dubbed my pencil case Sharky.

One afternoon, near the end of Year Two, the class was herded into the Dinner Hall and onto benches, where, before plastic-chair-seated parents, we sang. After the ceremony, amidst the huddle of adults and children, I happily reunited with Mam, who'd been in conversation with Ellen.

"She thinks you're great," said Mam fondly.

Touched but rather humbled, I wondered why Ellen should afford me this level of esteem.

My seventh birthday fell on the last day of term. Mam arranged for Ellen to join us for cake, cherryade and Passy the Parcel – set, naturally, to the *Very* album.

That sunlit evening, in the living room, amidst strips of wrapping paper and the lively conversation of someone not usually here, I felt somewhat mournfully drained.

On introduction of my main present, an eighteen-inch, battery-operated talking Ultimate Terminator, I'd mentioned to Ellen my acquaintance with the film of its inspiration. Exposure of a film classified "15" to anyone below that age, Nana (mistakenly) believed, was illegal.

I now forlornly dreaded that Ellen might mention to her parents my watching of *Terminator 2*, and that my parents might face legal consequences. Embarrassed to mention my most sensitive fear of separation from my parents, I kept it to myself.

Dad astutely surmised that I'd found things "a bit hectic."

Horrible

While I didn't logically suppose it would be any less tedious than its predecessors, the occasion of starting Year Three cheered me with a sense of exploration.

Walking John and me to school, Mam urged me not to rouse the wrath of Mrs Swan, whose shout was said to be severe. Six years previously, James, on closure of the Alnwick Convent, had resumed Year Three at Rothbury First School. Scorned by his peers, his indignant self-assertion had angered Mrs Swan. On days when James was deemed to have been "good," the teacher had awarded him a gold star.

Mrs Swan looked to be somewhere in her fifties. Short, grey-flecked brown hair and broad spectacles framed a handsomely aged face. Her coarse, Standard-English-accented voice might often forego primness for a genial smile.

Much of Year Three was devoted to discussion of the Ancient Romans, which in turn required our filling in of worksheets, occasional illustration and sticking gold paper to cardboard Legionnaire helmets. Occasionally, Mrs Swan treated us to readings of Hugh Lofting's *The Story of Dr Dolittle* (1920).

Having learned, by James's example, a solemn respect for the monumental figure of Jesus, I grasped the need for some kind of amicability towards classroom taunters, yet wasn't dissuaded from meeting their scorn with a rebuke.

Mrs Swan read us illustrated retellings of Gospel passages: Jesus's fasting in the wilderness, appointing of the apostles and eventual crucifixion. The message I retained from these readings, rather than of self-sacrificial compassion, was of the paramount virtue of obedience. While Mrs Swan didn't mention hellfire and damnation, I got an impression of God as supreme judge of all life. It was from Mrs Swan that I learned the Devil's real name – Satan.

Mrs Swan read to us Nigel Hinton's *Beaver Towers* (1980). Protagonist Philip, forbidden to fly his new kite until the weekend, hears an inner voice urge him to do so now.

"Who was the voice?" Mrs Swan briefly paused from her narration.

"Satan," droned several girls.

In assembly, Mrs Hunter, from the book of *Genesis*, read to us of Cain's murder of his brother Abel.

"You've killed him," read the Head Teacher. "His blood is crying out to me from the earth." Cain pleads to be spared ostracism, and God "marked Cain with a special mark."

Hell was no longer the wondrous underground cavern depicted in *Scrooge* (1970), but a fiery torture chamber of eternal condemnation. Chilled to the core by thoughts of what divine retribution might potentially be visited on my family, my agitated imagination involuntarily professed such self-destructive claims as to "despise" God. I cautiously began to constantly recite pledges of devotion.

"I like God, I like God," I kept silently repeating, and later, "I do not despise God."

Involuntary repetition of the latter incantation would stay with me into adulthood.

Against me, Keith Dobson continued his occasional campaign of scornful impudence. My retorts sometimes seemed to genuinely annoy him.

"Fatty Four-Eyes," he scolded.

If, during lesson time, I should gripe at a classmate's jibe, Mrs Swan would swiftly quash the spat. Deep, heavy and sharp, her shout filled the air. Its volume numbed me with fright. Its booming contempt crushed my chest with shame.

Mrs Swan's fine curls, huskily soft voice, dainty face and modest, long-skirted attire cast an image of unimpeachable gentleness and wisdom. On her eminent authority, I was obscene.

What a Growler, I thought, in allusion to *Beaver Towers'* bestial antagonists, *what a Snarler*. My attempt at disdain was futile – I couldn't deny my disgrace.

One afternoon, Mrs Swan had us row our chairs before her desk. Once this was done, I found myself seated by Emma Hadley.

While she was never one of my taunters, I sometimes sensed in Emma a faintly barbed aloofness. Often sat with a teaching assistant, her quiet voice emerged in prim defiance. We'd differed on certain subjects, but with no outright vitriol.

I raised my hand.

"I don't like sitting next to Emma," I said.

I considered this a polite note of my mild aversion to my neighbour, with a request of alternative seating arrangements.

Mrs Swan fixed me with a look of reproach.

"DO YOU THINK SHE LIKES SITTING NEXT TO *YOU?*"
The shout crushed my chest in stunned, frightened shame. This little old lady, this prim, caring custodian of children, challenged my defilement of the innocent.

I'd long recognised my perplexing tendency to get certain things wrong. My incompetence apparently stained my very soul.

Sometime later, a minor dispute with another classmate saw me reported to a passing Mrs Swan.

One needn't concern oneself, said the teacher, with the output of "horrible people."

Ghostbusters II

Around Christmas, it actually snowed. For much of Boxing Day afternoon, on the shared lawn behind the terrace, James, John and I plodged about in the snow, flinging balled lumps of it and rolling larger mounds of it into a snowman. While James went back inside, John and I lingered until daylight began to fade.

When we went back inside, Channel 4 was airing *Ghostbusters II*. My dismay at having missed the start, and therefore a chance to tape it in full, was, for now, soothed by exhilaration.

On-screen, I saw a hard-hatted Egon (Harold Ramis) drill into the road. Construction tools, the sudden shift to nighttime and Randy Edelman's shivering score lent a daunting air of seriousness.

On Ray's (Dan Aykroyd) dangling descent beneath New York, and into the experimental Pneumatic Transit subway, I re-encountered the ponderous river of pink-glowing Mood Slime.

The scene where the slime comes out of the bath tap and reaches for baby Oscar (respectively played by Will and Hank Deutschendorf), while no longer overwhelming, retained a chill. Dana's (Sigourney Weaver) horrified recount thereof then moves Peter's aloof dryness to gentle joviality, with which he soothes mother and baby.

During the climax, I cautiously averted my eyes and discreetly sought from James a commentary on the confrontation with the spirit of seventeenth century despot Vigo the Carpathian (Wilhelm von Homburg; voiced by Max von Sydow). I eventually braved a look at the screen to find Vigo to have reformed as a giant floating head, which, hosed by positively charged Mood Slime, splutters and growls at the purple deluge.

This saga of Particle Throwers, Proton Packs and ghosts was now imbued with parental tenderness and drenched in pink goo with the power both to summon angry spirits and make toasters dance with joy.

While enraptured at my reacquaintance with this relic from my infancy, I lamented my missed opportunity to capture it on video. When shopping in Newcastle, Mam and Dad made sure to keep an eye out for copies.

1995

Drugs

One Sunday morning, as John and I waited for Channel 4 to air *Adventures of Sonic the Hedgehog*, a continuity announcement previewed today's episode. While Sonic was in it, the animation was different – softer, darker and more detailed.

The advert reel finished, and the episode arrived. Through a lush, brightly detailed forest sped Sonic, to the exultant theme song "Fastest Thing Alive." Though a Sonic cartoon, this one was of perilous adventure. I was instantly thrilled.

From forest village Knothole, Sonic (still voiced by Jaleel White) and several other Freedom Fighters steal into the dark, mechanised streets of Robotropolis, ruled by Dr Robotnik. Voiced by the silken growl of Jim Cummings, this decidedly more sinister version of the character aims to convert the populace of Mobius into robot slaves.

Sally Acorn, the kindly if slightly strict squirrel depicted in the Virgin-published novels, is here approximated by svelte, booted Princess Sally (voiced by Kath Soucie). A computer whiz, she serves as the Freedom Fighters' strategist and is often exasperated by Sonic's impetuousness. Sonic's flirtatious banter with Sally often incurs aspersions on his brain.

While galled by her dainty superiority, I received her soft voice and fine features with a grudgingly embarrassed, tender respect. Her reconciliations with Sonic were always touching.

In the episode *Blast to the Past Part 1*, Sonic and Sally find the legendary Time Stones and travel ten years into the past, to the point just before Robotnik leads his machine army in a coup to convert Robotropolis into a mechanical dystopia. On this cliffhanger, the episode ends.

The following Sunday, before leaving for Barrowburn with Mam, Dad and John, I asked James to tape this week's crucial episode of Sonic.

I later returned home in a thrill of anticipation.

"I forgot to tape Sonic," James gently apologised.

For the next few hours, inconsolable regret knotted my stomach. In futile, unfair protest at James's honest mistake, I lamented.

"It's like a drug, son!" Granda Widdrington tried to rouse me from my funk. "People get addicted to telly!"

A Little Boy Like You

In school assemblies, Mrs Hunter discussed flood, famine, "the poor," Nelson Mandela and God.

Mrs Hunter eventually forbade students to bring crisps to eat at break time. Henceforth, only fruit was allowed. While I gave up break time snacks altogether, John brought in an orange and was stung by a wasp.

One morning, while Mrs Hunter addressed the assembly hall, I sat on the floor with everyone else.

As usual, my glasses kept sliding down my nose. I kept pushing them back up by contracting my nose and brow.

That afternoon, as the rest of Year Three went about today's task, I wandered in aimless bewilderment. The skin of my forearms, having been scorched by the blazing sun, now mildly stung. Mindful of the heatwave, Mam had equipped John and me with a tube of sunblock, which John had stored in Mrs Hunter's classroom.

Several minutes ago, Mrs Swan had left the room. I stole down the empty hallway to the open door of Mrs Hunter's classroom.

Just inside the door, on a shelf, lay the pink tube. Although designed to prevent rather than soothe sunburn, its cool touch would be welcome. I reached a hand about six inches into the open classroom, took the tube, squeezed out a cool white glob and applied it to my scorched arms.

From amidst the babbling throng, Mrs Hunter glanced at the doorway, noticed my presence and advanced.

She angrily led me to the office.

In the grey-toned room, I approached a leather chair and sat. Adopting a lower position, I thought, indicated my receptivity to whatever Mrs Hunter had to tell me.

"No, you're not here to have a nice sit down!"

I stood. Mrs Hunter levelled her face inches from mine. In a raised voice, she spoke for what felt like about fifteen minutes.

The message was that my lack of respect was atypically singular and grievously distasteful. Such disregard for civility, it seemed, was unheard of.

My fear, rather than overwhelming, was steady and stifling. It brought a wretched, utter disgrace. I'd considered myself a respectable member of society – quiet and unassuming. Okay, maybe reaching through the classroom door was a bit indelicate, but did it really warrant all this?

My misunderstanding of social boundaries, it seemed, was monumental. Just like my outsize appetite, my fear of toilets and inability to fall asleep anywhere other than in my mother's bed, my social incompetence was a baffling, gigantic outrage.

"*I don't think we* want *a little boy like you in our school!*" cried Mrs Hunter.

At home time, Mrs Hunter had a rather quieter word with Mam.

It seemed the teacher had been under the impression that I, in assembly, had been pulling faces at her. She'd interpreted my adjustment of my glasses as a gesture of derision.

Blood II

As the dinner period neared its end, I approached the Year Three classroom. In the gloomy corridor, Warren Raleigh jovially scorned my weight.

At my rebukes, Warren grinned and backed further away, leading me into the classroom. I shoved my hands against his torso and pushed. Warren fell, slid several feet across the wooden tiles and, against the metal leg of a table, banged the back of his head.

He remained slumped on the floor. Other students gathered around him. I realised I'd done something serious. Horrified remorse overwhelmed me. I hovered by Warren, apologising, and invited him to hit me in retaliation. Several Dinner Nannies arrived and escorted Warren to aid.

I wondered why I was never shouted at for this.

A wound in the back of Warren's head, I later learned, had needed to be stapled together.

Weeks later, amidst the back of his pale blonde hair, I saw a region of scalp to be bloodily uneven. I asked him how his head was. He politely said it was fine.

Henceforth, we remained civil acquaintances.

Snivelling

As summer dawned, break times allowed students onto the field. Beneath the fenced-off Bilberry hills, the field slanted and broadened to a tree-shaded fence, beyond which lay a branch of road. In glaring sunshine, children frolicked on the soft, bright grass.

I, as ever, was happy to wander indiscriminately and concoct disjointed fancies. To be able to do so on the field was lovely.

I wandered towards the bottom end, towards where John was gathered with some friends. Year Two Lucas Kidd was overseeing some kind of game, on whose boundary he forbade access. He angrily protested my intrusion. Despite his juniority, his throaty shout had fearsome volume and withering conviction.

In shocked, sorrowful humiliation, I attempted a shouted rebuke, apologised in advance and smacked him several times across the chest.

I then sobbed with humiliation and remorse, climbed to the edge of the field and gave two Dinner Nannies an account of my altercation.

"Stop snivelling on!" snapped Mrs Telford.

Positively Charged

One bright, warm afternoon, Mam and Dad, having been shopping in Newcastle, picked John and me up from school.

When we got home, Mam reached into a shopping bag and handed me a surprise – after months of searching, my parents had managed to find me a VHS copy of *Ghostbusters II*.

In pure delight, I absorbed the moment.

"I can't tell you how grateful I am for this!" I gasped.

An instant of silent darkness and a solemn orchestral jolt began the film.

For the first time in four years, I watched the poltergeist-propelled perambulator pursuit.

In the Manhattan Museum of Art restoration lab, Dr Janosz Poha (Peter MacNicol) supervises installation of the fearsome painting of Moldavian tyrant and sorcerer Vigo the Carpathian (Wilhelm von Homburg; voiced by Max von Sydow). Following Dana's (Sigourney Weaver) polite evasion of Janosz's flirting, he backs towards the painting, whose brow suddenly bulges forth – with a nervous thrill, I recalled this film's formidable scariness.

While I still didn't quite dare to behold the spectral mounted heads of Vigo's victims, I finally managed to see the full extent of the climax. Vigo, with his bestially deep voice, was scary, but no longer overwhelmingly so.

Amidst the threat of a seventeenth century despot and the flooding of New York with hate-infused, psycho-reactive Mood Slime, a tenderness permeates the film, epitomised in Peter's (Bill Murray) care for Dana and Oscar (respectively played by Will and Hank Deutschendorf) and Ray's heartfelt call for the goodwill which must surely remain in the jaded New Yorkers. On sudden inspiration, the Ghostbusters rig the Statue of Liberty with pilot controls, hose its interior with Mood Slime, and by the positive emotions of Howard Huntsberry's cover of Jackie Wilson's "Higher and Higher," pilot it through the city, where the crowd's joy weakens the shell of hate-infused Mood Slime around the museum.

The Ghostbusters, recalled from as far back as my third year of life, had returned to conquer the fiendish denizens of their wondrous world. A closing scene epitomises this – with the haunted portrait of Vigo blasted away, its canvas now bears a Renaissance painting, in which four archangels, who resemble the Ghostbusters, guard a cradled cherub, who resembles Oscar.

On solitary playground wanders, the beloved film fuelled my daydreams.

On reappraisal, however, my esteem for its heroes now courted a touch of nervous self-shame. I instinctively feared my disgraceful intrusion on Dana; her adult femininity had an eminence which, to me, seemed vulnerable to such outrage as I was apt to incur.

Serpent

In the summer holidays, one afternoon, we all had a run in the car to Tynemouth Sealife Centre. The hot blue sky, the anticipation of a car ride, the actual car ride, and whatever jolly sounds might emerge from the radio, all stoked my glee. There arrived a broadcast of Aswad's "Shine," which I liked (and would later love). I misinterpreted a lyric as "spreading your life/like the serpent you are."

Mention of snakes recalled both my fascination with the misunderstood creatures and the 1993 cartoon series adaptation of *The Animals of Farthing Wood* (1979). The anatomical precision and understated expressions of its multi-species cast evoked a reverence to which I'd felt hostile. Application to animals of such human values as law, with only Adder (voiced by Stacey Gregg) resistant to this virtue, had always somewhat jarred with me.

The softness of Adder's female voice reflected the prettiness of a world which disapproved of her. My illicit attraction to the character enhanced memories of the malignancy teachers seemed to see in me.

Mam bought a cassette of "Highlights from *The Buddy Holly Story*." While I liked it, John, for some reason, found it aggravated his carsickness.

Word came around of a live-action film adaptation of *Casper*. I'd seen a few episodes of the cartoon, and loved anything with ghosts, so the film was an obvious cinematic port of call.

Gigantic Whipstaff Manor pits widower therapist Dr James Harvey (Bill Pullman) and teenage daughter Kat (Christina Ricci) against madcap CGI ghosts. Casper (voiced by Malachi Pearson), the ghost of a young boy, becomes unrequitedly infatuated with Kat. Despite the improperness of my trespass upon femininity, approachably dry Kat had a touching kindness. To the heartfelt strains of "Highlights from *The Buddy Holly Story*," I, with forbidden fondness, idealised her acceptance of her spectral suitor.

The film stoked my fascination with stately buildings, houses almost as big as castles and filled with spooky secrets. There was such a building just outside Rothbury – distantly visible between the horizon-filling pines, Cragside House had been the first in the world to be lit by hydroelectricity.

Year Four

For our last year at Rothbury County First School, my class moved into the outermost classroom and under the care of Mrs Walker, who, relatively young, had arrived last year. Short black hair framed a thin, fine face, which while sometimes severe, savoured mirth and affection. Her Standard-English-accented voice might occasionally rise, but with nowhere near the frequency and volume of Mrs Swan.

Mrs Walker often read aloud to the class. Her spirited reading of Frances Hodgson Burnett's *The Secret Garden* (1911), complete with Yorkshire accents, was a highlight. In her merrily rambling class conversations, I was readily included. Quite happily, I mentioned to her what I believed to have been my reception of an electric shock but was probably just a burn from the hot living room lamp.

With several others, I queued by Mrs Walker's table to submit my worksheet for inspection.

"Andrew, look at my new tin," said Emma Hadley, seated nearby. Her remedial tuition had equipped her with a small bronze tin. Still galled by her past, adult-reinforced defensiveness, I found myself overborne by her demand for attendance.

"I'm not remotely interested in your new tin, Emma," I said flatly.

Having overheard, Mrs Walker, although not angrily, urged me to consider my own reception of such a response – such as my confidence to her of my supposed electric shock. The notion of such rejection was indeed shaming.

Mrs Walker read us an illustrated retelling of Moses's reception of the Ten Commandments. Their simplified interpretations included a commandment to "be faithful to your husband or wife." Concerned for my parents' evasion of divine sanction, I embarrassedly asked Mam if she and Dad were "faithful" to each other. Somewhat amused, Mam confirmed that they were.

While still on friendly terms with Ellen Miller, the passage of time waned our association. At break time, and in the lunch hour, I, as ever, wandered the yard in meandering contemplation.

At break times, Mrs Walker, sometimes with a small entourage of students, calmly patrolled the yard.

"Talk to me, Andrew," she said with a good-humoured smile, on occasional interception of my trajectory.

Esteemed, I wondered if her mild emphasis implied something amiss in my reclusive travels.

The approach of Christmas saw much lesson time reassigned to rehearsal of the songs which the school would communally sing for Christmas play *No Snow for Christmas*. Directed by Mrs Hunter, it concerned several children who, horrified by lack of Christmastime snow, consult Santa. He refers them to the counsel of Sally Snowflake, who in turn tells them to think about snow, whereupon it snows. There would follow a communal rendition of Frankie Laine's "I Believe," covered that year by Robson and Jerome.

Being heavily overweight, I thought I'd be a natural choice for the role of Santa. For some reason, it went to the only slightly portly Leonard Pringle. The central protagonists' decision to consult Santa would be followed by a troop of elves in sunglasses, who, fingers snapping, would chant a rhythmic verse in tribute to Santa's omniscience. I was cast among them.

On the evening of performance, Leonard, to indicate Santa's snowy residence, had to have his nose painted red. With mounting horror, I realised this was also required of those playing elves. Since age four, I'd feared facial invasion by gaudy, viscous fluid. In the hallway, Mrs Cross smeared each of our noses with a red-dipped paintbrush. I returned to the classroom, my nose heavy with thick moisture. Overcome, I sobbed and was allowed to wipe it off.

"We certainly can't have a tearful elf onstage," said Mrs Cross.

With somewhat diminished pride, I went onstage and intoned "Santa knows" with the others.

1996

A Real Effort

Mrs Walker assigned each of the class to write a story.

Thrilled, I wrote a scenario in which John, Joe the Border Collie (by now, I no longer feared bodily contact with dogs) and I, find, in the field opposite the Barrowburn farmhouse, a strange manhole cover. Beneath, a set of stairs leads to an underground metal chamber.

Inspired by *Are You Afraid of the Dark?* episode *The Tale of the Unexpected Visitor*, I wrote of a mechanical door which slides up to exude "blinding yellow light." This dims to reveal an Earth-like planet, down onto which the three of us float.

A talking basking shark warns us of this world's oppression by a fearsome tyrant. This fiend, who resembles one of the HR Giger-designed monsters from the *Alien* films, carries a barbed staff with which to zap people. In its castle, with a nearby shield, John and I deflect such a blast onto the zapper, and the three of us are automatically teleported home.

On a parents' evening, Mrs Walker apparently told Mam my story had been the best in the class.

Despite her occasional vexation at my apparent inability to listen, and gentle reproval of my occasionally stern reticence, Mrs Walker actively seemed to like me. Happily receptive to my attempts at geniality, she noted in my report that I'd "made a real effort this year."

Doctor Who

Years ago, James had mentioned something called *Doctor Who*. The name roused a mental image of a low-angle view of a daylit street, at whose end loomed a flowing-haired, intense-faced man. A supply teacher had hinted the show to have involved time travel.

One weekend, John and I lounged in the front room of the Barrowburn farmhouse. *Movies, Games and Videos* announced a long-awaited return from *Doctor Who*, an excerpt of which was then shown. Across a gloomy hall, a youngish, wild-haired, Standard-English-accented man called confrontationally to a man in high-collared red robes.

The North-American-accented captor implied himself and the Doctor to be from another planet.

Was the mysterious Doctor a traveller in space as well as time? Was *Doctor Who* British or North American? Was it a film, a series of films, or a television series?

One evening, BBC One aired a brief preview of the imminent *Doctor Who* TV movie.

I asked Mam about *Doctor Who*.

The series had been, I learned, on BBC One, when Mam was little.

What had it been about?

"Well," said Mam, "he fought the Daleks..."

The sound of the word gripped me instantly.

The Daleks, explained Mam, were domed robot-type-things. With protruding antennae, they glided across the floor, spoke in mechanical monotone and, with their "rays," sought to "exterminate" people. Their on-screen arrival had driven Mam behind the sofa in fear. On one of my drawing pads, she now sketched a simplified Dalek.

She then explained about the eponymous Doctor's time and space vehicle, a blue wooden phone box with the word "police" above the door.

"And it was really huge when you get inside..."

She now drew the police box.

Later, the Doctor she'd known in the seventies had been a wide-eyed, curly-haired, buck-toothed maverick.

A further BBC trailer described the Doctor as having a "new face." Apparently, on bodily death, his body transformed into another.

"He's a Time Lord," explained Dad, on a drive back from Barrowburn.

With a thrill of intrigue, I anticipated my introduction to a British fantasy series about time travel and mechanical space monsters, with a mad scientist as the good guy.

On Monday the 22nd of May, having spent the bank holiday at Barrowburn, I adjourned to my Sega Master System. Around eight, John called up the stairs that the film would soon be starting. Content to sacrifice my evening's progress, I switched off the console and telly.

In the living room, I put a blank tape in the video recorder. At ten past eight arrived BBC One's dark ident screen. Amidst dim vapours, a transparent globe held a "1."

"Now, one of BBC One's greatest heroes is back, and it's about time," said the calm announcer. "Action, adventure and some scares, nineties style, mankind faces total destruction – in *Doctor Who*."

The soft, Standardly Anglicised narration of Paul McGann's Eighth Doctor introduced a looming shot of a barren red planet – Skaro. I wondered if they'd used actual outer space footage.

"That's Mars," I said authoritatively.

A shot of Skaro's two moons blurred into the green-glowing eyes of Gordon Tipple's the Master. Against a black void, he stood imprisoned by a dome-shaped collar, from beneath which projected bars of light, forming a cage.

A distorted, high-pitched voice chanted something not quite intelligible. The cage exploded and was vaporised. Inwardly, I wondered if the voice had been that of a Dalek – was Skaro the Daleks' home planet?

Through the blackness of outer space, the title "Doctor Who," in shiny blue letters, loomed towards the screen. The midsection of Ron Grainer's theme tune, orchestrally arranged by John Debney, soared in benevolent triumph. Through a vortex of swirling colours, opening titles zoomed forth. These were followed by a spinning, rectangular blue box.

This, explained Mam, was the police box time machine: the TARDIS.

The scene faded to a spacious, candlelit chamber. By Sonic Screwdriver, the Master's remains were sealed in a chest. Sylvester McCoy's Seventh Doctor, a man in a checked green suit and red waistcoat, adjourned to an armchair for tea.

On either side of his head flowed wavy dark hair. A high brow framed a flexible face, whose eyes shone with genial wisdom. With his reserved intensity and slightly wacky hair, he naturally wore such a title as Doctor Who.

On sight of the mushroom-shaped, gantry-flanked TARDIS Console, Mam realised this place to be the "really huge" interior of the time machine.

The film was a magical introduction to *Doctor Who*. The Doctor gets shot, goes to hospital, dies and changes into a younger, entirely distinct man (Paul McGann).

His old enemy, the Master, having turned into a blob of transparent goo, dives down the throat of paramedic Bruce (Eric Roberts) and takes over his body.

With the initially reluctant help of cardiologist Dr Grace Holloway (Daphne Ashbrook), the Eighth Doctor regains his memories.

The subject matter of extraterrestrial physiology, bodily transformation, transparent goo and time travel had a sense of awed, fearful, joyous wonder.

To learn more of *Doctor Who*, I seized any opportunity. One Saturday afternoon in the nearby town of Alnwick, I found in WHSmith a small book, by David J Howe, simply called *Doctor Who*. An introduction of the series' history was followed by an essay on each of the Doctor's eight incarnations.

The cover of John Peel's 1993 novelisation of David Whitaker's 1967 serial *The Evil of the Daleks* featured Patrick Troughton's Second Doctor, the towering Dalek Emperor and a silver, black-domed Dalek – a sleek, domed box of wonders, its mechanical limbs teasingly implied identity.

While my concentration wasn't strong enough to absorb the story from start to end, I often read random passages. The impish, benevolently scheming Second Doctor, with the Human Factor, infects three Daleks. Amidst their fanatically murderous peers, to see these three faceless drones imbued with childlike glee was both comical and touching.

Steve Lyons' 1995 Virgin New Adventures novel *Head Games*, with its less familiar characters, was more of a challenge to grasp. However, its opening chapter offered a deliberately innocent, slightly comical and sincerely affectionate introduction to Sylvester McCoy's Seventh Doctor. Quaintly genial and detachedly jovial, he lands the TARDIS in the home of sixteen-year-old aspiring writer Jason and beckons him in search of green monsters and tea-hating despots. This, however, is a recreation of the Doctor conjured by the Land of Fiction – the following chapter shows the actual Seventh Doctor struggling with terrible guilt.

On Sunday mornings, I learned, UK Gold currently aired omnibus repeats of *Doctor Who* serials. I began with *Logopolis* (1981).

Typically about two hours long, early eighties serials were quite slowly paced. In contrast to the raw, contemporary wonder of the TV Movie, this era of the show sometimes rather strained my lax concentration. I determinedly persevered.

On the 18th of July, I reached the age of nine. Mam and Dad had got me a small trampoline, like Uncle Ross's.

Acquired by Aunty Jess on behalf of Nana and Granda, in a sleek cardboard presentation box, were two videos, respectively of the 1983 *Doctor Who* serial *The King's Demons* and 1983 *Children in Need* special *The Five Doctors*. The cover of the latter showed an actual Dalek.

Before going to school for the last day of Year Four, I watched half an hour of *The Five Doctors*. With the Fifth Doctor (Peter Davison), Tegan (Janet Fielding) and Turlough (Mark Strickson) holidaying in the Eye of Orion, the story had a jollier, more relaxed feel than recent UK Gold repeats.

In several scenes, a swirly CGI (this was the 1993 special edition) cone sweeps down from the sky and steals away the Doctor's previous incarnations.

In a silver corridor, the First Doctor (Richard Hurndall, standing in for the late William Hartnell) and granddaughter Susan (Carole Ann Ford), from round a corner, see a dome-shaped shadow. Into view glides a sleek black Dalek.

I giddily savoured the thrill of finally watching a Dalek in action. Its gunstick fired lances of green fire. Its voice, supplied by Roy Skelton, was a mightily rasping, mesmeric monotone. The First Doctor and Susan lead it into a corner, whereupon the Dalek's death ray bounces off a wall and, in a smart explosion, smacks right into it.

In the wrecked dome, a green mass of ovoid flesh angrily flails its tentacles. As I'd suspected, the Daleks were controlled from inside by living things.

Otherworldly

BBC One aired *Future Fantastic*. Hosted by Gillian Anderson, it featured commentary from authors and academics on the plausibility of such notions as ventured by science fiction, with occasional film excerpts and CGI animation.

The narrator wondered if drawing attention to Earth was wise – might the aliens be hostile?

To my delight, there followed a black and white clip of several Daleks.

The episode later addressed reported encounters with visitors from space. A succession of drawings culminated in the famous cover of Whitley Strieber's *Communion* (1987). The pictures encompassed the serene image of a bulbous cranium and large, slanted black eyes – the Grey.

ITV's *Strange But True* offered similar wonder. Eyewitness discussion of ghosts, cryptids, aliens or angels was often accompanied by brief, dramatised reconstruction – a table dragged independently across a floor and a hypnotised woman's approach through the void by an animated ghostly Grey.

In his bedroom, James kept an impressive collection of books, including several A4 softback titles of the *Marvels and Mysteries* series: *Marvels of the Mind, Life After Death* and *UFOs*. James freely let me browse.

Life After Death introduced the account of a young girl, Durdana, who, on revival from brief, terminal unconsciousness, had, from her earthly body, flown to the stars.

In a garden where everything shone independently, she met her deceased grandfather and an as-yet unknown woman. At the call of Durdana's father, she was taken to request God's permission for earthly return. Her later painting of God depicted, amidst the heavenly foliage, what appeared to be an earthward concentration of deep blue sky.

One Saturday at Barrowburn, Mam, in today's newspaper (I think it was either the *Journal* or the *Mail*), showed John and me an article about life after death. Illustrated by the doctored image of a man from whose prone body seamlessly rose a transparent projection of the same body, its interviewee claimed there to be "no heaven or hell as such" – discarnate souls rather found themselves in realms which, progressively, proportioned their earthly deeds.

I can't remember precisely when Mam told me about the figure she saw on the bedroom wall when I was two. On sight of a white-robed, radiantly glowing being who resembled my two-year-old self, Mam had been calmly astounded. While her informal religious observance fluctuated, Mam seemed in no doubt that the gently smiling being was my guardian angel. Over the years, the notion would give me a deep, simple reassurance – a persuasion that, despite my inhibitions and the misery they might cause others, I was, on the authority of a brief glimpse of the ether, here to do something worthwhile.

Night Out

Mam urged me, at weekends, to take walks with Uncle Ross.

We usually climbed the steep Cemetery Bank, walked along the tree-shaded farming estate of Whitton and out onto a road which bordered the wilderness. Enriching as it was, the steep climb was a bit of a strain for one of my weight.

At home, while I loved to read, my lax concentration barred me from doing so for very long.

In the Tyneside borough of Gateshead, above a vast concrete plane, stood the Metrocentre. Three years ago, seeing *Jurassic Park* with Dad, Granda Tait and John had introduced me to pitch-dark auditoriums and towering screens.

This year, Dad, John and I saw *Loch Ness*. Its lush scenery and Nessie-hunting staged gentle, wonder-flavoured drama. With Mam and James, we later saw the long-awaited film version of Roald Dahl's *James and the Giant Peach* (1961), a commendably faithful adaptation.

A new film lay on the horizon. Its poster showed a high-angle shot of New York, over which the sky was filled by a vast circular structure of what might have been stone. Its central point opened in huge doors, to emit a beam of white light. The object was mind-bogglingly big – could it possibly be some kind of spaceship?

"Might be good," said James as we passed the poster.

During Channel 4's broadcast of *Daleks: Invasion Earth 2150 AD* (1966), the advert reel included a preview of a new film with fifteen-mile-wide spaceships and exploding buildings. I asked Dad what this new film, *Independence Day*, was supposed to be about.

"It's about an alien invasion," he said.

I dearly hoped the BBFC would award it a classification permissive to one of my age. Alas, it was classified "12."

In Gateshead's Toys R Us, cardboard frames with a silvery *Independence Day* logo and a superimposed photo of a huge, crested, skeletal head, held clear, figurine-displaying boxes. In several were figurine specimens of the film's aliens; skeletal pelvis and insectoid legs mounted a huge, pointed head, which, at the pull of a rear lever, opened to reveal a small, jellyish biped. In their visceral weirdness, *Independence Day*'s aliens were awe-inspiring.

One night, Mam, Dad and James went to see the film and returned at around eleven. I raptly awaited their recount.

Mam and Dad had brought back some souvenirs – for John, a photo-illustrated storybook version of this year's film version of *James and the Giant Peach*, for me, a glossy softback release of

Doctor Who: The Script of the Film, and for both of us, Dionne McNeff's junior novelisation of *Independence Day*. While I eagerly read bits of it, my lax concentration wearied attempts to read it all the way through.

One afternoon at Barrowburn, Mam supposed that a stranger might be led to believe that I was twelve years old. While Mam fished, Dad, on the four-wheel motorbike, returned from the hills.

I approached and announced the long-awaited conclusion. Such was my excitement that I clumsily forgot to wait until he had finished speaking to Mam. While his reprimand was gentle, his utterance of the subject of my preoccupation, *Independence Day*, roused a twinge of fearful shame at my raucous imagination's vulgar demands.

It was decided that I should get a chance to try to see the film. Back home, Mam applied gel to my hair and lent me James's old denim jacket. Sometime later, I sat in the front seat of the Subaru alongside Dad.

Months ago, Mam had bought a CD, *Junior Party Mix*, and copied it onto cassette, which now played on the car stereo. A favourite track was a gently rousing ode to the benefits of going on holiday.

At the box office, Dad managed to persuade the ticket seller that my hiding behind his back wasn't due to me being underage.

After a reel whose trailers included those for *Chain Reaction* and *Star Trek: First Contact*, the screen blackened with the familiar BBFC insignia – only this time, a pink circle held a red number "12."

To David Arnold's softly awed score, the opening scene, on the moon, established a sense of fearful wonder at the mystery of outer space. Throughout the first twenty minutes, Jeff Goldblum and Bill Pullman, respectively familiar from *Jurassic Park* (1993) and *Casper* (1995), guided me through a frenetic build of political upheaval, mysterious satellite signals and giant spaceships.

"*This is where everything goes on fire*," whispered Dad as each City Destroyer readied its Primary Weapon.

Mam had been scared, James had said, when "they were operating on the alien." While I caught a glimpse of the huge, glistening skull, I didn't quite dare see it prised open to reveal the smaller alien's biomechanical cockpit of gooey tissue.

Will Smith's Captain Steven Hiller flew the crashed Attacker Ship into the vast, turquoise-lit interior of the orbiting Mother Ship, which Jeff Goldblum's David Levinson infected with a computer virus. I savoured a clear view of one of the small aliens, a translucent, glistening figure with Grey-esque almond-shaped eyes and a broad, tilted, disc-shaped cranium.

With tenderness, fearful awe, stunning spaceships and gooey aliens, the film was a glorious, forbidden thrill.

As we rode home through the night, I noted the aptness of Metro FM's airing of the Four Seasons' "Oh, What a Night."

Year Five

At the top of Garleigh Bank, on the edge of the village, the Middle School sat before the wilderness. At the back of the building's gloomy central hallway, the large Year Five classroom was divided by a windowed central wall. Behind this, Mrs Graham taught 5G. Before it, Mr Wood taught 5W.

I was in 5W. A tall, dark-haired man somewhere in his thirties, Mr Wood's deep, Estuary-sounding voice had a merry, bubbling quiver. On our first encounter, he met my raised hand with a surprised-sounding "hello!" Noticing my shark-shaped pencil case, he promptly seized one of its rubber teeth and frantically let go, as if bitten.

Still on friendly terms with Ellen Miller, I had the advantage of getting a lift with her mother up the steep Garleigh Bank.

At break times and in the lunch hour, I resumed my indiscriminate wanderings.

Mr Wood taught most of our lessons. For Science, he took us next door into the gloomy Science Lab. The tables, he warned, had borne spillage of potentially dangerous chemicals – after this class, we should always wash our hands.

For Maths, our classroom was overtaken by Mrs Bell, a small, stout Scotswoman with short, silvery blond hair. In our first lesson, my attempt to grasp the worksheet's numerical directions was like trying to pull a needle out of a soggy bale of hay whilst wearing boxing gloves. As ever, one number's pursuit of its fellows was instantly lost.

Near the lesson's end, I took my exercise book to Mrs Bell. She sadly surveyed my scant writings.

What could I tell her? That I wasn't very good at Maths? Surely a singular understatement – like an armadillo claiming not to be very good at mortgage broking. But wait – hadn't a few long-ago isolated incidents seen my successful apprehension of some basic sums? Could I really tell Mrs Bell in total, precise honesty that I wasn't very good at Maths? Or would such a statement hold a tiny hint of inaccuracy? If I knowingly spoke thusly, would I be guilty of lying? Was lying a sin? In cautious dread of sin, I chose a more general phrasal.

"I don't really... like Maths," I murmured.

This was safer – futile attempts to grasp the unfathomable were undeniably counterproductive to my contentment.

From her chair, Mrs Bell peered up at me.

"If you don't like Maths, then what *hope* is there for me?" she pleaded softly.

For Maths, seating arrangements were changed. Halfway through one lesson, I returned to my seat and was greeted by my neighbour, Anthea Heatley, with what seemed to be annoyance. I heatedly protested. Anthea retaliated. This exchange sowed a tradition of bickering that would recur throughout the next two years.

PE

A vast, L-shaped expanse of field bordered the school building's right and rear. The rightward field overlooked Cragside's miles of pine forest. Between the trees peeked a glimpse of the yellow stonework of stately Cragside House.

Behind the school, the broader stretch of field faced the distant, pine-crested mound of the Bilberry hills, beneath which lay the village.

Across these fields, PE lessons were held by portly, jovial Mr Logan, of whom James had spoken highly.

I wasn't very good at PE.

For one thing, PE lessons required a lot of running around. Throughout the school, while one or two kids had a mildly noticeable excess of flesh, I, by quite a distance, outweighed them all. When last I'd stood on a set of scales, they'd claimed me to weigh eighteen stone. Beneath my dark blue school jumper, my obese bulk swelled in a broadly rounded silhouette, but wasn't so obvious on the rest of my body. With my height and breadth, opined Uncle Ross, I carried my weight well.

My fear of getting hit in the face with any kind of ball further barred my PE ability. When a spherical, bouncing missile came anywhere near me, I, overwhelmed by dread of its potential violence, fled. I realised none of my classmates seemed to have such reservations.

My lax concentration rather dissuaded my receptivity to teamwork. In between avoiding balls, I would stand in a world of my own, letting my mind wander to themes more inspiring than whatever the National Curriculum currently sought of me.

Join in With the Other Children

As ever, at mid-morning break and lunchtime, I indiscriminately wandered the yard, stared vacantly ahead and randomly concocted fleeting, disjointed stories.

While most of my peers seemed to hold me in generally civil regard, some of their proffered conversation felt slightly... off. Classmate Len Wardle epitomised this. My replies to his functional pleasantries brightened his eyes with a knowing impudence. Sometimes, his jocularity heightened to an outright jibe.

Several older children took it upon themselves to talk to me. I could seldom be quite sure whether they sought genuine fellowship or secret amusement at my weight and introversion.

Jeff Howie, while outwardly civil, spoke with a bright-eyed mirth which seemed to offset his reception of my replies.

Dan Laidlaw's amiability seemed perfectly genuine.

Carla Limb seemed quite in earnest, but this implied something other than conversation – a conscientious effort to include the outsider.

Mrs Bell occasionally patrolled the yard. She peered amusedly down at me.

Didn't I want to join in?

To her smiling insistence that talking to people was pleasurable, I politely conceded. She assigned several of the aforementioned older children to make a point of talking to me, and returned for a satisfactory report that I was talking back.

Silly Voice

One morning, when Mr Wood took the register, Calvin Burcombe confirmed his presence with a comical pronunciation of the word "yes" – "yars."

Mr Wood stopped the register and solemnly demanded an explanation for "that silly noise."

Seconds passed. No explanation came.

Abruptly, the air was filled with Mr Wood's angry bellow.

"GET. OUT. *NOW*."

The sound shrank my insides with fear. I dreaded the thought of getting on the wrong side of this teacher. I wondered if anyone else reacted with such solemn dread as I did to a raised voice – perhaps I just had sensitive hearing.

Fancy

By the door, 5W had a small bookcase, stocked with youthfully geared fiction. Atop this, a miniature bookcase held thinner books. On several covers, a rectangular blue box, headed "Impact," held a genre designation. I was particularly drawn to those dubbed "horror."

Ritchie Perry's *Haunted House* (1994), sees Mr Bates, devastated to have just shot dead his wife and children, bewilderedly realise the house to have somehow made him do it. He then kills himself.

Next day, by the ambulance and police-surrounded house, teenage Maria learns of the recent murders. Maria scoffs at the idea of ghosts and is dared to go in. In broad daylight, she delves into the house.

Haunted House was one of the few books I ever read that genuinely unnerved me. Stephen Player's naturalistic, monochrome illustrations stoked the brooding menace.

In the plastic draw beneath my table, I kept the book for an extravagant while. Not only because I was riveted by the chilling story, but because I could barely stop looking at Maria. In the shadowed depths of the house, her soft features had an endearing vulnerability. While I shunned the thought of infatuation, Maria and her legs roused a soothing thrill.

"Are you *still* on that book?" hissed Anthea Heatley.

Following my introduction to *Doctor Who*, Dad heartily recalled *Star Wars*. I had some familiarity with it – throughout the early nineties, each Christmas Day, ITV's successive broadcasts had made a devotee of James.

This Christmas, Mam and Dad presented me with my own VHS copy of the first *Star Wars* (1977), later subtitled *Episode IV: A New Hope*. Happy to be included in its grand tradition, I watched.

Distantly recalled droids, zooming spaceships, deserts and lightsabers now came together in a thrilling yarn of tyranny and mystic powers. Perilous predicaments roused the heroes to a nervy intensity which somewhat daunted me – I instinctively feared to impose my feebleness and incompetence on such burdened toughness. Carrie Fisher's Princess Leia, with her blend of refined vulnerability and fierceness, was particularly daunting. I rather sympathised with C3P0 (Anthony Daniels), whom people kept telling to shut up.

1997

Promises to God

These last two years, my nervous, self-destructive tendency to guilt-inducing thoughts had necessitated such frequent, silent recitations as "I do not despise God."

This constant fear of guilt now drove me to pettily wholesome gestures – often picking up stray paper towels from the floor of the boys' toilets. Even a gesture of no obvious moral excellence – such as touching a table or opening a door in a certain way – offered redemption.

Urges to do so were accompanied by a silent voice which, while imagined, felt involuntary. It urged me to pursue any form of duty, however basic. I trusted it, in my fretful piety, to be the omnipresent voice of God. In my nervous quest for worthiness, I found myself forced to make a silent, involuntary promise, addressed to "God," that I would fulfil each compulsion. My compulsions, thus sanctified, offered splendid moral kudos – or should I break such a promise, grievous moral failure.

Destroy

James bought a second-hand Atari, a games console similar to the Commodore 64 he'd owned back in the eighties. The Atari took the form of a beige plastic keyboard, to be connected to a television set. The purchase came with a box of several floppy discs, which stored vintage computer games, including the legendary *Ghosts 'n Goblins* (1985).

I'd been cautioned against using the Atari to play my *Independence Day* Mission Discs. One afternoon, as John and I sat alone in James's bedroom, my rational judgement was overruled by a detached, audacious optimism.

On insertion of one of the blue-cased floppy discs, the Atari froze and became unresponsive.

On the day of the damage, James reserved his ire for when John and I were out of the room. Mam later told me he'd been sorely aggrieved, saying "why can't them two just... not destroy things?"

I received this with some disheartenment. In recent years, his amiably reflective rapport with me had relaxed and broadened.

I wondered what indeed had relaxed my senses of logic, caution and consideration.

Dad took the Atari to its supplier, who soon fixed it.

Storytelling

In his English class, Mr Wood introduced a definition of fairy tales as stories "with very good characters and very bad characters." He had us draw and annotate a character of our own invention, who was either very good or very bad. A villainess, he suggested, might be depicted with "a really tarty dress on..."

I drew an anthropomorphised golden Labrador, wearing a suit of armour. With a reserved smile, he surveyed the borders beyond my exercise book. I named him Silky.

We were then told to biograph our respective characters. My attempt at this never quite seemed to satisfy Mr Wood. With solemn urgency, he sought Silky's residence, acquaintances and lifestyle. In a house near a wood, I had Silky living with a wise old man. The more Mr Wood asked what life was like there, the more daunted I felt by further characterisation. In my exercise book, a frustrated comment referred to Silky by name. At address by disapproving authority, my conception of a kindly, unassuming, anthropomorphised dog felt chastised, my pretension to eloquence rebuked.

Mr Wood's English classes entailed communal reading of Christine Nostlinger's *Conrad the Factory Made Boy* (1975). Mr Wood would read some and frequently stop to select a student to take over. One day, Dale Harris hadn't been paying close enough attention.

"Where are we?" he murmured.

"What do you mean, 'where are we'?" said Mr Wood in smouldering indignation. The tension nearly suffocated me.

When my turn finally came, I clearly and enthusiastically emoted each line of dialogue. A delighted Mr Wood half-seriously suggested I take his place as lead reader.

While I'd been scared of his ferociously powerful shout, I came to appreciate Mr Wood's genuinely kind intent.

"He wants to be your friend," Dad advised, after one parents' evening.

At the back of *Conrad the Factory Made Boy* was a list of other books. Andrew Davies' *Conrad's War* (1978) concerned a boy keen on war, army, guns and killing.

I later found it in the school library. Conrad Pike is intermittently transferred to the Second World War, where he finds himself flying a Lancaster Bomber. Mindful of John's fascination with army type stuff, I rented and took the book home. We both ended up enjoying it hugely. Highly-strung, ambitious Conrad, his dozy father, dismissive mother, vomit-obsessed sister Florence and Towser the terrier wove a hilarious, emotionally layered story.

As we lay in our beds, I read it aloud to John. For Conrad's interrogation by a Nazi officer, I affected a German accent. In my delivery of his dialogue, I processed a tiny flicker of what felt like angry support. This was roused by the officer's imagined perspective, and not based on any views I'd ever had. However, I briefly guiltily feared that I'd condemned my fellow nationals.

One evening, as I entered the kitchen, Mam, with fond amusement, said John had been "singing your praises, Andy."

This slightly relieved my general fear that I might fall from grace with God. However, my guilt-ridden adherence to my compulsive promises prevailed.

Miss Hammond, who'd taught James the piano since he was seven, also had some experience in Maths teaching. It was decided that I might benefit thereby.

Each Friday evening, when seven o'clock neared, Dad drove me up the sloping main road, a little way out of the village, and to a tree-shaded recess where stood the tutor's small house.

Aged around mid-fifties, Miss Hammond kept a dog, a cat and a poster chart of British spiders. Warmly dry and understatedly affectionate, she would later put me in mind of a female Terry Pratchett. With tireless guidance, Miss Hammond actually enabled me to grasp some basic equations. She discreetly opined to my parents that I might have dyscalculia, the mathematical equivalent of dyslexia.

On Friday evenings, BBC One aired repeats of *The Black Adder*. While the humour didn't yet fully register with me, I was glad to join my family in further acquaintance with a saga which had shaped James's childhood.

Before the sprawling edifice of what we proudly knew to be Alnwick Castle, the power-hungry fumbling of Rowan Atkinson's Prince Edmund, with the cunning aid of Tony Robinson's Baldrick and the not-so-cunning aid of Tim McInnerny's Lord Percy, offered a disarmingly frivolous affirmation of the human struggle.

Blackadder II and *Blackadder the Third*, with more emphasis on Edmund Blackadder's withering similes, examined a sympathetically struggling yet ruthless schemer. As I began to grasp the humour, I found myself laughing very hard indeed at his emboldening ruthlessness.

Seahouses

In several weeks' time, Year Five would spend four nights at a hostel in the coastal village of Seahouses. My attendance seemed clearly unfeasible – I still couldn't fall asleep unless lying in bed alongside my mother.

Dad wondered if I could travel to the hostel each day, without having to spend the night. This turned out to be easily manageable.

At the end of the first day, I was directed back to the minibus.

"Your carriage awaits!" laughed Mr Wood.

One warm, overcast morning, the class processed in loose huddles through Seahouses. Behind me, a jar of novelty green slime was passed around. Adele Brogden made a point of casually wiping her slimy hand on the back of my anorak.

In a darkened museum corridor, behind a red rope, stood a wooden boat, the *Grace Darling*.

Further on, a wide, brightly lit area housed an expansive, open-roofed tank, about two feet high. Its clear water held several living shapes, mostly stingrays, but also, I marvelled, a dogfish. Its thin snout had a sore-looking red blotch.

The class was escorted to a region of rugged coast and given forms to fill in. The low, locally accented voice of Mr Foggon, Technology teacher, imparted lengthy instruction.

I raised my hand and requested a point of clarification.

"If you'd *listened*…" Mr Foggon said wearily.

I winced.

I saw little of the Seahouses hostel, other than its living room. Lack of windows lent a peaceful gloom, complemented by bluish walls. On entering, the central far wall bulged forth in a rectangular lintel, which held an open fireplace.

However, when I entered the next day, the far wall, including the ceiling-high lintel and the hollow of the fireplace, appeared not to be across the room but fixed to the wall by the door through which I'd entered.

Next day, the lintel and fireplace appeared to be back on the far wall.

Carefully guarded against fancy, I noted this incongruity with utter, confounded perplexity. It looked exactly as if the room had been seamlessly rearranged overnight. Throughout the whole trip, I found no explanation.

Never Survive at School

One morning, after PE, Mr Logan had several of the class sit on the wooden stage of the assembly hall. While the rest of us looked on, Mr Logan warned this band of miscreants that they were unlikely to "survive" at school. Wary of Mr Logan's solemn ire, I was smugly glad to have evaded it.

However, several days later, after another PE lesson, Mr Logan approached me in the empty hall. I hadn't realised the class had been meant to assemble on the field as opposed to in here. Year Six, Mr Logan told me, involved several classes in various classrooms. It was probable, he warned, that I wouldn't manage to "survive" Year Six.

Sorely humbled, I wondered what he wanted me to do. Pay closer attention, I supposed – exercise greater self-discipline in my attendance of instruction. The old song – *"listen!"*

Teachers generally seemed to feel that, with brusque encouragement, I would be able to force myself to listen. I wondered why I alone seemed to need such correction – why I couldn't force myself to stop being hungry, couldn't force myself not to be scared of minor things and couldn't pay attention. While supposedly traceable to bad habit and laziness, the impairment remained a mystery.

Belief

Sometimes, on reflection, I found myself to lack an assured persuasion of the actual existence of God. This worried me intensely. The concept of God embodied goodness, imbued existence with eternity, and thereby rendered immutable all worthy aspiration.

One evening, I steeled myself to tell Mam of my concern – the subject, with its ceremony and reverence, was delicate. With some amused surprise, Mam spoke reassuringly. Like James, she acknowledged the religion of our heritage, albeit informally. Her belief in its actuality, she said, sometimes wavered.

Around this time, it was finally accepted that the largest bedroom, currently occupied by James, would be more suited to a share between John and me.

Shortly after moving in, I found, on the large shelf above where James's bed had been, a large hardback – *The Illustrated Children's Bible*. Its bare, brown cover held an etching of a roughly hewn wooden cross.

To my relief, I found myself able to believe its simple account of God's separation of light from darkness.

Science Fiction

With John still at the First School, Mam took him to its occasional book fair and brought me back a surprise – a paperback, whose cover showed a night sky, before which a young boy stared up at a looming, orbital egg.

In Robert Swindells' *World-Eater* (1983), eleven-year-old pigeon breeder Orville Copperstone deduces a new planet to be some kind of giant egg. The global effort to avert a gestating space predator's apocalyptic breakfast was staged with thrilling solemnity. Bullied, anxious Orville made for a touching protagonist.

Late at night, with John long having fallen asleep, I read random excerpts – I couldn't quite force my concentration to grasp, in successive order, different scenes.

The Rothbury Library now offered for rent a selection of videos. From an issue of *SFX*, I recognised the 1953 version of *The War of the Worlds*.

"Oh, that's brilliant!" said Steven Bridget, on a class trip to the library. "They breathe human air and die."

Another video held the final three episodes of *Doctor Who* serial *The Daleks* (1963).

Back home, it introduced me to *Doctor Who*'s black and white origins – telly from when Mam and Dad were little. Its slow pace wove a brooding tale of nuclear devastation and ethnic cleansing. I savoured the domed, faceless, gliding Daleks. To William Hartnell's sternly horrified Doctor and Carole Ann Ford's fretful Susan, they ranted of their determination to nuke the pacifist Thals.

The War of the Worlds, in sumptuous technicolour, wove a tale of hovering death machines, glistening Martians and, in Earth's ecosystem's conquest of the invaders, a hint of divine purpose. Dad told me the film was based on a book – it was by HG Wells, writer of *The Time Machine* (1895). I was intrigued. It was arranged for Aunty Jess, on one of her Newcastle visits, to get me a copy.

One Saturday afternoon, as John and I re-watched the *Are You Afraid of the Dark?* episode *The Tale of the Hatching*, Jess came in with a copy of *The War of the Worlds* (1898). Thrilled,

I delved into it. While reverently fascinated, my brief concentration often murked my grasp of the narration.

Dad also mentioned *Jeff Wayne's Musical Version of The War of the Worlds* (1978). From one of their Thursday night shopping trips, Mam and Dad brought me back a cassette copy. Mike Trim's awesome cover illustration, in which a Martian Fighting Machine zaps the ironclad *Thunder Child*, showed the original Martian killing machines to be giant, three-legged vehicles.

I put the tape into my Walkman and was instantly enamoured – an ominously cataclysmic score, with Richard Burton's brooding narration, presented the story in clear, doom-laden awe.

Offered a cheap order by a new catalogue, Mam, as a small surprise, got me *The Ultimate Encyclopaedia of Science Fiction* (1995). On its numerous articles, I feasted. Comprehensive commentary, written in bite-size chunks, was perfectly suited to me.

My tenth birthday fell on the final day of term. In replacement for last year's trampoline, for which my weight had proved a bit too much, Mam and Dad had got me a new one.

From James, I unwrapped a video of the 1974 *Doctor Who* serial *Death to the Daleks*.

For school, as a parting gift to Mr Wood, Mam supplied me with four cans of beer.

That afternoon, my old acquaintance and fellow school passenger Ellen joined us for Action Man birthday cake and assorted tasties. With John, we watched the opening episode of *Death to the Daleks*.

"False rock!" said Ellen, of a boulder which suddenly fell towards Jon Pertwee's Third Doctor.

While Ellen was always good company, inclusion in my home life of a schoolmate felt a bit exhausting. As the bright evening slowly dimmed, I felt a strange, weary sadness.

With its surprise boon of Dalek action, James's splendid present introduced me to 1970s *Doctor Who*. Jon Pertwee's stern yet warmly genial Third Doctor and Elisabeth Sladen's nervy, plucky Sarah Jane Smith underwent a solemn adventure, with danger, destruction and wildly ambitious concepts. The black-eyed Exxilons bore a satisfying resemblance to the Greys.

From the Metrocentre, James acquired a newly released VHS of the first three episodes of an old favourite of his – Rob Grant and Doug Naylor's BBC2 science fiction sitcom *Red Dwarf*. I distantly recalled, from the smooth grey walls of a spaceship set, an argument between two identical men.

To John and me, James recalled the mining ship *Red Dwarf*'s vending machine cleaners Arnold Rimmer (Chris Barrie) and Dave Lister (Craig Charles). One day, a radiation leak kills all of the crew except Lister, frozen in a stasis booth. Ship computer Holly (Norman Lovett) brings Rimmer back as a hologram. Together with Cat (Danny John-Jules), a life form who evolved from Lister's cat, they all try to get back to Earth. One evening, with James, we sat down to watch.

Rimmer and Lister's lively bickering, detachedly dry computer Holly and jovially egomaniacal Cat evoke the dry whimsy of *Blackadder*. I laughed heartily.

In the face of such odds as Future Echoes, hallucinogenic mutant pneumonia and the unfathomable isolation of deep space, the dysfunctional crew has a robust camaraderie. Lister's infatuation with, and attempt to revive as a hologram, Clare Grogan's Kristine Kochanski, offered a forbidden, touching glimpse of adult tenderness.

Computer

As James neared his GCSE exams, it was decided that a personal computer might be a worthy investment. From a shop in Alnwick, Dad bought a Windows 95. On a rickety old wooden table with a wooden bench, it was installed in the corner of our upstairs landing.

Drumnadrochit

In the northern Scottish village of Drumnadrochit, by Loch Ness, the five of us, as well as Nana, would spend five nights. This would be the longest John and I had been away from home. The idea of going to Loch Ness, with its cryptozoological reputation, was fantastic.

The journey lasted about five hours. On my Walkman, *Jeff Wayne's Musical Version of The War of the Worlds* sustained me for much of the way. I often switched off to listen to, on the car stereo, the soundtrack of the 1996 West End version of Tim Rice and Andrew Lloyd Webber's *Jesus Christ Superstar*, whose symphonic richness and raw emotion paid heartfelt tribute to the Gospels.

A vibrantly bustling village, Drumnadrochit lay in a serene backdrop of steep, rugged hills and lush forestry. Atop a steep bank lay a district of holiday chalets. Inside ours, sunshine lit freshly scented light brown walls. Through French windows, a small garden overlooked, leftward, the forested hills, and rightward, bits of the village, bordered by the silvery surface of the enormous loch.

While I shared a double bed with John, I, as at home, had to wait to swap sleeping arrangements with Dad before I could get to sleep. As I got up the next day, Dad, James and John would return from the village, with talk of the misty air's peace and refreshment. I regretfully pondered my ineptitude at early rising.

The vibrant village held two Nessie museums, each with a looming replica of the legendary monster. One bright day, Dad took John and me on a boat tour of the loch. With his usual effortless zest, Dad conversed with the driver.

On more relaxed afternoons, I lounged in the chalet's living room, patio or in my bedroom.

I was occasionally troubled by realisations that my imagination, for the moment, seemed to lack an assured persuasion of the existence of God.

One early afternoon, I entered mine and John's small bedroom. I forcibly calmed my mind, disclaimed any conceptual or emotional persuasion and fell forward onto the bed. With some satisfaction, I currently seemed not to register conviction of the absence of God.

A twenty-minute drive back down the road took us to Inverness, from whose Waterstones I bought Jonathan Gems' novelisation of his screenplay for *Mars Attacks*.

The chalet had a guest book. Towards the end of our stay, Dad and James each wrote an entry. I saw a previous entry to be accompanied by a small drawing of the Loch Ness Monster. With my entry, I included a similar illustration.

On sight of my contribution, Mam was shocked.

"It's not a picture book," echoed Dad, solemnly.

"Spoiled that woman's nice book," said Mam.

Horrified, I feebly sought dignity with an attempt at indignant protest. I retreated to mine and John's bedroom and sobbed. Soon enough, Mam came in, apologised and reassured me that Dad would get some Tipp-Ex from the newsagent's.

Come *On*, Andrew! *Do* – *Get* – *That* Finished!

Two classrooms, divided by a thin, doored wall, housed Year Six.

The furthermost class, 6BL, was taught by Mr Logan. Mine, 6DK, was taught by Mrs Kilburn. Short, wavy dark grey hair framed large, tinted spectacles. Her vowels rose in an Estuary-sounding twang. At the start of term, she and Mr Logan explained the joint classroom situation, and that the two of them sometimes liked to "have a cuddle." In demonstration, they staged a loose embrace.

Mrs Kilburn had both joviality and easy, urgent authority. Her serious indignation, she forewarned, would be heralded not by shouting, but by a low-voiced restraint of her wrath. Graffiti on homework diaries – such, she said, as "Calvin loves Lorna forever" – was forbidden.

Most lessons were held here in the form classroom. Science and Information Technology were taught respectively in the Science lab and IT block, albeit by Mrs Kilburn, and Technology was taught in the Technology room by Mr Foggon.

In the form classroom, I once more found myself seated beside Anthea Heatley.

On failure to grasp Mrs Kilburn's instructions, I was often reduced to glancing at my hostile neighbour's work, in search of clues as to what I was meant to be doing. While I was slightly ashamed to do so, this was the only alternative to asking for further instruction.

My unwholesome tactic fuelled Anthea's assertions of my ridiculousness. She seemed to trace my stupidity to maleness. I, she snarled, lacked a *"brain* to *think* with!"

While severe irritation fuelled my dismissal of Anthea's jibes, a meek humiliation held her contempt to be just. I was indeed fat. My inability to grasp instruction did indeed seem out of place. Did both stem from ill-discipline?

An episode of ITV's *You've Been Framed* prefaced a montage of comedic home videos with a display of a boy and girl in school uniform, the former with his tie at half mast, the latter dressed neatly.

Host Jeremy Beadle declared girls to usually do better in education. Boys, he added, were typically more suited to such adventure as depicted in the following scenes of all-male buffoonery, set to Deniece Williams' "Let's Hear it for the Boy."

While I loathed claims that maleness was less suited to intellect than femaleness, I dreaded that they might amount to more than chivalry. While Anthea's bluster held no fear, the fineness of her features, lightness of voice and softness of hair lent her wrath a humblingly earnest bravado.

Much of the work was still, to me, barely comprehensible. I typically worked very slowly, often because I didn't fully understand what to do. As I worked on the monotonous tasks, my mind was inclined to stall. To stare into the distance offered soothing relief from the burden of concentration. The overheated classroom, and lack of sleep, lulled me further.

Mrs Kilburn frequently swept down to level her face with mine.

"Come *on*, Andrew," she urged, "*do – get – that* finished!"

If I asked for guidance on how to "get that finished," I supposed, Mrs Kilburn would realise that I hadn't listened to her instructions. She'd wonder at my laziness, my obstinacy, and my inattentiveness. She'd try to dissuade me from such behaviour. She'd almost certainly be cross. She might even raise her voice. I lived in instinctive dread of the tumultuous fright and humiliation of chastisement, of teachers' lamentation of their persecution with my uncooperativeness.

Over in the newly refurbished Music block, Mrs Kilburn, in preparation for a statistical exercise, asked how many dogs people had. Keen to show support for dogs, I mentioned my father's work-based custody of five sheepdogs.

Mrs Kilburn then more formally repeated the query to each student. When my turn came, I began a repeat of my earlier description. Halfway through my conversationally worded offer, Mrs Kilburn interrupted.

"HELLO! AN-DREW!" she yelled, not quite at the top of her voice. "ARE YOU WITH THE *HUMAN RACE?*"

While jovially exaggerated, her volume and fierceness staggered me. The query was, she explained less loudly, in search of pet ownership.

Cartoons

Granda Tait, who came over to babysit on Thursday evenings when Mam and Dad went shopping, shared mine and John's enthusiasm for the channel Cartoon Network, his favourite being *Batman: The Animated Series*.

"By, he can fairly sort 'em!"

In the living room, with Mam in the kitchen and Dad not having yet returned from Barrowburn, John and I watched Nickelodeon and Cartoon Network.

Dexter's Laboratory saw the frustrations of its eponymous boy genius (voiced by Christine Cavanaugh). While Dexter's egotism and petulance, somewhat dispiritingly, implied partial justification of his persecution by sister Deedee (voiced by Allison Moore), the show acknowledged the vulnerability of its hero, and relentlessly tantalised my desire to see him come out on top for a change.

Nelvana's adaptation of *Beetlejuice* (1988), with its titular spectral prankster (voiced by Stephen Ouimette) and softly-spoken goth Lydia (voiced by Alyson Court), merged madcap whimsy with genuine tenderness.

Around this time of day, a slow, distant crash of the front door announced Granda Widdrington.

"Hello," came his heavy voice.

Granda drifted into the room and lowered himself into the armchair opposite the door.

"What sort o' day y' had today, then?"

He might lament the chaotic brutality of the modern world, how some bastards or other just wanted bloody shot, or the devastating inevitability of mortality. After a protracted silence and a look of weary sorrow, his low voice rose to an almost musical note of resignation.

"By, it's hellish when you get old," he said. Youth, he warned, would be washed away by the sea of time on which we fecklessly sailed.

On his arrival, if a cartoon happened to be on the telly, I grew increasingly reluctant to allow its exposure. In a room ruled by Granda Widdrington, the telly's fanciful, emotive sights and sounds felt a vulgar intrusion. Memory of his playful scorn for such frivolity warned me that I ought not to let it pester this ancient, life-hardened figure.

New Year's Eve

Mam and I still had yet to discard our custom of sleeping in the same bed. Without the reassuring completion of Mam's arrival in my bed, the quest for sleep would be fearful and elusive.

New Year's Eve saw a reiteration of Mam's occasional weary frustration.

1998

Bed

As the year dawned, I tentatively aimed to have several nights in bed alone. To my mild amazement, I found myself falling asleep without incident, albeit usually around one o'clock in the morning. To Mam's undoubted relief, I managed to keep this up.

The Illustrated Children's Bible

Unsure whether the scriptures actually prescribed weekly attendance of church, I began to read a portion, each Sunday, of *The Illustrated Children's Bible*.

Downstairs, beneath the living room windowsill, lay a Gideon's New Testament, one of which, in the 1970s, had been presented to each member of Uncle Gordon's class. Here, I read Jesus's citation of the two greatest commandments: "Love the Lord your God with all your heart, all your soul and with all your mind... love your neighbour as yourself" (*Matthew 22: 35–40*).

I sometimes feared my failure to obey the first of these – to the being described in *The Illustrated Children's Bible*, I felt no intense emotional attachment. With no access to such analysis as offered by CS Lewis's *Mere Christianity* (1952), which urges the aspiration to act lovingly rather than to try to force emotion, I could only offer urgent reverence.

Dance

One afternoon, Mrs Kilburn, along with a visiting Mr Logan, lent an afternoon lesson to one of their prolonged, informal discussions.

"What about you, Andrew," said Mr Logan with a playful smile, "who do you fancy?"

"Nobody," I said truthfully.

With a broadening grin, Mr Logan wondered if I was sometimes known as Hot Lips Tait, a title as perverse to me as it was revolting. Sexuality, with its messy, brazen flamboyance, was among the least dignified things I could imagine.

Mrs Kilburn and Mr Logan concluded that my not fancying anyone was due to my having "never had a cuddle."

They resolved to amend this here and now. With genuine trepidation, I asked them not to. Grinning remorselessly, the two teachers hurried towards my chair. Ensnaring each of my shoulders with their arms, they pressed their torsos against my head.

Several mornings a week, the two Year Six classes were herded into the assembly hall, where, under Dinner Nanny Mrs Baines, Mrs Kilburn and Mr Logan led us in Country Dance. While I abhorred its brazen grandeur, obligation made it relatively endurable.

Dual partnerships, however, were worse. Assigned to Ellen, the degrading evocation of romance stifled my movement. Mr Logan wearily bemoaned my determination not to join in.

Mrs Kilburn, at the start of last term, had told us of her legal prohibition from, bar emergencies, bodily contact with any of us.

As the class now pranced in a leaping procession, Mrs Kilburn, positioned behind me, saw me take a wrong turn. By way of steering, she swiftly smacked me around the back and chest.

Diet

Having, throughout First School, undergone food limitation programmes advised by magazines, my torso remained mountainous as ever. Apparently, diets – or at least those I'd tried – didn't work.

At the village surgery, Dad booked me an appointment with Dr Allan. A tall, silver-haired man with a Standard English accent and gently jocular smile, he prescribed me something rather more specific – a prohibition of certain nutrients.

For weeks, I adhered. Then, one Friday evening, I slipped.

Mam and Dad had been shopping at the Morpeth branch of Lidl and had bought several pots of chicken and mushroom flavour Snack With Noodles – a favourite of mine. Noodles, bits of chicken, sweetcorn and croutons were all ready at the boil of a kettle – and, unlike Pot Noodles, no peas. However, my new diet forbade some of their content.

Since I'd been so good, Mam supposed a mild breach wouldn't hurt this once.

Next morning, I awoke feeling queasy. In the kitchen, this worsened to a bout of nausea. I hurried to the kitchen sink but could only retch.

At some point in the next few seconds, conscious awareness left me.

I woke up and realised I was lying on the floor by the sink. I was vaguely worried to hear Mam sobbing. The voice of Granda Widdrington was sternly reassuring her.

"But my little Andy's never done anything like that before!" sobbed Mam.

Granda, it seemed, had caught me just as I'd fainted.

With Mam reassured – and advised by Granda against "bloody diets" – she told me to relax in the living room and "put Stanley Ipkiss on."

As suggested, I watched the first twenty minutes of my video of *The Mask* (1994).

Indecent Exposure

Outside the school back door, I queued for lunch. Several places ahead of me, Arnold Ainsley and Mark Cowens amused themselves with irreverent aspersions on my masculinity.

To rebut their derision, I decided on a new approach.

I would wield an audacious gesture whose irreverence would pale theirs.

I could offer proof, I retorted, that I wasn't, as they claimed, a girl.

I unzipped my fly, reached into my underpants and... well, you get the idea.

Mark and Arnold reacted with amused incredulity. My point proven, I sheathed my secret weapon.

Later in the lunch break, I was approached by several older students, who requested a repeat of my spectacular gesture. It was a simple request, and they meant no obvious harm, so I complied.

A few minutes later, one of the Dinner Nannies summoned me to the school office. Overwhelmed with fear, I prepared an unconditional surrender.

Behind the office desk was North-West-accented Mr Ledstone, with whom I was on agreeable terms. In Year Five, he'd approached me at break times and asked how James was doing.

He now calmly noted what had been brought to his attention. I gibbered a denouncement of my reckless stupidity.

He solemnly explained that such behaviour was in fact against the law. While seemingly assured that I wouldn't do it again, he had no choice but to report the incident to Mr Henderson.

Back home, I told Mam what I'd done. Solemnly shocked, she confessed her surprise.

"What the hell did you go and do a stupid thing like that for?" said James. He later approached me with an apology for his sharpness.

Two days later, after assembly, to locally accented Mr Henderson, I stressed my repentance, which seemed to appease him.

However, my place in school folklore was cemented. For years to come, easy sport was ready-made in a request for my confirmation of the time I'd... well, you get the idea.

The Seventh Doctor

While five nights' lack of sleep usually compelled me to sleep through UK Gold's Sunday *Doctor Who* omnibus, I had, this last month, caught some of Sylvester McCoy's first season.

Having aired in 1987, the year of my birth, it had a thrilling modernity. Across a black background, metallic closing credits flashed amidst the shivering chimes of a synthesised version of the theme tune. Beneath them swirled a purple CGI galaxy, through which tumbled the blue block of the TARDIS. At the credits' end, sleekly squared letters spun around to form a silver, red-glowing "WHO." Above them, in a streak of CGI gold, appeared a loopy, diagonal "*Doctor*."

In the second half of the four-episode serial *Paradise Towers*, I became more closely acquainted with Sylvester McCoy's Seventh Doctor. While recognisable from the TV Movie, his wavy dark hair was shorter and topped by a Panama hat. A genial sense of fun offset his solemn, excitable urgency. His merrily lilting, Scots-flavoured Standard English and distant, impassioned gaze embodied the mysterious danger I'd first scented in the title of *Doctor Who*.

What was more, this era of the show was closer to television as I knew it – faster pacing, a more colloquial range of diction – such as Sophie Aldred's Estuary-accented Ace – synthesised music and digital animation. I looked forward to seeing the Seventh Doctor face the Daleks...

In the living room, I found John watching UK Gold. This week's *Doctor Who* serial, now in its fourth and final episode, was *Remembrance of the Daleks* (1988). High above the Coal Hill School yard descended the Imperial Dalek Shuttlecraft. A square hunk of beige metal, the model's bulk hinted slightly but noticeably more advanced effects work than earlier serials.

In the school, over the shuttle's roar, Sylvester McCoy's Seventh Doctor bellowed at Sophie Aldred's Ace to get away from the window, which soon shattered. His urgency cautioned my thrill at this near-modern Doctor's contest with the Daleks – any hint of ire deterred my sense of fun.

Out of the shuttle hatch, onto brightly daylit streets, glided the Imperial Daleks. Gleaming white with golden limbs, these models were bulkier than their forebears.

The bluish grey, similarly smooth Renegade Daleks met them in battle. From gunsticks flew jets of respectively green and amber fire which, with stunning explosions, smacked into Daleks left and right.

The Seventh Doctor discreetly aids the Imperial Daleks' capture of the Hand of Omega. In the school basement, via a rigged television, he contacts the Dalek Mothership and goads Davros (Terry Molloy) into using the Hand on Skaro's sun, which, instead of becoming a source of unimaginable power, explodes.

I found myself feeling quite sorry for the panicked, ranting Davros.

Special Needs

One hot afternoon in Mrs Kilburn's classroom, I stared at a sheet of mathematical instructions. While the rest of the class buzzed with chatter, I had even less idea than usual of what to do.

When the sheet's allocated session finished, Mrs Kilburn addressed the class in mention of a task everyone else had apparently completed, but with which I was totally unfamiliar.

As the general chatter resumed, I approached Mrs Kilburn and meekly explained that on the day of the task just mentioned, I must have been absent.

The task to which Mrs Kilburn referred, she now told me with a yell, was the one she'd just given the class half an hour to complete. While delivered with her comically affected wail, the lament held no mirth. Staggered with fright and numbed with shame, I returned to my seat.

Promise

In *The Illustrated Children's Bible*, I read a simplification of the story of Samson. Cutting his long hair, he explains, would break his promise to God, and he would therefore lose his miraculous strength.

I dreaded the prospect of such a moral burden as having dishonoured a pledge to God. When my fretful imagination urged me to make a promise to God, I made sure to keep it. One lunch hour, having promised to remain in the same spot until the bell rang, I spent twenty minutes standing on a manhole cover outside the Information Technology block.

From some of these sanctified obligations, I devised ways of freeing myself. When compelled to make a promise, I added to my mental vow the word "perhaps." If I promised only the possibility of my doing something, I reasoned, then I wasn't obliged to go through with it.

At the far end of the school, in a long, gloomy workshop, Thursday afternoons saw what used to be called Woodwork lessons but were now called Technology lessons.

At the start of each lesson, Mr Foggon said something about our current task and let us get on with it.

Several weeks since he'd assigned it, I still didn't know what it was. Something to do with sheets of plywood. Mr Foggon's mention of each implement had failed to correlate in my understanding and instead registered as a drone of gobbledegook. At the time, I hadn't asked for further instruction; he'd surely be cross that I hadn't listened. I dreaded to think how he'd react if I asked for further instruction now.

As the weather warmed and brightened, Year Six neared its end. One Technology lesson, I, as usual, wandered aimlessly between the workbenches. Across the bare floor lay numerous chips of sawn wood – which a familiar, fretful urgency drove me to constantly rearrange. I kept promising God that I would, with my foot, shift bits of wood into particular positions.

I pondered my intrusive, tedious task. Surely my classmates lacked such hindrance. I now devised a means to evade the endlessly repeated obligation. I made a promise to God that from now on, the only objects I would kick would be footballs.

Throughout the next few weeks, I reflected that, for the rest of my life, if I kicked any other object than a football, I would bear the guilt of dishonouring a commitment to God. The prospect of a lifelong burden, and the threat of lifelong guilt, began to rouse in me an intense, mournful dread. One afternoon, I feared that I may have already broken my sacred promise. My despondence began to show.

In the living room, Mam asked what troubled me.

Mention of my reverence of God was somehow embarrassing; I felt both as if I were intruding on something too important for me and spouting frivolous fancy.

"I'm... frightened of God," I paraphrased meekly. I was burdened by a lifelong commitment, I explained, and by fear that I may have already broken it.

Mam confidently dismissed my need to worry.

"God likes nice little boys like you," she said. Her confidence, for tonight, alleviated my sorrowful fretting. "You should put a nice film on," she soothed, "a film of your choice."

We watched James's old *Ghostbusters* video. While I found comfort in its lifelong fellowship, at the edge of my mood, sorrowful guilt continued to fester.

Each day, over the next few weeks, my mood sank into miserable, guilt-ridden worry. The memory of my promise refused to let me be.

On my first few entreaties for reassurance, Mam managed to console me.

John, often present when I confided in Mam, would chant in a mockingly prim, high-pitched voice, "rel-igious boy! Be good for God!" Any fear of divine retribution, he tried to reassure me, was baseless, as his deliberately blasphemous utterances failed to incur any lightning bolts.

Mam now introduced to John and me a prayer she'd learned when attending middle school at the Alnwick Convent. While not formally religious, she soothed me with an account of the power of prayer to clear the mind and urged me away from promises to God. Inwardly, I automatically promised not to promise.

"If you've got a problem," said Mam, sitting close by me on my bed, "don't keep it bottled up, because then it becomes ten times worse."

I promise I won't, my mind's voice promptly pledged.

Next day, I found myself compelled to make another promise, thus breaking a promise to my own mother and resulting in another attack of conscience.

I'd never known anything quite like this relentless, fearful remorse. It swamped me in boiling, helpless misery. I therefore defined it as depression. I was depressed, I told myself.

One morning, a wave of guilty sorrow drove me to ask Mrs Kilburn if I might be allowed to visit the office and ask to go home. As a faint strain gripped my torso, I could honestly say I wasn't feeling very well.

Mrs Kilburn acknowledged me to look a bit under the weather. My face was blotched red – although that might have been at least partly due to the hot day and overheated classroom.

I went to the school office and asked if I might be allowed to go home, as I was feeling "stressed."

"Ooh, you don't get stressed at your age!" said school administrator Mrs Chiswick with an encouraging smile. I left the office.

With the lesson over, my classmates poured into the hallway. I passed them with the ignominy of a crumpled face but was well past the point of caring.

"What's the *matter*, Andrew?" crooned Len Wardle with a look of concern so pained as to seem genuine.

Depressed

Over the next few weeks, I repeatedly sought consolation from my parents.

"Nothing is gonna happen to you if you break a promise," said Mam desperately.

I feared not divine retribution, but the burden of obscene guilt I'd have to carry for the rest of my days.

That evening, we rode up to the joint two fields in which Granda Widdrington and Uncle Ross kept several cows. Beneath a hot blue sky, well-nourished grass gleamed with daisies. Behind the others, I dragged my heavy frame up the sloping field.

"Nothing is gonna happen to wor Andy," said Mam. Encouraged by the robust endorsement, I could almost believe I could stop worrying.

Back home, as we sat on the sofa, Mam held me close for several minutes and whispered reassurance as my sobbing subsided.

"Have I broken my promise to God?" I whispered.

"No," whispered Mam.

Ultimately, Mam was powerless to relieve me of my guilt. On its driving of my mother to despair, my guilt feasted.

Professional counsel, Mam seemed to feel, would be a terrible thing to have to resort to. If we took that path, she said, "you'll go to doctor after doctor," only to be referred, eventually, to a psychiatrist. Without exaggeration, the idea seemed to genuinely frighten her. A lifetime of listening to Granda Widdrington, I suppose, who scorned "bloody quacks."

"I," said Dad gently, "think God is another word for nature."

"It's just a *belief* to comfort people, son," urged Granda Widdrington. "Some people worship the *sun*; some people worship the *moon*..."

Mam, with renewed calmness, argued that I was taking religion too seriously for someone of my age.

After a temporarily soothing talk with Mam and Granda, I resolved to present to the world a demeanour more befitting a ten-and-three-quarters-year-old. I forced an approximation of carefree glee, filled my XP65 Super Soaker, took it onto our small, concrete back yard and, in hearty squirts of boyish innocence, discharged the liquid ammunition.

I soon realised what a cheap attempt to fool myself this was.

At my age, in the 1940s, Granda Widdrington had run wild with his brothers and friends, fighting, footballing and playing such tricks as teaching a parrot to say "dorty bastard" or, from atop a tree, urinating onto the head of an unsuspecting priest.

"You'll hang, Neville!" the cleric had warned. Issues of conscience and religion, I supposed, had been as far from the ten-year-old Granda's mind as the computer games against whose ill he now warned me.

I, on the other hand, was fat. I was overwhelmed by fear at the prospect of getting hit in the face with a ball. I couldn't seem to force myself to listen to school instruction. And now, I devised worries whose insolubility drove my mother to despair. Some kind of innate or deeply ingrained tendency seemed to steer me away from common standards of acceptability, a retreat from certain forms of logic. As I desperately yearned for some kind of absolution, I could only blindly wonder what was wrong with me.

Daily, the guilt lingered. Its unamenable ache would occasionally flare to burning, desperate misery.

One bright afternoon, we had one of our occasional drives to Lordenshaws, a smoothly rounded hill which loomed above the village. As the purple Frontera sped past climbing sunlit fields, the thrill of travel lifted my mood to a point where I could envision indefinite relief from guilt. I numbly realised, however, my inevitable reacquaintance with my iniquity.

In the heat of July, Mrs Kilburn handed out end-of-year reports. By this point, the passage of time had begun to persuade me that my pangs of guilt might eventually wear off.

The report addressed my ineptitude in almost every subject but English, where, Mrs Kilburn said, I had "no real weaknesses."

However, her closing comments noted my reclusiveness and my tendency to "totally ignore others." She closed with a prescription for me to "begin to conform a little more to basic requirements of social living."

St James's Church, Morpeth, was to host a performance of the King Edward VI school choir. While sitting through the whole thing might require some discipline on my part, I decided to attend – any outward venture offered diversion from my sorrowful fear.

"It's a bit like a reverse of the TARDIS, this church, Andy," said Dad as we took a pew. "It's smaller on the inside!"

In the soft, stone gloom, amidst the service and choral performances, my fearful guilt lay in a numb ache.

At one point, after a lapse of conscious awareness, I found myself lying on the floor beneath the pew – I'd fainted again.

Dad drove us to Ashington Hospital, where, after a brief examination by a kindly smiling young doctor, I was given sugared milk and a Custard Cream.

It occurred to me that a promise wasn't necessarily morally immutable – what if one promised to do something bad? In which case, couldn't a promise be countermanded by a contradictory promise? And didn't Jesus urge not to swear by anything? (*Matthew 5:34*)

The City of Thoughts

My incessant anxiety finally mellowed, and I began to eagerly anticipate my eleventh birthday. The display box of my red pullback Dalek figurine, acquired last year in Eldon Square's BBC Shop, listed manufacturer Dapol, Llangollen, Wales, and how to order a merchandise catalogue. From here, I'd selected my requested presents. The parcel's inscription with a birthday message from the place's staff touched and humbled me.

On Saturday the 18th of July, I unwrapped some of the finest presents I'd ever been given. A plastic-windowed box displayed a set of seven Dalek figurines, complete with Dalek creator Davros. A small plastic figurine faintly but aptly evoked the profile of the Seventh Doctor. Of *The Daleks* (1963) and *The Dalek Invasion of Earth* (1964), I now had David Whitaker and Terrance Dicks' respective novelisations (1964 and 1977).

While James was in Italy with Morpeth's school choir, Mam, Dad, John and I went to the Metrocentre to see the new version of *Godzilla*, which would sow my intermittent but fond acquaintance with the saga.

On a family wander of the shops, I saw, in WHSmith, something of which I'd known for a while. A rectangular display box held *Destiny of the Doctors* (1997), a *Doctor Who* computer game designed to run on a personal computer. For weeks, I'd guiltily dithered over the extravagant price of twenty pounds. Dad now offered to buy the game for me. Both humbled and thrilled, I accepted the kind offer.

Henceforth, much of my free time was devoted to *Destiny of the Doctors*. Filmed footage of Anthony Ainley's the Master, enthroned amidst the orange vapours of Siralos, was followed by sturdily detailed digital sets, including, primarily, the TARDIS.

With the arrow keys, I drove the Doctor's robot friend Graak past yelping Daleks, hissing Ice Warriors and growling Sontarans, in search of items to secure the Doctor's release.

Clicking on part of the TARDIS Console replaced the scene with the City of Thoughts, an encyclopaedia of *Who* lore. Its concise but detailed articles, highly accommodating to my lax concentration, frequently enticed me.

A Brilliant Mind

For Year Seven, my form class moved into the care of music teacher Mrs Avery, who held my older brother James in fond regard. Around her early fifties, mousy neck-length hair framed a face whose locally accented voice was apt to good humour and, at admittedly severe provocation from certain levels of classroom buffoonery, weary frustration.

I thought it best not to mention that, even after two years, I couldn't read music.

Having failed to absorb her instructions one lesson, I murmured to Sean Moreau a request for information on what we were supposed to be doing.

"Oh, *Andrew!*" a nearby Mrs Avery said loudly.

Mrs Avery also taught us English.

"He's got a brilliant mind," she said bluntly, on reception of one of my observations.

I inwardly glowed at the candid praise.

My class was now taught Maths by Mrs Webster, school librarian and English teacher. With black, grey-flecked hair and a Standard English accent, she looked around her late fifties and had a reputation for severity. She seemed quite affable, inspecting my early attempt at a worksheet with a word of sing-song warning at the mistakes.

"Oh *dear...!*" I mimicked.

With a chuckle, she echoed in agreement.

After Science lessons, I always went to the boys' toilets, to wash my hands, as Mr Wood had urged back in Year Five, as the tables, having been covered in sundry chemicals, were "filthy."

This detour, to Mrs Webster's mild vexation, sometimes made me late.

I often proved unable to grasp her instruction.

Wary of admonishment for not listening, I resumed my traditional approach: I sat at my table, staring ahead, occasionally at the worksheet and, very occasionally, making an attempt to respond to instructions whose numerical invocations had all the clarity of a dishwasher instruction manual translated into Ancient Egyptian.

Summons to Mrs Webster's desk for progress inspection soon established my tectonically slow work rate. In addition to which, I might mislay the right worksheet.

"Everyone has to look after you!" said Mrs Webster.

Anticipation and reception of her ire stoked a heavy, mournful tension. Could mathematical worksheets, I wondered, really be worth all this strife? What if tomorrow saw an attack from outer space?

Wrong Thoughts

In autumn, with the spectacle of my religious anxiety having long faded, I found a new moral worry. Sometimes, when I thought of my parents, the recollections weren't accompanied by a surge of affirmative affection. I feared that this might mean I was guilty of not loving them.

The year neared Christmas. One weekend afternoon, Mam, Dad, John and I walked the bustling, brightly lit Metrocentre. On a plastic bench, we sat down. I opened the plastic wrapping of my HMV-bought issue of *SFX*, Britain's leading science fiction and fantasy magazine.

An article introduced Rage Software's PC computer game adaptation of *Jeff Wayne's Musical Version of The War of the Worlds*, a copy of which I'd requested for Christmas. A still from the game showed a digital rendering of a Martian Fighting Machine, as featured in Mike Trim's album cover illustration. The article included a small monochrome imprint of the game's interpretation of an actual Martian – on a thick bunch of tentacles stood a tall, bulbous, bodiless cranium, with two Grey-esque slanted black eyes.

We rounded off the afternoon with a visit to McDonald's. To its upstairs section I followed my family. As I neared the table on whose benches they sat, I realised something: I might be technically guilty of hating my parents. I prided myself on my positive relationship with my parents.

Should a momentary thought of my parents rouse the slightest twinge of disquiet I now feared this to constitute hatred of those who had birthed and raised me. My fretful imagination imbued the thoughts with an assertion of angry rejection.

For now, I kept my worries to myself and, without incident, had my usual lettuce-free McChicken Sandwich.

Back home, throughout the evening, the worry churned within me and demanded eventual release. Around ten o'clock, John and I, in our bedroom, had changed into our new Bart Simpson pyjamas. Mam came in to say goodnight, noticed my unease and invited confidence.

Somewhat demeaned by open discussion of hate and love, I tentatively articulated my fears. My guilt swelled, and I sobbed.

Mam laughingly consoled and reassured me, with note of my bodily moisturising of the progressive images of Bart.

The cartoon image would feel no objection, I said.

"He'll not have to," said Mam.

She embraced me for some time. I went to bed reassured that there was nothing wrong with me.

Throughout the next few weeks, my fearful guilt returned. Again, I repeatedly sought reassurance from Mam. At my incessant distress, she began to despair.

One night, we both sat on my bed; the darkened room tinged with the dull yellow light of my bedside lamp. Mam gently tried to reason away the cause of my worry. My voice choked with sobbing. I abased my excessive woe, which I supposed might be seen as disproportionate to such global horrors as disease and famine.

Left of the door, the wall held a large monochrome poster of Elvis Presley. Bought on a whim by John at a jumble sale, the deceased songster's soulful gaze now frightened him.

"Oh, Elvis," said Mam, in mimicry of Elvis's Deep South drawl, "what are we gonna do about Andy?" Christmas, she noted, was nearly upon us. "And you do like Christmas, don't you?"

As a rule, I did like Christmas. But at this moment, I felt no thrill at its mention. I wanted to say yes, but feared I would be guilty of lying. I felt remorse at the very question, as if I had already cruelly rejected Christmas and made it sad.

As the big day loomed ever closer, I intermittently sank into despairing sorrow.

"It's the season to be *jolly!*" said Granda Widdrington.

I explained to him that I feared myself to be guilty of the obscene sin of hating my parents.

"Your mam is your *best friend*," he reassured me.

"Andy, you could murder someone," said Mam, "and I would visit you in prison."

Mam reassured me that my feelings of supposed hatred were merely due to chemicals in my growing body called hormones.

Sometimes, the emotional disease I'd brought into the house looked promisingly to have been subdued. Other times, I sagged into despair and sought further reassurance.

One afternoon, I accompanied Mam and Nana on a walk. By the Cemetery Bank, Mam and Nana inspected a gravestone.

When we got home, they realised that they'd inadvertently walked on the soil above this person's grave. My fretful imagination conjured disapproval and directed it at my mother. With irresistible, self-punishing compulsion, I willed it to constitute hatred.

As Mam, James and I watched the 1970 Albert-Finney-starring musical version of *Scrooge*, I dwelled on my fresh transgression. Inspired by the film's darkly comic scene of Scrooge's visit to Hell, my fretful imagination fleetingly affirmed my agreement to sell my soul to the Devil, should Old Nick be telepathically listening. Thankfully, this worry didn't last long – I had plenty to distract me.

On Christmas Eve, at around six, I went along with James, John, Nana and Dad to the Crib Service.

In All Saints Church, numerous candles soothed the gloom. The current priest, a jolly man with thinning grey hair, maintained one of the best carols to be "Happy Birthday To You."

The five of us settled into a pew at the back. The service began, and we all stood to sing "Once in Royal David's City." As I looked at my copy of the sheet on which the lyrics were printed, a swell of sorrow choked my voice. The intolerable shame of supposedly hating my parents, the helpless misery my bizarre worries caused Mam and my dismay at having thereby ruined Christmas mounted in immutable, horrified woe. I tried to join in the song. Hot tears poured down my face.

Dad quietly escorted me out of the church and back home.

"I thought we'd sorted out all our problems?" soothed Mam.

Throughout the evening, my woe gradually subsided, helped by the anarchic humour of a BBC Two broadcast of Aardman Animations' *Rex the Runt*.

At the kitchen table, I wrote out a Christmas card to Mam and Dad and stressed to Mam that it was a "very special" one.

"Well, it's from a very special boy," said Mam.

I woke to the darkness of early morning. Christmas Day was here. I felt no sickly waves of distress. So far, so good. John soon woke to join me.

The two of us went downstairs. Eventually, Mam, Dad and James joined us.

I unwrapped a smooth rectangular cardboard box, on whose cover a Martian Fighting Machine blasted the ironclad *Thunder Child*. Eager for CGI rendition of Wellsian Martians, I triumphantly noted my definite glee.

From the Metrocentre's Gadget Shop, John and I now each had a glow-in-the-dark Grey mask.

I was surprised to find my largest present to be a PlayStation. Months ago, Mam had asked if I fancied one. I'd been uncertain. In 1995, on release of the revolutionary thirty-two-bit console, I'd resented such hardware's eclipsing of older consoles like the Mega Drive and Master System. This had later faded to general indifference.

With daunted excitement, I saw my extravagant present to be housed in a large black cardboard box and equipped with two games.

My ever-ready conscience had me pledge to share it with John.

While Dad connected the PlayStation to the telly, John and I took *The War of the Worlds* to the upstairs landing and switched on the Windows 95.

Two discs, blue and red, respectively played the game from a human and Martian perspective. I tried the red disc first.

Across the dead, rusty surface of Mars, a Martian Tripod, to a remix of Jeff Wayne's "The Red Weed," marches into a pyramid-shaped building. In smooth, heftily detailed CGI, the Martian Elders, in softly echoing monotone, discuss their need to invade Earth. While thrilled by the loving rendition of the seminal space monsters, I found the following strategy game a bit fiddly to manage.

After sitting on the cold landing for an hour, I decided to inspect my PlayStation. Before the telly, it lay on the floor, its box on a nearby armchair. The two games, like CDs, came in square plastic cases.

One of the games was something called *Crash Bandicoot*. Its cover bore a digital cartoon image of an anthropomorphised orange mammal. Bushy black eyebrows, green irises and a slightly pointed snout framed an impudent grin. Above a bare torso, he wore fingerless gloves, blue trousers and sturdy black boots.

The disc was installed. On a dark screen, with a twinkling chime and an electronic shiver of music, the PlayStation logo arrived and faded. To opening titles, the game's digital score tumbled and bounded. Across a jungle-shaded beach, Crash Bandicoot (voiced by Brendan O'Brien) pelted towards the screen, gave a yelp of alarm and ducked as the game's title crashed into place behind him.

Joypad in hands, I selected the "START" option.

On the first level, N. Sanity Beach, I drove Crash left, right, into somersaulting leaps and a *Taz*-esque tornado spin to repel assailants. Along the sand, I guided Crash onto a pathway which tunnelled through a jungle. With smooth sand, brightly detailed foliage and heavily textured stone ruins, this world had both the expressionism of a cartoon and a weight which approximated solidity.

Smashing the numerous wooden crates typically yielded Wumpa Fruit, an extra life or a floating Aboriginal mask, which materialised to protect Crash from minor attacks.

Crash, the instruction manual narrated, had been genetically engineered, along with several other inhabitants of three southeastern Australian islands, by vengeful Dr Neo Cortex, to build a world-conquering army. Crash, having escaped brainwashing, set out to thwart Cortex.

The other game was *Tekken 3*, a beat-em-up in the vein of *Mortal Kombat*. To my slight amazement, Granda Widdrington seemed enthralled.

"Gan on, Johnny, hit the bugger!"

That afternoon, I found myself once more dragged down by my relentless guilt, the misery it caused my mother and the collective pollution thereof of Christmas Day, that special day when everyone is supposed to be happy.

Not yet despairing, I resolved to channel my efforts into something worthy. In the cool air of my bedroom, I read from *The Illustrated Children's Bible*. In pursuit of religious devotion, I, for about forty-five minutes, read solemn, simplified accounts of ancient conflict.

Downstairs, as my sorrow swelled, I devoted my attention to the intrigue of *Crash Bandicoot* and sought comfort from the moral kudos of frequently letting John have a go.

At some point, Mam discovered the return of my bizarre, insurmountable distress. Her miserable frustration poured into the Christmas atmosphere.

By evening, the emotional fires had mellowed. The day ended in peace.

On Boxing Day, I came downstairs shortly after ten. While not quite content, I wasn't yet despairing. For breakfast, I had some leftovers from yesterday. In the living room, John was watching a broadcast of *Super Mario Bros* (1993).

As the day unfolded, my unfathomable, miserable guilt returned to poison the house, as it would throughout the next week or so. My search for reassurance, for persuasion that my infinitesimal and imagined twinges of emotion didn't constitute hatred of my parents, drove my mother to despair.

Several times, Dad took me up to his and Mam's bedroom for calmer, but still ultimately fruitless, counselling sessions.

In my search for peace of mind, I tried the option of going next door. In the living room, Granda Widdrington sat alone. He welcomed me heartily.

It hadn't escaped his attention that my young mind was burdened with something or other. Reassuringly confident, he was unfazed. His words didn't actually banish my worry; they rather stressed, with infectious confidence, its absurdity.

Eventually, Mam joined us on the sofa. Granda sagely advised that instead of drawing pictures of extraterrestrials and such like, I should cultivate an interest in "nature" and draw pictures of that.

"Aahl the different bords..."

1999

Crash and Coco

Throughout January, my sorrowful guilt began to fade.

In *Crash Bandicoot*, I became entranced – its digital cartoon realm amazed not only with sumptuous colour and detail, but in the leaping, flitting manoeuvres of its innocently impudent hero. Getting to know Crash and his world nurtured my days with fun.

On return from Barrowburn one evening, Dad, having stopped at a friend's, now gave me some second-hand issues of *Official PlayStation Magazine UK*. One of them had an article about *Crash Bandicoot 3: Warped*, released only last month. In this third title, Crash was joined by his "now playable sister Coco."

Furthermore, one of the magazines had come with a book of cheats and secrets, including, for *Crash Bandicoot*, the Super Password. With this combination of triangles, circles, squares and "X"s, the game offered access to every level.

Before a burning Castle Cortex, Crash, atop a blimp, evaded and deflected spherical bolts of fire from the ray gun of a Rocket Sled-mounted Dr Neo Cortex (voiced by Brendan O'Brien). With Cortex vanquished, Crash, held aloft in the embrace of she-bandicoot Tawna, grinned at the screen, raised a hand in farewell, and the two bandicoots flew off into the sunset.

Heartened and emboldened by my fellowship with a new saga, I felt a blooming desire to explore the sequels.

One evening, on a visit to Asda, I decided to take the plunge and bought a copy of *Crash Bandicoot 2: Cortex Strikes Back* (1997). John used his own savings to buy *Crash Bandicoot 3: Warped*.

On the ride home, I removed the box's plastic wrapping and took out the instruction manual. About halfway through, a monochrome digital portrait illustrated a profile of each character.

Curious about Crash's sister, I turned quickly to Coco Bandicoot. The young computer whiz would use her laptop to hack into Dr Cortex's space station to reveal to Crash the devious doctor's plans.

By her round face, large eyes, sweeping blond ponytail and soft smile, Coco shone a femininity which seemed gentle and welcoming, all the more so for her kinship with Crash. Was it time for me to start fancying people?

In *Crash 2*'s introductory sequence, Coco (voiced by Vicki Winters), woke Crash from his snooze and sent him to bring her another laptop battery.

In the Warp Room, she later interrupted the giant hologram head of Dr Cortex (voiced by Clancy Brown), and warned Crash not to trust the allegedly reformed mad scientist.

On the back cover for *Crash Bandicoot 3: Warped*'s instruction manual was a small, superimposed full-colour illustration. Astride Pura the Tiger, Coco beamed a particularly soft smile. Her white tee shirt, denim overalls and pink trainers evoked a casual adventurousness. Her abundant blond hair, tied informally in place, and warm, bright-eyed smile had a gentle vibrancy.

The sight, sound and narrated attributes of this cartoon figure inspired in me a nurturing glee and tender fondness.

In its own weirdly soft way, infatuation was rather fun.

In *Crash 2*, I guided Crash through jungles, snowscapes and storm-lashed ruins.

In the Warp Rooms, Coco's hologram-projected head fed my hunger for her.

In *Crash 3*, while Crash leapt through Time Portals to various points in history, Coco, on the central floor of the Time Twister, attended a giant computer screen. On attempt to enter certain Portals, Crash fell flat, whereupon in leapt Coco, onto the Great Wall of China to mount Pura the Tiger, or onto Caribbean seas, to ride her jet ski in search of Crystals and Gems.

As I played each game, its digital worlds, joyous as they were, began to reveal their limit. The figure of Coco encompassed digital animation, a few lines of recorded voice acting, a brief biography and illustrations. Her loveliness was a flicker within a high-tech bit of fun.

My love weighed in a nervous loneliness. On the jet ski levels of *Warped*, should I drive into a skull-marked floating bomb, the jet ski would explode, and Coco would be sent flying into the air, to land and forlornly float in the water. Even though she would be instantly transferred to the start of the level for another try, and although I didn't really suppose her digital body to be sentient, guilt compelled me to lean towards the screen and softly offer reassurance. I dreaded to think what the game's makers would think of such a display.

In my devotion, I succumbed to pangs of helpless dismay. One night, as Mam sat by me on my bed, I, in embarrassment, explained my fancying of a computer game character. Mam, in heartened compassion, assured me that there was nothing wrong with this. I showed Mam the back cover of *Warped*'s instruction manual.

"Well, she's quite attractive," soothed Mam.

Reassured and thrilled by this endorsement of my love, I took heart.

Attempted Murder

With decline of my involuntary compulsion to make promises to God, other fears now frequently compelled me to perform brief, empty rituals.

At break and lunchtimes, as I stood on the yard by the school's back door, I would avoid walking to a certain region of yard. My rebellious imagination decided that if I did something in a certain way, it was with the intent to "hurt" Coco. I feared the guilt of betraying her. I hadn't a clear conception of what hurting her actually involved. I took the precaution that her imaginary person, whose presence lingered in my own imagination, might, in the unknowable depths of infinity, yet feel sensation and emotion.

My fear of being guilty of trying to do bad things took further forms. Between school hours, as I hovered around the house, I made, towards people's backs, hand gestures. No, not the kind involving one or two raised fingers. These gestures required minimal effort. I would flex my hand slightly and ease it in the general direction of someone's back. My rebellious imagination imbued these gestures with an attempt to kill their unwitting recipient.

Having realised the ease with which my hands might fall into this manoeuvre, and afraid of the evil with which I might imbue it, the forbidden intent now came frequently.

My harsh taskmaster of a conscience decided that I was now guilty of several accounts of attempted murder. With each empty, compulsive little gesture, I found myself unable to suppress reckless assertion that I willed the motion to kill whoever stood before me.

I realised how absurd it was, but logic seemed to hold that I'd willed physical action to result in death. I couldn't seem to stop doing it. While the deed's blatant mundanity stayed any overwhelming horror, the undeniability of my transgression weighed on me in a numb, burning sorrow. Not just for the attempted murder, but for the stress my irrational guilt once more caused my mother. Mam could only dismiss the absurdity of my guilt and urge me away from such fanciful self-flagellation.

By my own confused but seemingly irresistible logic, I'd sunk as morally low as a human being could.

Furthermore, my infatuation with Coco, afloat on a sea of transient recordings, was doomed to abandonment. The loneliness simmered with frightening urgency.

One week, on the basis of a slight cough, I managed to steal a few days off school.

Mam offered firmer counsel. The only cause I had for despondence, she said, was my weight. My latest irrationality, however, drew attention to more obviously untoward behaviour – teachers' observation of my reclusiveness.

"Don't you want any friends?" Mam implored softly.

The honest answer was a resounding no. The comfort of my own imagination, my limited concentration, and common perception of me as a harmless misfit, to be kindly indulged or discreetly mocked, outweighed any desire to engage with my schoolmates.

However, the phrase "don't you want" had a unique power to make me feel guilty for cruelly rejecting whatever it offered.

Wasn't anyone at school into PlayStation?

Well, Sean Moreau, I supposed.

Could I perhaps bring in a PlayStation magazine, to kindle a shared interest?

I agreed to give it a try.

Sean

Having moved last year from Gosforth to Rothbury, Sean was withdrawn, although not to my extent, and manifestly a decent sort. Although Scots-born, his mild voice had a general northeastern flavour. Several inches shorter than me, his slightly protruding ears framed thin dark hair.

Into school, I brought an issue of *Planet PlayStation* and showed it to Sean. Our shared delight in the Power of PlayStation begat conversation and, in turn, fellowship. While we lacked the casual openness I had with John, Sean and I became a fixture of each other's daily routine. Our general focus was on PlayStation, films and television.

I understood that after school, classmates sometimes accompanied each other home. I wasn't keen to try this with Sean. The prospect felt like a tiring intrusion of the ritual of school into the peace of home. I guiltily confided this to John. He sympathised – his relationship with his "school friends," he said, needn't extend to his home life.

Wrong-footing

My fretful, self-punishing imagination sought new ways to earn me guilt. Walking the pavement with John, I, whilst lowering a foot, imagined its collision with his heel, perhaps tripping him, whereupon he might even fall, perhaps fatally, into the road. While desperate not to will such an outcome, I couldn't stop the imagined intent. My conscience would then pronounce me guilty of attempted murder.

While the guilt ached with a dull, fretful sorrow, I trusted in the possibility that my ill-intent might be illusory.

On a stack of bedside plastic drawers, John often kept a glass of water. Sufficient pressure to the draws, I imagined, might dislodge the glass, which could fall, from about a foot, in the direction of John's head. What if it should hit his temple?

Whenever John had fallen asleep with the glass in place, I made sure to take it off the draws and put it on the desk. Surely attempted life-saving cancelled out attempted murder?

On school mornings, into Mrs Avery's Year Seven form classroom, I took my paperback copies of David Whitaker and Terrance Dicks' respective novelisations of Terry Nation's *Doctor Who* serials *The Daleks* and *The Dalek Invasion of Earth*. While unfamiliarity with the latter's supporting characters and settings stayed my concentration, I happily browsed random scenes.

The Daleks had begun their twenty-second century invasion by bombarding Earth with meteorites and had then massacred much of the populace with an artificial plague. This genuinely horrific concept sat well with the Daleks' technological fancy. With mild unease, I hoped no hostile aliens would telepathically tune into my brain and get ideas.

Characters

One Maths lesson, I strove to grasp today's task. Getting any further with it would mean asking Mrs Webster for help. She would, I suppose, realise that I hadn't listened to her instructions. I could ask for help, take the heat for not listening or sit it out here, feign concentration and escape a reprimand for slow work rate. Perhaps. My instinct was to keep things as simple and peaceful as the situation would allow.

To ease the tedium, I recalled the filmed opening of BBC Multimedia's *Destiny of the Doctors* (1997) in which the Master (Anthony Ainley), on capturing each incarnation of the Doctor from their respective time streams, watches a montage of, and mocks, each Doctor.

I now envisioned such a showcasing for various computer game heroes. The older Sonic the Hedgehog might be seen as equivalent to William Hartnell or Patrick Troughton. Crash Bandicoot seemed an apt parallel for Tom Baker. And sly Gex Gecko might serve as a basic approximation of Sylvester McCoy. I mentally superimposed each cartoon face onto the swirling orange mists of the planet Siralos.

"Andrew," called Mrs Webster.

I braced myself and, to her desk, brought my exercise book.

The page devoted to today's task was blank. Mrs Webster supposed my mind to have been elsewhere. She asked what I'd been thinking about.

While easily cowed by the authority of teachers, I did realise there to be boundaries. To my private thoughts, surely I had some kind of right?

"Erm, with all due respect..." I murmured.

"Oh, no, Andrew," she said with dangerous calm. "You do not 'due respect' me. I don't 'due respect' you."

Presentation of such names as Crash Bandicoot or Planet Siralos to Mrs Webster was inconceivable; the authority of her disapproval would be mind-crushing.

"Erm, different, um, characters," I said.

"Well," she said, in stern solemnity, "you may want to consider what use they'll be to you when you need to pass your exams in order to get a job. These. *Characters*."

I returned to my table. Humiliation swamped me with a rare level of fretful sorrow. I realised Mrs Webster hadn't meant to make me feel so low, but my private joys, so vulnerable to disapproval, had been pummelled with utmost authority.

Toilet III

While not outright scared of toilets, prolonged contact with them daunted me, doubly so for school toilets. Around age nine, I'd found some mastery over this hesitation. Now, for whatever reason, the comfort of postponement had reclaimed my inclination.

Rumour spread, to the particular delight of Len Wardle, of my incontinence.

Whatever perversion bloated my belly, addled my conscience and sensitised me to petty fears was now, in the most foul way possible, comedy gold.

I gradually forced myself to adopt more prompt toilet use.

Porn

An issue of *Total PlayStation* had a several-page article on the much-hyped *Tomb Raider III* (1998).

In promotional digital artwork, gun-toting explorer Lara Croft, with her finely strong features and thin ponytail, had a stern prettiness. The artwork's wryly extravagant focus on her private parts shamed me away from closer engagement.

Sean had impudently asked if I liked "porn." What was porn? Pictures of naked ladies, apparently.

I emphatically did not like porn. The thought of my intrusion on female nudity, in its secrecy and sanctity, roused a saddened, frightened shame. I understood women's breasts were known to delight heterosexual men; in such media as *Brookside*, young men hailed any hint of "knockers." I wanted no part of this. Bare breasts' bulbous swell, in diversion from bodily identity, depressed and slightly revolted me.

Tomb Raider III's artwork, with a slightly mocking exultancy, offered Lara's famously sizeable bust. Her detached calm mocked the illicit thrills her frame was known to entice. It made me feel slightly dirty.

Her legs, however, were a delight.

The Wrath of Keith

As summer dawned, Sean, I and the rest of our class awaited Mrs Avery to arrive for afternoon registration.

At one point, Keith Dobson wandered over. Throughout lessons, Keith often offered irreverent commentary on his immediate environment. Sean, with his quiet manner, was often fodder for these routines. I couldn't help but laugh at their giggling audacity, although I apologised to Sean and stressed that my mirth wasn't at his expense.

In Keith and Sean's current conversation, I noticed a hint of disagreement – Sean had offered a jocular remark of his own. Keith suddenly flew into a flurry of movement.

With unwavering energy, he repeatedly hurled his fists at Sean, who rose to his feet but barely managed to lift his arms in resistance. He was shoved against the wall, where he slid to the floor. Having forced him into this position, Keith continued to pound his face, before something made him relent and back away.

Sean's face was blank. His lower lip, and the skin beneath, were bloodied. Many of our classmates gathered around. I spoke reassuringly to Sean and went to the office.

What had I done when Keith went berserk?

I'd blankly watched.

It wasn't that I feared a share in the beating. As much as anything, the violence confused me. I had no idea how to reasonably react to it. Its turmoil, its demand for fervent response, numbed me. Its brutality, contestable only by similarly heated emotion, had me in a dazed lull.

Pig

For my twelfth birthday, I requested the PlayStation game *Gex: Enter the Gecko* (1998).

One afternoon at the Metrocentre, Dad slipped into HMV. As Mam, Dad, John and I continued to wander the shops, it occurred to me that Dad had probably recently bought my birthday present. By my proximity thereto, I feared the occasion to have been sullied.

Eventually, as we left a Currys electronics shop, Dad admitted to having discreetly bought the requested game.

At the revokement of birthday mystique, I felt an urgently sorrowful sense of having sullied my own innocence. I briefly sobbed.

In disgrace, I went with my family back to the car. On the way out of Gateshead, we stopped at Toys R Us, to get me some other birthday stuff.

Throughout the Sunday morning of my twelfth birthday, I was relieved to succumb to no significant pangs of despondence, although the prospect thereof cast a manageable gloom.

My presents included two paperback books. At school, I'd distantly seen Adrian Wilson reading a copy of one. Above a cartoonish illustration of a bespectacled boy standing by a steam train, a dark pink border bore the title *Harry Potter and the Philosopher's Stone*. The other, blue-bordered book, *Harry Potter and the Chamber of Secrets*, held a slightly more naturalistic illustration of a flying car, in which sat two boys and a caged owl. Seemingly part of a series, both books were credited to one JK Rowling.

"They're supposed to be *really* good," said Mam.

On the back cover of *Philosopher's Stone*, an esteemed quote compared Rowling to Roald Dahl. This, of course, implied something special.

As the day dragged, I had a brief look at the first chapter of *Philosopher's Stone*. From the gentle prose, I gathered the story to entail a film director named Vernon, whose sister-in-law knew people who dressed peculiarly. The casual, genial prose had a comforting cosiness.

This last year, my anxieties had drawn more prolonged bedtime visits from Mam. Intrigued by the *Harry Potter* books, she took to sitting on my bed to give us nightly readings of *Philosopher's Stone*.

Following Mam's reading of a few pages, I took the book from my bedside drawers and read some more. I now realised Mr Vernon Dursley to be a firm director, rather than a film director.

Towards the end of the first chapter, when Professor Dumbledore addressed a map-reading cat as Professor McGonagall, I supposed a similarly comedic quirk to the game show *Pets Win Prizes*, one of whose hosts was a cat termed "the Professor." However, when the cat changed into Professor McGonagall, deputy headmistress of Hogwarts, I realised this story not to be a frivolous romp, but a modern tale of wizardry.

The promisingly sinister villain Voldemort, having murdered baby Harry's parents, had, on attempt to kill Harry himself, unaccountably vanished. On a flying motorbike, half-giant Hagrid arrives to tearfully leave Harry on the doorstep of his Dursley relatives.

In the next chapter, nearly ten years later, Harry's Uncle Vernon and Aunt Petunia have him sleep in the cupboard under the stairs, dress him in their son Dudley's old clothes and hold him in general contempt. A few months younger than his cousin, Harry is told to fry bacon for Dudley's eleventh birthday breakfast.

Having noted the one-year-old Dudley to have kicked his mother up the street in screaming demand for sweets, the narration now notes his excess weight, hatred of exercise and love of punching.

At Dudley's disquiet at only thirty-seven birthday presents, Harry fears an imminent tantrum, against which Aunt Petunia insures with offer of two more presents on today's birthday outing. In calculation of the prospective quantity, Dudley shows comical difficulty. Unable to leave Harry in the care of neighbouring Mrs Figg, the Dursleys have no option but to bring him along.

Dudley, on obtrusive protest of his Knickerbocker Glory to be too small, is bought a second, with Harry allowed to finish the first. The next chapter establishes Dudley to be leader of a gang of bullies.

In written stories, hinting a character's badness by note of their weight was nothing new. However, whereas *The Snow Spider* (1986) briefly mentions bully Dewy Davis's weight, *Harry Potter and the Philosopher's Stone*, while clearly aiming for such comic excess as that of *Charlie and the Chocolate Factory's* (1964) Augustus Gloop, imbues Dudley with some naturalism. Seemingly for credit of prettiness and sensitivity to one so ungainly, his mother's adoration is mocked. Dudley's appetite seems to stem from the same source as his self-entitlement: parental indulgence.

Engrossed in the story, I tried to suppose Dudley to be scorned more for his bullying than his weight, and that he was probably fatter than me, anyway.

However, in Dudley, I saw something of myself - or rather, what I feared, and what some seemed to suspect, to have sown my inhibitions.

The outrageous size to which his ungoverned appetite has bloated his body echoes the feebleness of his difficulty with numbers. With their house invaded by innumerable duplications of a letter addressed to Harry, the Dursleys, with Harry, flee across the country. At a smack round the head from his panicked father, Dudley snivels – beneath his blubbery body and bullying bluster is a wailing child. Dudley is coddled by his mother, Dudley is greedy, and Dudley is fat. His lack of restraint on his appetite, and the resultant body his mother so adores, lend Dudley the immobility and heedlessness of infancy.

This characterisation recalled the childhood transgressions which continued to shame me. I'd lashed out, sometimes at minimal provocation, sometimes at none. I'd been, and continued to be, scared of silly things, like crossing stepping stones, getting hit in the face with a ball and shouting. I'd slept in my mother's bed until I was ten. I couldn't absorb instruction at school. And I couldn't seem to force myself to stop being hungry. Was all this because I was lazy?

Having sheltered in a sparsely furnished island hut, the Dursleys are woken by Hagrid, who arrives to deliver in person Harry's summons to Hogwarts School of Witchcraft and Wizardry.

Hagrid openly sneers at Dudley's weight.

Hagrid, Keeper of Keys and Grounds at Hogwarts, friend of Harry's parents and soft-hearted narrator of Harry's tragic history, is a figure to be admired. His treatment of Dudley is implied to be an overdue dispensing of justice.

I wondered if Rowling realised that overweight readers might feel unwelcome in her world of magic.

Scorn from schoolmates who couldn't really be expected to know any better was a mildly irritating fact of life. Hints from an adult, an author, no less, that society oughtn't really to be bothered by such flab as mine roused in me a numb despondence.

When Uncle Vernon insults the name of Albus Dumbledore, Hagrid loses his rag, waves his magic umbrella, and Dudley, with a howl of pain, has a pig's tail protruding from the base of his spine. The Dursleys flee into the far room.

Ah, yes. Pig. A recurring figure in illustrated children's storybooks, *Sus scrofa domesticus*, for his appetite and reputed filthiness, is a playful symbol of untidiness and gluttony. The term "pig" denotes unfettered excess. It charges loutishness and slovenliness. It does so by comparison of a human being to a creature often thought to live among its own faeces. Like I was. By my rampant appetite, the term innocently reduced me to degenerate infancy. Eats like a pig, lives like a pig, manners of a pig. Stinking, snivelling, selfish pig.

I somewhat identified with bewildered, isolated Harry, who finds himself part of a secret magical community. His quaint yet contemporary tale of mystic wonders, ancient secrets and thrilling scares had me increasingly enamoured. I felt rather pressured into disapproving of Harry's arch-enemy Draco Malfoy. I found myself involuntarily asserting wordless gestures of support for his sneers at Ron Weasley's poverty.

At mention of plump Mrs Weasley, slightly overweight Neville Longbottom and jolly Hogwarts ghost the Fat Friar, I clung to the possibility that should Rowling clap eyes on me, she might not dislike me. However, I feared, should they behold me in person, Harry, Ron and Hermione would probably find me an unsavoury imposition.

Shortly after we'd reached "The Mirror of Erised," Mam got a dishwashing job (soon to rise to the role of chef) at nearby pub the Newcastle House, from which, usually tired, she often returned late. I continued reading *Philosopher's Stone*. Bedtime was a period which required me to remain in place. The hours in which I lay awake reinforced my concentration, making reading easier.

One warm afternoon, on return from a walk with Uncle Ross, John and I visited SPAR. John decided to get an ice cream. Would I indulge?

"I don't need fattening anymore," I quoted Hagrid, in airy pursuit of a sliver of absolution from Miss Rowling.

The *Harry Potter* books roused such attention as to make the news. *Newsround* introduced thirty-four-year-old Joanne Rowling. With a sober, weary face and soft, unassuming voice, she related her divorce, parentage of a young daughter, struggle with poverty, and, by the power of storytelling, succession thereof with fame and fortune.

"I'm pleased for her," said Mam.

How's the Diet Going, Andrew?

In September, my form class became Year Eight and transferred to the school library for the care of Mrs Webster, who would also take us for English.

One registration, Mrs Webster allowed a few minutes for reading. Between desks, she inspected respective titles.

"Ah, and he's the man at the moment," she noted of my copy of *Harry Potter and the Prisoner of Azkaban*.

In the Dinner Hall, I found myself seated beside Mrs Bell. Buoyed by her genial conversation, I shared my aim to make a serious attempt at weight loss.

"Well, to do that," she said, her gaze gently amused, "you need to eat lots... and lots... of *fruit*."

I didn't suppose it would do to mention that, save for berries, I couldn't bring myself to eat solid fruit.

The following week, back in the Dinner Hall, I once more found myself seated by the Maths teacher. With my usual urgency, I swept forkfuls into my maw, chomped briefly and eagerly repeated the process.

"How's the diet going, Andrew?" said Mrs Bell. Her indulgent geniality was gone; this was a demand. Perhaps an encouraging challenge. It barely occurred to me that it might be a deft sneer.

Slugs

With Miss Ordway absent, Mr Logan took a Science lesson. Through the fire exit at the front of the large, gloomy classroom, he sent us onto the school field, in search of live specimens. Equipped with plastic white boxes, we wandered the rear slant of the huge field.

Sean and I peered between blades of grass in search of slugs and beetles. When we found them, I couldn't bring myself to touch them. I didn't quite dare the shock of invasion of my flesh by such exotica.

While disheartening and baffling, the shame was manageable. Sean did the work of picking them up.

Adrian Wilson got wind of my inhibition. He and his friends shared a few wry chuckles – nothing nasty, just a gentle ribbing.

Word reached Mr Logan that Andrew was scared of touching creepy-crawlies. With the class quietly seated, Mr Logan stood behind the front bench, cupped a beetle in his hands and, with his edgily playful smile, invited me to touch it.

Trying to make light of the situation, I airily declined.

Mr Logan's smile broadened. He coaxed me further.

I forced a smile and tried to humourise my repeated refusal.

The beetle held in his cupped hands, Mr Logan took a hasty stride towards me. I swapped decorum for self-preservation, stood and hurried backwards. Proffering the beetle, Mr Logan followed. I led him in a lap around the tables.

The class laughed. I tried to make my flight seem like an appeal to Mr Logan's renowned sense of fun, but I really was that desperate not to touch a beetle.

Scared of shouting, scared of jumping into water, scared of getting hit in the face with a ball, and scared of creepy-crawlies. My disorderly appetite and bulk, yet again, were matched by my inordinate timidity. With numb despondence, I supposed that I must be what was commonly called a wimp. Not for the first time, I recalled Enid Blyton's short story "Boo! Boo! Boo!", in which Uncle Jim scorns eight-year-old Harry's cowardice.

The term "coward" implied something not just laughably feeble but immoral, an infantile retreat from responsibility.

In assembly, Mr Patrick, on the projector, showed us a propaganda image from the First World War, in which a young woman scornfully offers a young man a white feather. Even if, in retrospect, the image's message was implied to be contemptible, its power prevailed.

I sought to prove my valour elsewhere. One weekend visit to Barrowburn, John and Sean jumped, quite easily, over the stream.

For something like half an hour, I stood over the two-foot ledge and stared into the clear, flowing depths. Three feet away and two below lay the opposite bank. I desperately sought the will to jump, but the threatened turmoil of brief adjacency to such a drop decisively overwhelmed me.

Resident Evil

Having last year seen a televised advert for *Resident Evil 2*, which noted the PlayStation game's BBFC classification of "15," I was curious about its 1996 prequel, *Resident Evil*, also classified "15." Sean lent me his copy.

The title sequence saw, from behind, a man walk down a darkened corridor, turn around, and cry out in terror. The scene then cut to a spurt of digital blood.

A monochrome live-action film, in which an uncredited cast flee the Arklay Forest from several Zombie Dogs, is followed by the STARS Alpha Team's arrival in the nearby Spencer Estate's huge hallway. Each digital character had, in their clothes, a fluid detail. Their faces, while inanimate, were a brief yet fine affectation of naturalism.

Early on, I tried the game both with Chris Redfield and Jill Valentine. To a softly brooding score, each searched a stately labyrinth of rooms, looked for such items as keys and shot Zombies. The bald, pale grey animate corpses shuffled through the corridors and groaned ominously. Should he get hold of you, a Zombie seized your character and gnawed at their neck with digital spurts of blood. Should this happen once too often, your character, with an anguished gasp, would fall down dead.

The macabre threat and brooding atmosphere lent early plays a tense chill. As I persevered, this mellowed to intrigue. Due to loose translation from the original Japanese, dialogue sometimes sat oddly with its context.

One afternoon, while a dialogue scene played, Mam entered the bedroom. At my imposition of emotive fantasy, I felt an embarrassment which didn't quite force me to turn off the telly, but which brought to my face an awkward grin.

As the nights darkened, a Halloween issue of *Planet PlayStation* supplied a paperback guide to several horror-themed games, including *Resident Evil*.

The fine digital features and soft, bright voice of Jill Valentine lent me an emboldening comfort. Brought by friendship with Sean to this quest of life-affirming terror, I generally felt quite at peace with the world.

2000

Stones

As the new century began, I was relieved to find myself generally innocent of prolonged bouts of irrational worry. On the way to school each morning, however, I frequently met a moderate but persistent hindrance.

Out of the central village, John and I, by the main road, walked the increasingly steep pavement.

As I lifted, drove and lowered my feet, I often noticed, cluttering the path beneath me, tiny stones. In flight, one of my shoes might often hit one, knocking it several inches forward.

It occurred to me that someone might trip on a stone. Might this in turn send them falling into the road, thereupon to fatally collide with a moving vehicle? Or perhaps the fall alone might result in a fatal blow to the head. I didn't suppose any of this to be likely, but its seriousness and notional possibility forced me to afford the idea a solemn urgency.

Might my foot knock a pebble into a position where it might derail some unwary future pedestrian? As I pondered this, I involuntarily willed my moving feet to sow this precise outcome. Should my foot knock a pebble, and if my imagination decided that I wanted it to kill someone, my conscience decreed me guilty of attempted murder. In search of redemption, I halted and eased, with my foot, the stone into a less dangerous position.

With John waiting for me to catch up, I often forced myself to abandon my mission of redemption. Instead, I uttered a short prayer in request for prevention of any danger.

Throughout the school morning, I sometimes found myself dissatisfied with my redemptive efforts.

In school, I helplessly pondered my guilt. As far as I could tell, I'd wantonly sought others' deaths. What was this self-punishing tendency of my imagination to force myself to will such things?

Throughout the day, my guilt eventually wore off – perhaps my conscience simply couldn't run on such meagre fuel as a nudged pebble accompanied by bad thoughts. As I worked through the day, my pangs of guilt seemed to die of old age.

Survival Horror

Of Calvin Burcombe, with whom I was on distantly friendly terms, I requested to borrow his copy of *Resident Evil 2* (1998). In exchange, he would require a loan of one of my own games. I lent him *Crash Team Racing* (1999) and borrowed *Resident Evil 2*.

The game opened on the nightly streets of Racoon City, beneath the flaming wreckage of the lorry which had crashed into the police car hastily vacated on either side by Leon Kennedy (voiced by Paul Haddad) and Claire Redfield (voiced by Alyson Court).

In this open-aired necropolis, a constant assault of groaning Zombies proved almost overwhelmingly scary. I briefly wondered if this game might be too much for me. However, with persistence, and the help of *Planet PlayStation*, I guided both Leon and Claire past the Zombies and into the research facility beneath the police station.

While I cherished Coco Bandicoot as my inductor into infatuation, acquaintance with the respective heroines of the first and second *Resident Evil* games roused a milder tenderness. Guidance through fearsome odds of each leggy, sweet-voiced heroine proved a balm to lurking loneliness.

Sean's introduction of me to the world of Survival Horror had fortified our alliance. On many a weekend, Dad took him, with John and me, up to Barrowburn. We rode old spare bicycles and had brief rides on Dad's four-wheel motorbike, or the quad, as a delighted Sean termed it.

School Disco

Year Eight had a new member, Scots-accented Leanne Moffat. With some risqué levity, but in total earnest, Sean confided to me his infatuation with her. We were at an age, it seemed, when fancying people began to lose its stigma.

One May assembly, Mr Henderson announced a school disco to be held on Friday evening.

On Friday afternoon, as Sean and I walked down the steep bank, he voiced his desire to attend. His aim, he said, was to meet with Leanne Moffat in some sort of observance of his attraction. Some thirty feet behind us, Leanne walked with several friends. As I continued down the hill, Sean, grimly determined, hurried back up. Further down, he caught up with me, his face aglow. He'd done it.

Would I go with him?

While touched by his request for my support, I had trepidations – school discos really weren't my scene. However, I decided to tag along.

At seven, Dad drove me up to the Middle School.

In the murky entrance hallway, I descended the few steps towards the windowed assembly hall doors, before which, at a table, Mrs Chapman sold tickets.

Inside the assembly hall, the towering blue curtains were drawn. Through the darkness, multicoloured spotlights flitted across a bounding crowd of Year Sevens and Year Eights. At ear-crushing volume, current pop hits thundered through the gloom.

I found Sean, with whom I exchanged barely audible shouted greetings.

For much of the night, I hovered by the door. My classmates, I supposed, would be leaping around each other in amorous fraternisation. A few friendly faces looked in on me and asked if I cared to join the pubescent rite.

"I'm going to save that sort of thing for when I'm fifteen," I said.

I couldn't really suppose I'd want anything more to do with it in two and a half years' time than I did now. Romance seemed an obscenely brash, overbearing arrangement, whose grandeur could only further shame such a bloated misfit as I.

The deafening music stopped. Mr Henderson, in a mood of alarming levity, took to the floor. It was time, he announced, for a game! If we would bring several of the stacked chairs into a row, the music would briefly resume. In round one, the boys would chase the girls, select one and bring her to a chair, thereupon to sit on his lap. Round two would involve the same principle, but with the genders swapped.

The music exploded back into the air.

Barely manageably embarrassed, I loped indecisively with the bounding boys and darting girls. I really didn't want to pester any girl with anything resembling amorous intent.

Mrs Webster, with a frightening grin, ran past me.

"You've got to pick a girl, Andrew!" she shrieked.

I forced myself to approach a hapless Year Seven and led her to a chair.

When the disco resumed, a slower song drew several couples into an improvised waltz, Sean and Leanne among them.

Outside, in the mild, darkening evening, as parents arrived, Sean caught up with me.

"I did a slowy with Leanne!" he said.

Online

From Rothbury's fairly new computer shop, Dad bought a modem. Our Windows 95 personal computer now had access to the World Wide Web. This new computing marvel, access to limitless worldwide pages of digitised images and print, was finally in our grasp.

Our Outlook Express internet provision was accessible on weekdays after 6 pm and throughout weekend days. Online connection barred the telephone from making or receiving calls.

Finally online, I found some interesting *Harry Potter* rumours. The BBC official *Doctor Who* website included an episode guide assembled from various reference books. Amazon UK exhibited for order just about any kind of commercially available item. Of books and films, I happily browsed customer reviews.

Pudding

Mrs Bell now taught my class Maths. While she lacked Mrs Webster's severity, I seldom dared to approach Mrs Bell for further instruction. As I tried to grasp them, her mathematical terms quickly dissolved into impenetrable gibberish. Requests for repeated instruction, I feared, would incur increasingly impatient urges for me to pay closer attention – something I didn't know how to do. I simply couldn't grasp each symbol's numerous designations. One might as well try to teach knitting to an octopus.

Occasionally, I took a stab in the dark and interpreted a worksheet's instruction into something that might, possibly, imply at least an attempt to fathom it. Mostly, I just stared at the photocopied ink, in hope that I might yet find an iota of meaning.

Mrs Bell leaned over.

"It's no good sitting there," she said, "like a pudding!"

She uttered the word with a playfully slow emphasis. Having read JK Rowling's Hagrid to use the term in protest at Dudley's excess weight, I wondered if it was now meant as a jibe at my own flab. I'd have thought such vulgarity to be beneath Mrs Bell. Comparison of me to a glutinous foodstuff implied, by way of my imposing bulk, a witless inertia. Mrs Bell's prim blue eyes and cooing voice sanitised the jibe (if such it was). Even to professional adults, the sight of me, apparently, was an imposition. I had it coming.

In the final week of Year Eight, the hot sky glared deep blue. For a task whose beginnings I could just about grasp, Mrs Bell lent me a plastic protractor. The plastic semicircle was loose, flimsy and on the verge of fracture. Before long, it came apart in my fingers.

I reported the damage to Mrs Bell. She grimaced. Her soft voice, in earnest bluster, bid me stay behind after class.

When the rest of the class had left for dinner, I remained seated. Mrs Bell loomed dramatically over me.

"*Right*, Andrew *Tait*," she railed of the broken protractor, "*that* is *criminal vandalism!*"

Her haughtily pinched face and modestly raised voice cowed me with manageable fright: not at the fury of her wrath, but by the innocence which sanctified it. I was really quite shocked to have incurred, by breaking a piece of flimsy equipment, such retribution.

Bewildering as her tirade was, right was irrevocably on her side. Her cooing voice lent matronly eminence and scholarly gravitas: if she decided I was a threat to civilisation, I had no means to deny it.

Tongue

As summer dawned, I was comfortably confident that I could meet my thirteenth birthday without any pangs of inordinate sorrowful fret. Now well acquainted with Calvin Burcombe's borrowed copy of *Resident Evil 2*, I was to receive my own.

Harry Potter and the Prisoner of Azkaban had ravenously whetted my appetite for further exploration of JK Rowling's saga. This last year, the media had lifted the first three *Harry Potter* books from momentous popularity to international phenomenon. On Amazon, the new book's red-framed cover showed the now-fourteen-year-old Harry, astride his Firebolt, speeding past a fearsomely detailed dragon. After *Azkaban*'s grotesque Dementors and touching family revelations, I excitedly wondered what lay in store for Harry and friends.

A few days before my birthday, I chose the wrong moment to enter the living room and saw, lying on the sofa, a copy of the book ordered from Amazon. Having sullied my birthday present with early exposure, I felt a moderate sense of loss.

Later that evening, in consideration of its relative cheapness, Mam and Dad decided to gift the book to me independently of my birthday. My dismay at early exposure was overwhelmed by delight at finally starting the new *Harry Potter*.

I knelt across my bed and devoured the ominous revelation of refuge in the abandoned Riddle House of Voldemort and Wormtail, and Harry's subsequent alarm at a sudden twinge of his lightning-bolt-shaped scar.

The narration then turned to more Dursley comedy. Dudley, in protest at having been forced to go on a diet, has chucked his PlayStation out of the window.

Throughout the past three books, Rowling's descriptions of Dudley's weight had made me wonder if my own weight might rouse her to a lesser degree of the same moral outrage. Despite his mother's protests that he's a growing boy who needs his food, the fact remains that Dudley's waistline exceeds the sizes of the Smeltings school knickerbockers. Despite his shouted protests, and his mother's tearful refusal to see anything wrong with his body, necessity confines him to a diet.

From my implicit share in this satire, I hid behind supposition that I wasn't as fat as Dudley, and that Dudley was scorned not merely for his size, but for his bullying.

Even if a lesser specimen, I was of the same breed as Dudley: I was fat because I ate too much – or rather, as I'd one day learn, because I already had eaten too much. With Dudley's anti-diet tantrums, Rowling, in *Goblet of Fire*, still seems to equate his outsize appetite with parental indulgence.

Beneath my engrossment in the story, I felt a mournful, resigned alienation. My parents did not overindulge me. On noticing my excessive appetite, my mother had tried to dissuade it. She had never refused to acknowledge my weight. She had tried to help me lose weight. And if obesity stems from parental indulgence, then why, please, weren't my two brothers obese?

To take Harry for a stay at their house, Arthur, Ron, Fred and George Weasley materialise inside the Dursley's blocked-up fireplace and temporarily demolish the chimney. While Arthur makes awkward conversation, irrepressible pranksters Fred and George go to get Harry's luggage.

Fred then slips Dudley a Ton-Tongue Toffee, which magically grows his tongue to a size which chokes him. His sobbing mother pulls at her son's engorged tongue. Having teleported to the Weasleys', Harry and friends have a good laugh.

While I clung to Rowling's favourable depiction of other fat characters as a disclaimer of her contempt for the overweight, their excesses of flab were either lesser or briefly mentioned.

While comical, Dudley's engorged tongue is portrayed as a grotesque, uncomfortable threat to Dudley's immediate safety. It reflects the outrage of his weight – an imposition on others and a hindrance to him, but induced by feckless greed and deserving of derision.

I recalled my own mother's sobs of fright when I awoke on the kitchen floor after trying the wrong diet.

I ploughed through the rest of the book, but always with the underlying impression that my frame was a decadence-honed eyesore that Harry and friends oughtn't really to be bothered with.

Slow

The bright, hot morning on which I turned thirteen found me encouragingly relaxed. My very own copy of *Resident Evil 2* marked the occasion with anticipation and pride. The day had fallen on the second last day of term. To observe the departure of Year Eight, the Middle School had arranged a day trip to Newcastle's newly opened Life Centre, followed by dinner at a pizzeria.

On the hot concrete of the school yard, Sean presented me with a diarrhoea-themed birthday card.

Having learned from Mam "ferme la bouche" to be the French equivalent of "shut your mouth," and from Dad that "head" translated to "têt," I imagined I could now say "shut your mouth, you shithead" in French. For the last few weeks, 8B had hosted several French exchange students. Fletcher Wrenford now urged me to greet one of our guests with the irreverent instruction. He steered our group to the attention of a tall, tanned French lad.

Fletcher and friends urged me to speak. With severe reservations about the accuracy, comic value or civility of my linguistic titbit, I faced the young Frenchman and forced myself to utter my humorous apprehension of his language. My fears of our mutual embarrassment, and that I was once again being lured into comedic self-exhibition, were overruled by something I didn't quite understand – to a need to accommodate others, logic and self-assertion fell.

At my fumbled delivery, the lad smirked.

"*Slow*-er," he urged with a smile.

I was relieved to give up; he seemed not to have a clue what I was on about.

Year Nine

On the first day of Year Nine, I woke early. Downstairs, in my white shirt, red and white striped black tie and black jumper, I stood before the mirror. With a semi-ironical salute, I observed my approach towards adulthood.

Left of our house, I climbed to the library and crossed the road to a steep region of the sloping green, before which lay the bus stop's flagstones. Hereabouts lingered several others, including Sean.

Nervously keen to observe protocol, I showed the driver my bus pass.

After the half-hour ride to Morpeth, the bus pulled up by a street marked "Dawson Place." As I disembarked with the others, I made sure to show my pass again. It would be weeks before I was dissuaded of the necessity of this.

In chill air, the babbling procession crossed the quiet district, turned left to a forested roadside and, through the towering school gate, climbed the steep bank to the King Edward VI School, or KEVI for short.

Through teeming corridors, I followed my timetable to the Lower School and up several flights of stairs to the D Floor, where lay my form classroom.

My form tutor was Mrs Willis. A tall young woman with long straight ginger hair and a mild Standard English accent, her kindly reception of me lent some much-needed reassurance – this place was massive. She too, it turned out, was from Rothbury.

That night, at home, I perused my two-week timetable. Tomorrow included Music, as taught by Mr Ford, James's old choirmaster and friend. After four years of attending Music classes at Middle School, I still couldn't actually read music. Now, with the curriculum geared ever closer to exams, I wondered what consequences awaited my inability to learn. I briefly sobbed.

A fellow bus passenger I dimly recognised was Rhoda Patterson. Having been in Year Nine when James was in Year Thirteen, they'd been in the school choir together. Dark brown hair framed fine, bespectacled features, from which issued a peaceable Standard English voice. At the end of one of the first days of term, she, I and one or two others walked down the bank away from the bus stop.

With inclusive familiarity, she asked if I found KEVI agreeable.

Bodily and emotionally weary, I longed for an evening in which to forget my new obligations.

"I don't really want to talk about it just now," I said politely enough, I thought.

That evening, I recounted the exchange to Mam and Dad, who both seemed dismayed at my dismissal of such kind consideration.

With a shock of shame, I realised myself to have retained the unwittingly unwholesome approach to society that in my youth had caused such upset.

English classes, held in my form classroom by Mrs Willis, quickly proved the highlight of the week. As in registration, I sat by Sidney West, a brightly civil boy with curly dark hair. We were given photocopied sheets of the poem "A Martian Sends a Postcard Home," in which the eponymous visitor, in cryptic detail, describes commonplace terrestrial phenomena. Our task was to write a similar account. I had great fun with this.

At the end of the day, I joined the thriving procession down the school bank, past a small church, across the road and to the bus station.

The open-walled bus station bridged a pavement, which, before Morpeth's Co-op, bordered the busway.

While waiting for the bus, I sometimes went inside the Co-op, in search of some such delight as a bottle of coke. As I turned through a crowded aisle, the bulky holdall hung across my waist bumped abruptly into a small boy. He began to sob with shock. Stunned, I blurted a manic apology to his mother, who smilingly absolved me.

Inspired by *Ed, Edd n Eddy*'s Double D, I cultivated the cautious habit of walking with my forearms raised to my sides.

Friendly

In Biology, Chemistry, Physics, History and PE, Sean and I became acquainted with a boy named Craig Burdis, generally known as Burdy.

I'd never known anyone quite like Burdy. Nearly six feet tall, impudent mirth frequently crinkled his face and buoyed his booming Morpeth voice. There wasn't a malicious bone in his body – as I would later learn, he had an industrious capacity for generosity – but he seemed constantly delighted by dryly indelicate description of select schoolmates. One boy with a slightly heavy brow and pale skin tone, Burdy giggled, looked like "a little green Martian!"

I was terrified he was going to get us into trouble. In assembly, Head of Year Miss Knox's mild London-sounding drawl, usually affably jocular, rose to solemn tirades against bullying.

"Ah, shuddup man, Burdy," I moaned, should his targets be nearby.

Save for classroom navigation with Burdy and Sean, I often walked alone.

I turned into the corridor which bridged the Lower School Hall. In a broad rightward alcove, a row of benches faced the Lower School boys' toilets. On the front bench huddled a recurrent host of older students. One, a thin-faced boy with short blond hair and glasses, brightly greeted me. One day, his amused smile came with a salute.

Never quite sure to what extent such greetings fed a secretly derisive mirth, I habitually humoured them and returned the salute. I quite enjoyed the eminence, however ironical, of militaristic gesture.

My offer of it on our next encounter seemed to delight the older boy and his pals. In the corridors and in the yard, I received grinning requests for a salute.

I realised my presence, to them, was a comedic exhibition. But what if their smiles also held genuine fellowship? Might they intend me to share in their fun?

During the half-hour bus ride to and from Morpeth, on the headphones of my cassette Walkman, I listened to songs recorded from James's Abba and Status Quo CDs. One rainy morning, at the front of a double-decker Arriva bus, I sat on a backwards-facing bench. On the opposite-facing bench were two older girls.

The girl opposite my right had a neck-length bob of wavy, mousy blond hair, soft, merry features and a black Adidas jacket whose sleeves were streaked with white stripes. With apparent recognition, she brightly noted me.

I endeavoured to respond civilly; she seemed genuine. However, one could never quite be sure. She now requested a brief listen to my headphones.

To me, this seemed suspiciously forward. In case her request was innocent, I tried to word my refusal politely.

"Sorry, but, uh, no," I said.

On the second floor, in a region which merged the Lower and Upper ends of the school, lay the Art classrooms. At the window, I sat by Julian Biggs. Several inches shorter than me, spiky blond hair topped sharp, fine features. With a hint of fun, his level voice plied me with conversation designed to expose, for his amusement, my eccentricities.

He seemed to find everything about me illicitly amusing, from my brotherhood of a man of drinking age, to my disclaimer of any desire for romantic relationships.

On the PE field, I, as ever, instinctively fled whenever the ball was launched anywhere near my vicinity.

"I'll pass the ball to you, Andrew," called Julian, with his none too convincing air of innocence.

The Egg

To my delight, Mrs Willis assigned a creative writing project: a short story, of our chosen theme, geared toward someone of our own age.

I envisioned a scene in which a family, relaxing one starry evening by a lake, see a meteorite land on the water. To central protagonist Philip, I imparted vague notions of my own attributes, although in my mind's eye, he more closely resembled James. To Philip's year-younger brother Jim, I broadly assigned my brother John's occasional stridency.

My envisioning of their fictional parents was much more vague. I didn't quite dare presume to defile adult eminence with my frivolous narrations.

I felt a conscientious pressure to pander to media assertion that women could indeed have traditionally male jobs and know about stuff. While I would never have dared to give the mother a name or visual description, I noted her knowledge of astronomy.

To my delight, Mrs Willis pronounced the story "gripping" and compared the scene of the Egg's hatching to *The War of the Worlds*.

Exercise

I continued to fall asleep at an average of around two in the morning. When daylight came, my weariness burned.

"You've just got to force yourself," said John, who usually fell asleep around twelve.

After a bittersweet goodbye to softness, warmth and stillness, I forced myself out of bed. The time I took to wash my face, get dressed and eat usually left about ten minutes before the bus would leave. Dad, on his way to Barrowburn, was happy to give me a lift.

The Frontera carried me up the sloping three hundred yards of road and stopped outside the library. Into the cool morning air, I heaved my tall, broad, obese frame.

To those already gathered along the sloping green above the bus stop, I wondered how I must look. The bus stop was about a minute's walk from my house. Was I so lazy to demand a lift from my father? Couldn't I force my bloated bulk up three hundred yards of road? Didn't I blatantly need the exercise?

Well, I was tired from lack of sleep.

"'Cause you *don't go to bed*," Granda Widdrington would insist. My weekend lie-ins, he'd warned Mam, were to blame for my weight.

While it seemed unlikely that a brief uphill walk could make much of a dent on my weight, the supposed power of exercise to burn fat, coupled with the shame of work-shyness, was a hard persuasion to resist.

Legs

In the evenings, Sean would sometimes phone for an agreeable ramble, mainly pertaining to recently seen or anticipated films. While I'd admitted my aversion to nudity, our occasionally jocular friendship was solid enough for me to confide my partiality to legs.

One morning, as the bus prepared to leave for Morpeth, Sean and I sat near the front. Near the door, bolted to the bus's inner right wall, was a bench. Sean glanced at it.

"Here, Andrew," he murmured with a smirk, "what d'you think of *them* legs?"

On the bench, with several others, sat Adidas Jacket. I'd seen her legs before. However mockingly, Sean's appraisal hinted their splendour; their fine pallor and slim curvature were of a body two years older than me.

So far, I'd considered the attention of Adidas Jacket a mild, if probably well-intentioned intrusion; I supposed the usual kindly, conspicuous need to assure me of my inclusion, which, I feared, might hold a touch of mockery.

142

Each day, I henceforth cherished every glance at her bare legs. In her wavy, mousy blonde hair, high brow, light blue eyes and soft, mellow features, I began to see a sensual gentleness. I suddenly yearned for her airily merry voice to once more grace me.

But for whatever reason, her focus on me seemed to have been exhausted.

I sought at least to learn her name.

One afternoon, I sat directly behind Adidas Jacket, who, with a friend, shared a set of earplugs attached to a personal stereo.

"Lorna!" said Adidas Jacket in mock-grumpiness when her earplug slipped. As the bus rolled on, I listened.

"Faye!" Lorna suddenly laughed indignantly.

Footsteps

Over the years, Mam had occasionally been perplexed to hear, from the vicinity of the stairs, what had sounded like the voice of a young boy.

"Hello, there!" it had called brightly.

Our house, during the Second World War, had apparently housed several evacuees from Newcastle.

One afternoon, I wandered down from the bus stop to find Mam and John in the kitchen. Shortly after John's return from school, Mam now told me, she and John, in the kitchen, had heard the front door open and close. This had been followed by the sound, from across the stairs, of hasty footsteps.

Mam had investigated – and found no one in sight.

Firstlings

My lifelong cautious regard for electronics had by now mounted to frequent guilty fears that I, with careless intent, had moistened an electric socket, either by brushing it with my foot or spitting on it. I was overall persuaded that this hadn't in fact happened, but fear of the prospective guilt pressured me to do my utmost to ensure safety.

As I eased my way through heaving corridors, I would stoop over an electric socket, sometimes for nearly a minute, and repeatedly touch it with my fingers in desperate pursuit of undoubted dryness.

As my form class dispersed, I joined the crowding procession, which filed into the corridor and across to the stairwell.

As I neared the stairs, I found myself directly behind softly-spoken Lilly Rogerson.

I lifted my foot. I suddenly found myself arrested by a fretful, reckless urge to flout safety, and to drive my foot so swiftly as to risk its contact with the back of Lilly's heel. I envisioned a scene in which such a nudge might trip her, perhaps even fatally, down the brief flight of stairs. My desperation to avoid such horror was overruled by an addled, self-punishing recklessness. I drove my foot blithely on.

Unable to stop myself, I willed the lowering of my foot to pursue potentially fatal contact.

At most, my toecap nudged fractionally against the heel of her shoe.

I was now, I feared, guilty of attempted murder.

While never unmanageable, the guilt stifled me, for weeks, with awed sorrow.

Desperate to believe I hadn't really meant Lilly to fall to her death, I clung to the possibility that my irresistibly affected malice hadn't really been an attempt at murder. Perhaps eased by the absurdity of the allegation, my conscience gradually relaxed.

The evenings darkened. From the bus stop, I descended the pavement past a sloping row of attached houses. Through a brightly lit window, I saw the relaxing head of an elderly woman.

With fearful caution, I pondered how easily it would be to bang on the window. If the elderly woman had a heart condition, doing so, I imagined, might prove fatal. If I wasn't careful, I could kill someone.

As I walked downhill, I feared my horrified fascination might rouse me to bang on the glass. On one occasion, the ease and danger of doing so were sufficient to persuade not my logical memory, but my emotive imagination, that I might indeed have banged on the window without fully realising it.

For weeks, I carried the fearful guilt. Not a stark panic, but a murky, mournful dread. Again, the allegation succumbed gradually to logic and ran out of steam.

In English, Mrs Willis took us through Macbeth's soliloquy, in which the murderous king vows henceforth to act on impulse. By this point, surmised Mrs Willis, Macbeth has acclimatised to his guilt – it's basically worn off.

I regretted not having been able to avoid incursions of guilt, but eventual desensitisation to them was a relief. I dared to wonder if the guilt was even deserved. I clung to the possibility of my innocence.

2001

Pipes

In the first floor Chemistry classroom, beneath my desk, a thin metal pipe protruded from the floor.

How easily might my shoe nudge it?

How fragile might it be?

Could my incaution result in a lethal explosion?

Might my unconscious mind hold some insidious urge to deliberately cause such disaster?

If incautious, might I succumb to such urges?

What if I kicked the pipe?

What if I already had?

On realising all this, I involuntarily imbued any innocent manoeuvre of my foot with an imagined will to rupture the metal and endanger my classmates and teachers.

My conscience frequently forced me under the table to ensure that the pipe was intact.

Fingernails

I shared several classes with Jeff Stobbs. One Chemistry lesson, he glanced at my hand.

"Irr," he murmured, "do you clean your nails?"

I made no comment. When the time came to wash my hands, I always made absolutely sure to do so. I now wondered why the need to clean beneath my nails had escaped my attention. I henceforth did so diligently.

"Irr," Jeff grunted on a similar occasion, "you're a *pig*, you."

Pig.

The jibe unified my outsize appetite, my past difficult relationship with toilets and the absent-mindedness which now gave an impression of my inept hygiene.

Cock

On the bus, one of the older girls, who seemed to be called Louise, asked what I was listening to on my Walkman.

Wary of opportunists out to lure me into exhibiting my absurdities, I pleaded ignorance of the current song's title.

"What does it go like?" she pressed.

I took the request for me to harmonise as a blatant indication of badly disguised contempt. Still, I wasn't entirely sure.

"Don't be so bloody nosy," I said, firmly but mildly.

With tender indignation, she protested a mere attempt to get to know me. I wondered if years of defensiveness really had made a curmudgeon of me.

On the way home, Sean and I, at the back of the bus, on a leftward-facing bench, sat huddled amidst several older students.

Two feet before us sat the occupants of the rightward-facing bench, and to our right sat those at the very back of the bus. Among them, a chortling older boy asked me comically inane questions.

"What *do* you want from me," he said, "apart from my cock?"

His increasingly blatant contempt roused in me a desire for self-assertion. A request for him to shut his face was unlikely to go very far. I launched myself diagonally from my seat and aimed my shoulder at him.

A manoeuvre of the bus steered me toward the opposite bench, where my hefty frame disrupted an arrangement of papers in the lap of a quiet, older, short-haired blond girl. She fixed me with a solemn glare and shouted a rebuke. Arousal to such fierceness of her fine features and soft voice reiterated the lifelong imposition on society of my confused, cumbersome person. Her solemn, innocent fury buckled me with frightened shame.

I tried to quell some of my humiliation with a ridiculous bellow of "Accident!"

Throughout the rest of the journey, I, ashamed of my feebleness, quietly wept at my righteously brutal rejection.

When the bus pulled to a stop, my face remained moist. Louise, who had herself been in tears a few days ago, happened to pass me. "Andrew?" she murmured. "Have a cup of tea."

Redwall

As the days began to warm and brighten, I arrived home to find John watching *Redwall*, a new cartoon. The woodland stone edifice of Redwall Abbey housed an order of anthropomorphised mice, who fed and sheltered various residents of the local countryside. Cluny the Scourge's (voiced by Diego Matamoros) horde of invading sea rats roused young novice Matthias (voiced by Tyrone Savage) to find the legendary sword of Martin the Warrior (voiced by Benedict Campbell).

Soft, richly detailed animation characteristic of Nelvana, Anglicised North American accents and a fluting, poignantly earnest score wove a gripping yarn. John and I became hooked.

Should Granda Widdrington arrive for his afternoon visit, I, with beseeching apology to John, would press a button to replace the cartoon with the blue screen of the TV guide. I realised I was being absurd, but I couldn't quite bear to allow exposure of *Redwall*, or any cartoon, for that matter, to Granda Widdrington – memory of his playful sneers at and pious scorn for television irrationally shamed my continued consumption thereof.

Faye

As summer neared, John and I, one free afternoon, strolled through the village's mild, sunbathed air.

Across the high street, the paved valley floor slanted down to Soulsby's emporium of postcards, stationery and toys. I glanced through the window and beheld a wondrously familiar bob of wavy, mousy blond hair.

The weather blazed ever brighter. On the way home, I, with the excuse of John's imminent birthday, stole into Soulsby's secondary room. I stared at the Airfix model aeroplane kits, for which John had a particular fondness. Dad, the aviation enthusiast, never tired of assembling them for us.

As I waited in the quiet gloom, I soon heard the momentous, but not altogether unexpected, sound of Faye's voice. With some urgency, she addressed the man behind the till. Her tone, I thought, threatened annoyance. Even though I was in no way bothering her, I shrank inwardly at the prospect of earning some of this ire. Both petrified and elated, I busied myself with staring at the displays. A moment later, Faye strode into the room and noticed me.

To my astonished relief and glee, her face and voice lit up in surprised elation. For a glorious moment, we exchanged pleasantries. The sunshine had brought her clear skin to a radiant pallor. And to cap it all, she had that skirt on.

Via lunch sitting orientation, I deduced Faye to be in Year Eleven.

In the kitchen, as Mam gave me a haircut, I steered the conversation toward the Year Elevens. While some might this year leave school, others would progress, as had James, to KEVI's Sixth Form, admission to which required five GCSEs with at least a "C."

While eager to learn as much as I could about Faye, mention of such delicacy as infatuation would shame my intrusion upon it. In reference to one of the Year Elevens, I forced myself to use the word "fancy."

Mam deduced that I was referring to Faye Preston, acquaintance of James. Mam received my confession with encouraging casualness.

Already buoyed by that evening's broadcast of Terry Jones' version of *The Wind in the Willows* (1996), I found myself encouraged to savour my blooming discovery of life.

Little Green Blobs

One Saturday afternoon at the Metrocentre, in WHSmith, I saw a plastic-wrapped issue of *TV Zone* to hold, in its top right corner, a thumbnail photo of a Dalek. Smooth, white and bulky, with gold limbs and orbs, it was an Imperial Dalek from *Remembrance of the Daleks* (1988).

I bought the magazine. "Little Green Blobs," an interview with writer Ben Aaronovitch and script editor Andrew Cartmel, observed the DVD release of *Remembrance of the Daleks*.

Halfway through the magazine, an A4 poster showed a doctored production shot. On a daylit school yard stood the Imperial Dalek Shuttlecraft. Before it, past the parked TARDIS, several Imperial Daleks were followed by the Special Weapons Dalek. Instead of eyestalk, plunger and gunstick, its scorched, grimy dome mounted a hefty cannon.

Leftward, a squad of bluish grey Renegade Daleks advanced upon their Imperial rivals. From the gunstick of an Imperial Dalek flew a jet of amber fire, which culminated, amidst the Renegades, in a superb explosion.

I hungered for reunion with this chapter of *Doctor Who* which, with synthesised score and touches of early CGI, had veered towards what I recognised as modernity. I searched in vain for a VHS release.

Fox Kids

With increasing frequency, John returned from school to retreat for several hours into our bedroom to attend his recently acquired PlayStation copy of *Command and Conquer: Red Alert* (1996).

I, meanwhile, savoured each opportunity to return to the corner of the landing, switch on the old Windows 95 and delve once more into the World Wide Web.

In a perusal of cartoon fanart, I found, on a welcomingly simple white screen, a collection of web pages dubbed Sailor Napper's Realm. Drawings by various hands, as well as Sailor Napper's digital "Poser" sculptures, all entailed the teenage heroines of a Japanese cartoon.

With cartoonishly large eyes and tiny noses, softly expressive faces headed anatomically detailed frames with miniskirted, adult-looking legs. Each girl bore the title "Sailor" followed by a designation of some respective solar body. The cartoon series from which they stemmed was called *Sailor Moon*. What was more: it was currently being aired on Fox Kids.

Having recently returned from school one afternoon, I selected "Fox Kids" on the Sky Box's digital listings, switched off the telly and stole upstairs to watch it on the portable telly in mine and John's bedroom.

The small screen held a world of soft, lushly bright colours, mainly peopled by North-American-accented teenage girls. Beneath expressively large eyes, the mouths were often a succession of pink triangles and circles.

Serena (voiced by Terri Hawkes), the titular Sailor Moon, peered into a mirror and applied pink lip gloss. In a soft, high, jovial voice, she counted her cosmetic preparations. Such gaiety roused a sense of my coarse intrusion.

Before long, John urged a change of channel. With the pretence of casual curiosity, I requested further viewing.

"Because you fancy Sailor Moon?" said John wryly.

I pursued further clandestine inspections of *Sailor Moon*. If the living room door opened, I immediately changed the channel. Others' exposure to my consumption of flamboyant, feminine fancy held an irrational shame which near-panicked me.

Quite Weird

My fourteenth birthday arrived on the final day of Year Nine.

Having missed the bus home, I sat on the short brick wall by the bus station and read my recently purchased copy of Terrance Dicks' *Doctor Who: The Eight Doctors* (1997). While I'd long enjoyed reading the blurbs of *Doctor Who* novels in WHSmith, my lax concentration usually deterred my commitment to unknown authors. However, I had some familiarity with Terrance Dicks, and this book opened immediately after the TV Movie.

Ever wary of the lonely futility of obligatory enjoyment, I did a fairly good job of it being my birthday, helped by my new VHS copy of *Doctor Who*'s second serial, *The Daleks* (1963).

"It would take somebody quite... *weird* to come up with *Doctor Who*," mused James as the protagonists sheltered in chambers housed within a phone box.

I briefly wondered if I'd corrupted my young mind with imagery so bizarre as to be somehow dangerous.

Llangollen

Along with two TARDIS pens ordered last Christmas, a merchandise catalogue had included a promotion leaflet for the *Doctor Who* exhibition in Llangollen, Wales. It occurred to Mam that since John had gone on his Year Seven skiing trip to France, I might in turn be afforded an extravagant excursion.

Moved by the generous offer, I proposed a visit to the fabled exhibition. Mam and Dad readily agreed and planned an overnight trip to Llangollen.

In preparation for the lengthy car trip, I recorded a new mixtape from James's Abba and Billy Joel CDs, Mam's Kirsty MacColl *Galore* CD and my *Best of Rolf Harris* CD, acquired for my fourteenth birthday from Uncle Ross.

On the night before the journey, I sneaked an online visit to Sailor Napper's Realm. Downstairs, Mam, Dad and James watched *Da Ali G Show*.

Around ten o'clock next morning, I sat on the left-hand side of the back seat of the Vauxhall Frontera. As we rode, the thrill of motion and the mixtape's music roused me to an ecstasy of anticipation.

In time to the music, I recalled and arranged fond mental images. *Sailor Moon* heroine Serena, her lively spirit tempered by lovelorn sensitivity, roused in me a nervously blooming affection.

After about four hours, we reached Wales. Broad, brownish green hills and dense forestry bordered lightly bustling streets.

After an hour or so, I saw, through the windscreen, a brown road sign, whose white print listed locations, numbers, and, wonderfully, a surprisingly detailed etching of a Dalek. A momentous levity shivered through the car.

Fifteen minutes later, Dad brought us to an open-spaced car park.

Leftward, a huge steam train engine guarded a museum devoted to *Ivor the Engine*.

Thirty yards before us stood a smooth, stark white building. High above the doors loomed a huge red and yellow recreation of the diamond-shaped logo as used in *Doctor Who*'s title sequence from 1974 to 1979. And what was standing sentry left of the doors but an actual life-size Dalek? Oh, we were here alright.

With Mam, Dad and John, I hastened for a closer look at the gorgeous thing. Delirious at sudden proximity to an interstellar cyborg, I noted its now-tangible details. A few inches shorter in height than myself, its bluish greyness implied its rank to be that of a Renegade Dalek, as featured in *Remembrance of the Daleks*. Its sturdy bulk had a coarse firmness. I reverently savoured my encounter with a shape whose recorded and broadcast image awed and delighted me.

"Shake hands with the Dalek then, Andy," laughed Dad.

With fearful caution, I gripped the broad black suction cup at the end of the smooth pole which projected from the Dalek's middle. We took several photos, which ended up showing me, in shorts and black tee shirt, with my fingers resting reverently on the Dalek's dome.

Through the doors, the first, broadly lit chamber was mostly bare, except for a rope-bordered, eight-foot-high windowed blue hut – the TARDIS. Attached to its rope barrier was a message, written from the perspective of the Doctor, with a request not to touch.

In the subsequent darkened corridors, tall, broad windows framed illuminated chambers, set with neatly mounted costumes as used throughout the show's history. With a solemn thrill, I beheld such sights as a Time Lord's wide-collared robe, Jon Pertwee's jacket and Sylvester McCoy's question mark pullover.

The Hall of Monsters displayed props, models and costumes which had contributed to the realisation of fantastical creatures. From the ceiling hung *The Power of Kroll*'s (1979) giant squid. Amidst stretching tentacles, a bright green, rounded body, a foot or so in length, sank into a circular maw rowed with teeth.

A glass-walled display of Daleks of various rank and colour included the Special Weapons Dalek and a model of a gunge-streaked battle-damaged Dalek.

In a concrete-floored hall, we saw Bessie, the Third Doctor's Edwardian car.

The exhibition concluded with a small, copiously stocked merchandise shop. The rows of DVDs included *Remembrance of the Daleks*, but no VHS release. Mam made a generous proposition. James, having enrolled at the Open University, would benefit from an up-to-date personal computer. As our old Windows 95 was getting a bit slow, we might as well get one that could play DVDs.

I was now able to buy a copy of the DVD.

Remembrance of the Daleks

Having stayed in a Travelodge, our long drive back to the North East took us first to the Metrocentre. Instead of a new computer, my parents chose to splash out on a DVD player priced less than a hundred pounds.

Back home, Dad lay across the living room carpet and fiddled with the relevant wires.

Eventually, beneath the Sky Box and video recorder lay a third rectangular box, this one grey, with a retractable disc draw.

I installed my disc.

Following an introductory CGI recreation of the 1970s time vortex, a grey screen held the options of "Play," "Episode Selection" and "Special Features." Beside this display played a clip I recalled from three years previously, of the chunky white Imperial Daleks gliding out of their cream-coloured Shuttlecraft.

The serial opened with a satellite shot of the planet Earth, accompanied by radio broadcasts from 1963. As the camera panned back, synthesised music brooded over the overhead arrival of a rectangular, cream-coloured Dalek Killcruiser. Like its *Red Dwarf* contemporaries, the model's size and detail easily invited suspension of disbelief.

The following title sequence, with its purple CGI galaxy, was followed by a brightly daylit London street. Opposite a school, away from the parked TARDIS, strode Sylvester McCoy's Seventh Doctor and Sophie Aldred's Ace.

Ace's badge-emblazoned jacket, East-London-leaning accent and bolshy enthusiasm lent a joyous edge of naturalism.

Sylvester McCoy's Seventh Doctor surveyed the scene. Beneath a Panama hat and wavy dark hair, his heavily browed face cast solemn stares and rapt gazes. His soft, high Anglo-Scots voice rose and fell in rumination. For his eminent mix of steel and whimsy, I felt a renewed admiration.

With a can of Ace's Nitro-9, the Doctor blows the top of a Dalek to smithereens. Between the fallen bricks atop its charred base peaks a domed mound of bright green flesh.

"Take it to Area 51!" laughed Dad.

A hieroglyph-marked floating casket houses the Hand of Omega, a glowing white ball, with which the Doctor tricks Davros into blowing up the Daleks' home planet Skaro. As in 1998, I had to feel a bit sorry for the poor nutter. The serial, charged with energy, affection and grandeur, was, by its end, tinged with melancholy.

The DVD rekindled my devotion to *Doctor Who*. I frequently browsed my copy of David J Howe's *Doctor Who: A Book of Monsters* and even forced myself to get up on weekend mornings for the odd UK Gold repeat.

Sailor Moon

I found myself increasingly drawn to secretly watch, and soon record, episodes of *Sailor Moon*.

Of its several fourteen-year-old heroines, central focus was on Serena.

Stylistically large eyes, a tiny nose and polymorphic mouth adorned a face whose high brow, broad cheekbones and blunt chin lent it a cherubic softness. In twin tresses, blond hair streamed from two spherical bunches, earning her the nickname Meatball Head. Her feminine gaiety, realised perfectly in a soft, high, lilting voice, blazed like the young summer.

I recorded a full episode. In James's small bedroom, to which he allowed general access, I eased past the enormous Yamaha keyboard and, by the airing cupboard, installed my tape in a video recorder atop a portable telly.

In this episode, *Sailor Mercury Moving On?*, softly spoken Amy (voiced by Karen Bernstein) prepares to leave to study medicine in Germany. At the airport, an extra-diegetic song, coupled with a montage of her smiling friends, heralds her change of heart. The celebration of female friendship was both daunting in its delicacy and touching in its tenderness. Initially, I countered my intimidation by mocking the sentiment, yet remained compelled to see more.

Funny Little Ways

By this point, my fear of electric sockets and gas pipes was, to my family, well known. In wretched embarrassment, I warned Mam, Dad, James and John that I might have "accidentally spat on" some plug or socket. This latest irrational fear was met with variably patient reassurance and exasperated calls for restraint of my disorderly imagination.

I recalled an illustrated storybook. Nanette Newman's *Spider the Horrible Cat* (1994) sees elderly Mrs Broom take in a stray cat. On finding Mrs Broom lying unconscious in the garden, Spider, disturbed to be suddenly without responsive companionship, leads a neighbour to his prone keeper, who is then taken to hospital.

All these years later, I was suddenly impressed by how vulnerable people of a certain age might be to sudden bouts of ill health. It occurred to me that failing to notice a suddenly collapsed oldster might well lead to their potentially preventable death. Sudden intimidation by this prospect set me on constant alert.

Wherever I went, I scanned my peripheral vision. Any unidentified arrangement of shapes might be someone in need of medical attention. My failure to provide it would amount, my conscience decreed, to murder. As I walked to school, or through the village, I would often halt in mid-stride to inspect any area that might host potential casualties.

Serena

Sailor Moon's lush colours, heartfelt music, softly vibrant voices and unashamed sentiment stirred in me a sweet, forbidden thrill.

I came to laud the saga of reincarnated Moon Princess Serena, upon whom were magically bestowed the miniskirted sailor suit and Moon Tiara of Sailor Moon. Daunt at Serena's gaiety had mellowed into affection, which bloomed quickly into aching, ecstatic infatuation.

Gaily styled blond hair, vulnerable yet happy eyes and a rounded face wove a soft vibrancy. A soft, high, merrily lilting voice unified the image.

Fan site *Castle in the Sky* revealed the voice to belong to Terri Hawkes. By a distant, monochrome shot of a dark-haired woman, a biographical blurb noted the actress to have recently given birth to twins. With a pang of inevitability, I saw time to have distanced me from the source of the beloved voice. Even so, further doses of *Sailor Moon*, with their recorded traces of Terri's vibrant, sensually sensitive voice, rekindled my intoxication.

Serena's flighty whims, giddy fret, naive bravado and sensitive devotion had me besotted. Her frequent admonishment for lateness, academic failure and disorganisation roused my sympathies. Her protection of time-travelling seven-year-old Rini (voiced by Tracey Hoyt) from the Negamoon Clan shone a touching compassion. Unexplained abandonment by boyfriend Darien (voiced by Toby Proctor) burdened her with valiantly managed loneliness, which culminated in her massacre of a cake buffet.

Even though she had a boyfriend and was composed of pastel drawings and the voice of a woman more than twice my age, her sorrows held me in forlorn euphoria and her joys buoyed me.

Any instant of contentment was now flavoured with the possibility of stolen moments with Serena.

With its clear air, open fields, distant pine-and-heather-swathed hills and the gentle rush of the River Coquet, the village park's timeless power to soothe and excite me now stoked memory and anticipation of my newfound joy.

Shut Up

My Year Ten timetable held two classes with "technology" in the title. One, from what I could gather, focused on designing.

The other, in some way, focused on mass-marketing. The latter was taught by Mr Pritchard. Bald, youngish and of medium build, his mild North West drawl enjoyed touches of understated levity. In venture of our familiarity with digital curvaceous explorer Lara Croft, he gently broke it to the lads that she wasn't in fact real, as no one with such a career could possibly keep their nails so nicely manicured.

Beneath my desk lay several electric sockets. One morning, I involuntarily willed a casual foot manoeuvre to fling in their general direction a discarded pencil shaving, with which, my restless conscience decided, I intended the electrocution of whoever next plugged in an electrical device.

Such was my guilty fear of such a prospect that I managed to face, at the end of the lesson, the humiliation of pestering Mr Pritchard with my fear that a pencil shaving may somehow have become lodged in the electric socket.

"How?" he replied.

The dry monotone implied a bemused exasperation.

Absolved of my guilt, I gibbered a retraction and left him in peace.

One morning, Mr Pritchard's dry banter offered the chivalrous view that girls were neater than boys.

I still resented claims of boys' innate slovenliness, loutishness and academic incompetence. With girls' supposed academic superiority lauded as overdue moral victory, my inability to learn was implicitly traced to my larger, coarser, supposedly more aggressive body.

Unable to disprove the fashionable view that girls were brighter, I continued to quietly hope it to be erroneous. That I, in my singular inhibition, should bear the further shame of being a threat to womankind, sorely galled me. Furthermore, one of the few things on which I prided myself was my fastidious neatness.

One piece of homework involved drawing something on a blank sheet of paper. For some reason, I failed to store mine in a folder. Mr Pritchard strode between the desks to gather each piece of work. He inspected my scuffed sheet.

"Are you a boy?" he droned.

"Yes," I said.

"Well, that's why your work looks like that, then," he grunted.

Appreciative giggles arose.

I was shocked into miserable, silent fury.

Of Mr Pritchard's instructions, all I could grasp was that the coursework had something to do with drawing diagrams or sketches or something and putting them in some kind of order.

Having failed to retain early instructions, I, with my usual naivety, resolved to muddle along in hope that the path to correctness would eventually reveal itself. Should I request further instruction, Mr Pritchard, I feared, would suppose I hadn't been listening. My laziness, or obstinacy, or both, would incur his bemusement, exasperation and annoyance.

The threat of a raised or sharpened voice of authority roused a queasy dread.

There came a point when the coursework required file storage of older work. Having long since discarded them, I couldn't file my earlier efforts, which I doubted had even fulfilled the tasks in question.

My chest in a vice of dread, I approached Mr Pritchard and tentatively explained, having discarded my work, my inability to fulfil today's task. Mr Pritchard flatly acknowledged my explanation and turned away.

I nervously followed and asked what I should do now.

"Well," he droned, "you've thrown all your work in the bin, so you better sit down and shut up before I lose my temper."

This taste of the kind of wrath used for troublemakers staggered and chilled me with sickly, frightened shame.

The other, marginally more comprehensible Technology class required written work. On absence of its teacher, a short-haired, North-West-accented ginger woman, we were left in the care of Mr Watt, a youngish, bespectacled man with an easy-going Estuary-sounding drawl.

The current task was to design a set of small, portable devices. Others seemed to be personalising theirs. In a brief delirium of bravado, I decided to draw some Daleks on mine. On finishing,

I brought my paper to Mr Watt for inspection. He peered at it encouragingly.

"Maybe some *Cybermen...*" he pondered.

Delighted at the endorsement, I added some.

At the start of the next lesson, the class's usual teacher assessed respective progress. With a gently pained sigh, she stressed the implausibility of my submission. On scrutiny of my frivolous fancy by scholarly eminence, I recoiled in self-disgusted dread.

Her weary drone went in for the kill.

"*All those Daleks...*"

Desperate to hear no more, I gabbled my contrite compliance.

"*Shut up* and listen to me," she interrupted.

The eminent wrath roused more sickly, self-abasing dread.

Novel

In Year Ten, while Mrs Willis remained my form tutor, my English class moved into the care of Mr Dolan. A few inches shorter than me, with thin brown hair and of indeterminate age, his understatedly jovial Berwick voice met my efforts with enthused esteem.

In my schoolbag, from a box set of science fiction novels Uncle Ross had given me last Christmas, I stored Arthur C Clarke's *2001: A Space Odyssey* (1968). At the awe of outer space, human ingenuity and the eerie inscrutability of whomever had built the Monolith, evenly paced prose wove easy wonder.

The mysterious Firstborn were revealed to have advanced their bodies to inhabit the energy of space itself. This notion of a union of matter and spirit was nothing short of moving.

With the blue crystal of Metebelis III, the ethereality of Regeneration and the implied sentience of the TARDIS, *Doctor Who* had also implied the transcendence of mind.

I sought to channel such grace through my own fancies.

In cold, rich air, evening skies darkened to deep blue and held the occasional star. On the frontward horizon, below the rocky, pine-robed edifice of the Simonside hills, miles of wilderness rolled down to the village. In a soft, mysterious glow, an occasional moon soothed all.

On renewed fellowship with *Doctor Who*, the eminence of its titular citizen of the universe stoked my story ideas. Infatuation with *Sailor Moon* dared my notions to reach for such tender idealism as its lovelorn heroine.

In a daydreamed story, young Philip found himself embroiled in the time-travelling machinations of the tentacular, telekinetically floating Greelashons of the lush, windswept planet Veeshah.

However, any attempt to write emotionally layered relationships stifled me with shame at my intrusion on such delicacy. Even so, a story was taking shape. I resigned to hope that someday I would grow out of my curious inhibition and, for now, kept scribbling.

Convention

Dad, John and I made a rare visit to the small shopping centre on Northumberland Street's Eldon Square. In a video shop, John noticed a small poster, whose logo seized my attention.

It was the *Doctor Who* logo as used in the 1996 TV Movie. Superimposed on the foreground was a distant shot of the film's huge, wood-panelled TARDIS Console Room. Above the Console, on either side, were two superimposed headshots of Colin Baker's Sixth Doctor and Sylvester McCoy's Seventh Doctor. A convention, Dimensions on Tyne, was to be held in the first weekend of November in a Newcastle hotel.

Dad spoke to a shop assistant, who kindly allowed us to keep the poster.

That Bloody Telly

On the Saturday morning before the convention, I rose around nine to catch UK Gold's *Doctor Who* repeat, *The Caves of Androzani* (1984). Aged nine, I hadn't retained much of the story, but had been impressed by its rugged solemnity and poignancy.

Around half past nine, John and I lounged on the sofa, still in our pyjamas, as the telly hosted the mounting perils of Peter Davison's Fifth Doctor and Nicola Bryant's Peri. Granda Widdrington, having arrived from next door, had assumed his position in the armchair.

I felt no desperate urge to hide from him the faces and voices which streamed from the screen and speakers. Foreign to his rule as were most broadcasts, *Doctor Who*'s exposure to earlier generations absolved it of raucous modernity. Furthermore, my scant familiarity minimised the threat of shame.

"Is this the one you're gan' to see tomorrow?" asked Granda of Peter Davison.

John and I left the room for breakfast and bathroom visits. Twenty minutes later, we returned to our broadcast. Noon was nearing, and we were still in our pyjamas. Our disorder suddenly roused Granda to urgency. His voice didn't fill the room but boomed fiercely.

"*That bloody telly wants* bombed!"

The sound swamped my chest with sickly, self-abasing dread. My engagement with the fancifully staged on-screen figures, suddenly a frivolous affront to Granda's peace, now felt raucous and selfish. My enthusiasm to watch any more just now was squashed.

Dimensions on Tyne

Early on Sunday morning, Dad peeked through mine and John's bedroom door and announced that it was time to get moving. The convention was to start at nine.

Having breakfasted, I hovered in the greyly daylit kitchen. As well as my phone and wallet, I equipped myself with a small plastic bag, in which I stored the inlay booklet from my DVD of *Remembrance of the Daleks*, which I hoped to present for the signature of Sylvester McCoy.

"Johnny," laughed Mam, "will you stop antagonising?" John, it seemed, had been framing the back of my head with two impudently raised fingers.

Having parked, Dad, John and I caught a Metro shuttle to the city centre. With a glance at the written directions, Dad led us along the quiet streets to a multistorey building, scaled by a flight of metal stairs. This was the place.

Through tall wooden doors, the carpeted foyer had a peaceful gloom. Between two halls on either side milled a substantial gathering of people.

Dad purchased our admission, which included a numbered card to designate our cyclical admittance to specific events. At the ticket prices, I suppressed my horrified guilt.

Before the first event, John and I wandered freely. Through the double doors of the leftward hall, several of the milling populace admired a five-foot motorised silver Dalek. Determined to make the most of today's extravagance, I put in a good bout of staring at it. Even if it wasn't an original prop, to see a Dalek in any form was always a joy.

A speaker-amplified voice announced today's first formal event. Instinctively compliant, I joined the placid crowd in the rightward hall.

Above the stage, a projector screen hung from the ceiling. A few seats ahead of me, a curly-haired woman sported a Tom-Baker-esque floppy hat and scarf. A man arrived onstage and announced the arrival of Nicholas Courtney. The significance of the familiar name was soon clarified by a montage on the projector of Brigadier Lethbridge-Stewart, fondly remembered for alliance with Jon Pertwee's Third Doctor.

Mr Courtney, a silver-haired man with a full, neat beard, took a chair onstage and, with the interviewer, hosted a conversational account of his time on *Doctor Who*.

The interviewer happened to mention Colin Baker, who, within this very building, was currently breakfasting. My proximity to two veteran actors suddenly felt an intrusion. Onstage was a man whose work had etched a character cherished across five decades, of whom my attendance consisted of sparsely viewed repeats and reference materials.

In a room upstairs, several tables held a hefty stock of on-sale merchandise. I snuck a look inside Terrance Dicks' novelisation of his own *The Five Doctors* (1983) but couldn't really afford anything. Mam had offered me some extra money, but I, wanting to be as little of a burden as possible, had declined.

I wandered to the hotel bar and bought a packet of Real McCoy's crisps. A tall man with thin, dark hair, balding at the front, passed a word of approval on the aptness of my choice of snack. Esteemed, I acknowledged the approval.

The rightward hall's next event, featuring several of the guests, was "Whoniversity Challenge." A host posed the question of which planet had been home to the Marsh Men. No one seemed sure. And then, from somewhere amidst the onstage huddle, electronically amplified, came a merrily lilting trill.

"I think it should've been Mallow," said the unmistakable voice of Sylvester McCoy. With surreal simplicity, I registered this weaver of wonder to be in the building.

A mounted monitor screen announced that several guests, including Sylvester, were now available to be photographed alongside convention attendees whose admittance card held such-and-such a number. This included John and me.

John, armed with dynamism and a decent budget, went to get a photo with Sylvester. While Dad escorted John upstairs, I remained seated. Ten minutes later, they returned.

"I've just had a conversation with Sylvester McCoy!" John grinned.

Hours remained before autographs would open to people with my registration number.

"Wouldn't you like to go and get a photo with Sylvester McCoy?" Dad asked me concernedly. I heartily affirmed but explained my low funds. Dad readily offered to pay. In the last few years, I reasoned, I'd lent John a few ten-pound notes, which he had yet to repay. I reasoned that I could now comfortably accept a counter-lone. I submitted my proposal to John. He readily agreed.

With Dad, I climbed the heavy flight of stairs.

Several floors up, halfway down a gloomy corridor, beside an open door, a man sat at a desk, on which lay an open cash box. I gave him two ten-pound notes. He handed me some change and a plastic white card, which bore a printed number seven. He offered a pen and a form for an address to which my photos could be posted.

"Well, Andy, he's in there!" laughed Dad.

I stepped inside.

Within the next few seconds, I registered a windowed room lit sparsely with overcast daylight. Left of the inner door, a few feet into the room, a diffuser umbrella loomed above a six-foot grey screen, which blocked much of the room beyond. Before it, a man sat by a camera. For an instant, I was confused; he didn't look anything like Sylvester. He amiably welcomed and directed me to my left. I returned his greeting and approached the other side of the canvas.

In the next instant, I felt a man's warm hand seize and shake mine with zealous speed and thoroughness. The gesture's energetic kindness roused to dazed ecstasy my regard for whom I knew to be its donor. Any fear of my imposition on this hard-working talent was toppled by a man whose performance flair was clearly matched by human warmth. The strange yet so familiar voice bid me a jovial welcome.

"Ah, you're number seven, like me!"

He sounded genuinely delighted by my visit.

The photographer directed me to sit with one leg across the small bench. Sylvester eased his left elbow across my shoulder.

"You're my favourite Doctor!" I managed to blurt.

"I bet you say that to all the Doctors!" said the voice, with its signature rapt drollness.

As the photographer worked, he and Sylvester chatted.

"What's your name?" said Sylvester. I thought he might be addressing the photographer, so shied away from imposing familiarity. At any time, a gaffe of mine was apt to shame my esteem for anyone, my savour of their splendour a noxious intrusion. Such a blunder with Sylvester would be like soiling a priceless painting.

"What's your name?" I heard Sylvester say again.

"Andrew," I said carefully, now reassured of his addressing of me, but still wary of my intrusion. With two flashes from the camera, and some terms of parting esteem, the session came to a close, and I went on my way.

Dazed with glee, I lingered in the gently bustling foyer. The euphoria was rather like that instilled by a kind word from Faye.

As afternoon arrived, John, whose ticket allocated different events to mine, attended an autograph session. His cardboard TARDIS plaque, bought on a whim from Forbidden Planet, was graced by the signatures of Carole Ann Ford, Anneke Wills and Deborah Watling, all sixties *Who* royalty.

In the rightward hall, the projector screen showed a brief CGI invasion of Earth by Hoverbout-mounted Daleks, set to Danny Elfman's *Mars Attacks* (1997) score. There followed a conference of several Big Finish personnel. These last three years, the production company, with original cast members, sound effects and incidental music, had recorded *Doctor Who* audio plays. Their covers merged superimposed photos of cast, props and CGI. While they looked fabulous, my overly cautious lack of commitment had so far barred me.

Those onstage now requested audience assistance on a current production. A scene in which an army of human rebels defied their Dalek overlords required numerous voices to shout, "Death to the Daleks!" If we would now shout the specified dialogue, it would be mixed with other such recordings taken from other conventions.

My lingering euphoria lent me a wholehearted enthusiasm. On cue, I affected a look of rage, delivered the dialogue at an impassioned volume and fisted the air. In the row before me, a boy of about five peered around the room, noticed my warlike gesticulation and gave a shy grin.

The screen then announced an autograph session open to those of both mine and John's registration.

Across a hall nearer the entrance, a sizeable crowd gradually condensed into a queue. Dad respectfully stepped back, and John and I got in line. The queue eventually moved and dwindled to reveal a long, white-clothed table, at whose far end sat a broad, white-haired man. I recognised him to be Colin Baker.

"You're very welcome," I could now hear him saying, in jovially functional monotone. Within a few minutes, he stood and strode towards the exit.

To his recently vacated right sat Sophie Aldred, now short-haired, but instantly recognisable. Sat to her immediate right was

Sylvester. His wavy dark brown hair had mellowed closer to grey, the ends flecked with silver. Tinted spectacles framed his broad brow and flexible face. A casually smart, dark yellow jacket evoked his Doctor's attire. Across the table before them stood the small boy from before, down at whom they beamed with unfettered glee.

"My name's James too," said Sylvester. "I've got lots of names."

"Do you like the *Daleks*?" said Sophie.

"Who's your favourite Doctor?" said Sylvester. I wondered if this had been inspired by our earlier conversation.

"Peter Davison," said young James, quietly excited.

"Is he your favourite monster?" said Sylvester.

On the table before Sophie and Sylvester lay several glossy photos of each, in varying degrees of character and promotional pose. I inched gradually to my left.

I heard Sophie's voice proffer gentle niceties towards John.

With nervous reverence, I took a fateful step leftward and met her welcoming smile. Two paragraphs in my DVD inlay booklet noted the respective careers of Sylvester and Sophie. I humbly requested Sophie's biography to be anointed by the signature of its subject. With a smile, she readily complied and inscribed, in golden ink, "To Andrew, love, Sophie Aldred. X"

With humble thanks, I inched leftward. I peered down at the table and found myself once more in the presence of Sylvester McCoy. Fuelled by the esteem of our earlier encounter, I confidently looked him in the face.

"Could you sign here, please?" I said with a proffer of the inlay booklet, my elation stayed by his apparent weariness. I laid the paper on the table. He peered down at it. "Could you just sign there, please?" I asked, indicating his biography. He took his pen and wrote across the paper. "Thanks very much," I said and moved on.

The next signer was a broad man with an abundance of curly brown hair.

"Please could you sign here?" I said, offering my booklet.

"Of course," he said with an easy smile and obliged. I later realised this man to be John Nathan Turner, *Doctor Who*'s producer throughout the 1980s.

Weeks later, as term drew to a close, school ended at midday for a ceremonial service in St James's Church.

Afterwards, I crossed the chill streets into Appleby's Bookshop, a favoured visit of James. The Science Fiction and Fantasy section held several BBC *Doctor Who* novels. I was promptly drawn to Robert Perry and Mike Tucker's *Storm Harvest* (1999). An aquatic blue cover merged Sylvester McCoy's worried-looking Seventh Doctor with a superimposed shot of what was clearly a lovingly crafted prop; a domed cranium, bulging eyes, turquoise hide and snarling maw recalled HR Giger's xenomorphs.

On a peek inside, fond descriptions of the Seventh Doctor and Ace's arrival on an otherworldly beach instantly entranced me. When I had the money, I would have to get this.

2002

Work Experience

Back at school, I, emboldened by her encouragement, confessed to Mrs Willis my attempt at a novel. My manuscript of around thirty handwritten A4 pages had reached the scene where Philip and his younger brother Jim have been escorted to relative safety by Neelreon, the floating, tentacular Greelashon, to the lush, windswept planet Veeshah.

Mr Dolan one day passed me with a friendly enquiry as to my endeavour, which I was humbly proud to agree to lend him for inspection.

That Friday, outside my form classroom, I handed him the manuscript.

"Good stuff, good stuff," he said thoughtfully.

Year Ten, the year of Work Experience, had assigned James to menial chores in some office in Newcastle. I was at a loss to see how my impaired powers of concentration and navigation would allow for such responsibility. My being set to work in an office seemed like a surreal, brutal joke.

I decided to relieve some Sunday evening monotony with an audacious endeavour: the preparation of saucepan-heated drinking chocolate. I'd watched James brew such luxury for himself, but I, so far, had been too daunted to operate the cooker.

I poured milk into a pan, placed it on a ring and twisted a knob. Perhaps I could do adult things after all. I left for a few minutes and returned to find the kitchen swamped with smoke. On the pan's rim smouldered coagulated milk. I cursed my recklessness and reported to Dad.

On entering the kitchen, his voice rose to sombre emphasis. While nowhere near a shout, it roused my inordinate fear of the few occasions when he had raised his voice.

I lurked upstairs for a while. I eventually risked a sneak past the living room.

"Andy?" called Dad from within. "Don't you ever do that again," he said. A comical drone softened his ire.

I resolved, in future, to, where possible, avoid doing things.

Peritonitis

On Monday morning, I arrived for breakfast unusually promptly. I suddenly found my enjoyment of a bowl of Weetos stifled by a very mild nausea, accompanied by a faint but consistent ache in my solar plexus. Determined to relish the chocolatey crunchiness, I persevered, but each swallow soon became a sickly burden. I admitted defeat.

Mam asked if I should perhaps take the day off. I conceded to the now slightly increased stomach ache, which gradually intensified.

The next day, I was in no doubt that school anytime soon was out of the question. A dull, ponderous ache weighed across my entire torso, movement of which in certain directions stoked the ache to a deep, sharp twinge. I managed to eat some toast, but my once-proud appetite was nowhere in sight.

Next day, I sat limply across the sofa, unable to do much else. I was in no state to lift, much less fetch the Gadget, so Mam steered the digital TV guide for me. At the Kids' listing, I directed her to Nick Junior's current broadcast of *Arthur*. The trials of a bespectacled anthropomorphised aardvark would now be quite welcome.

"Arthur," soothed Mam and pressed select. I felt somewhat embarrassed at sharing a cartoon whose name only John and I knew.

Mam arranged a house call from Dr Kay, a youngish woman who assessed my symptoms and assured Mam that my ailment would pass. Mam was unconvinced.

The day dragged into evening. I laboriously shifted myself upstairs and onto my bed, where I remained the rest of the night.

Daunted by my torso's crushing stiffness, wrenching aches and slicing twinges, I dwelled in mournful fear on the concept of pain.

The next day, Mam arranged a second opinion. Dr Carr was inclined to advise a hospital examination. My spirits lifted by the prospect of some kind of progress, I settled on the sofa to watch a Movie Channel repeat of *Bicentennial Man* (1999).

Minutes later, the gently hushed, Standard-English-accented voice of Dr Carr advised Mam to my hospital examination.

When Dad arrived home, he and Mam helped me into the Frontera, and off we went. While sharp twinges tweaked my belly with each bump, I salvaged some glee from the combination of motion and the cassette soundtrack of the 1999 version of *Joseph and the Amazing Technicolor Dreamcoat*, which I'd got Mam for Christmas.

Around eight, in a private ward, a small telly mounted high on the wall showed today's episode of *Brookside*. I was eventually brought a mug of Ribena, for which I was rapturously grateful. I was soon forbidden any more fluid. A drip was attached to my arm, which, a kindly male nurse explained, would supply me with fluid equivalent to the volume of a can of coke.

A doctor arrived to inform us that the nature of my condition remained inconclusive. Further investigation would tomorrow be made via a camera installed either by back passage or stomach incision. I very much favoured the latter. Astride a trolley bed, I enjoyed a feeling of invincibility as they wheeled me down the corridor.

"Have you got a girlfriend, then?" said the X-rayer, a jovially conversational young woman.

I meekly replied in the negative. My association with this delicate subject demeaned both it and me, but she was just making conversation.

From outside, distant street lamps bleached orange my small, cream-toned private ward. On each bedside were two small armchairs with footstools, which Mam and Dad were content to sleep on. With a wistful ache of thirst in my throat, I waited for the night to fade.

Next morning, the doctors, to my relief, had decided to use a stomach camera.

More staff helped me onto a wheeled trolley and pushed me along, while Mam and Dad closely followed.

The corridors' dim brown gave way to greyish green. Nurses helped me out of my shirt and into a green surgical gown. Humbled by the devotion being shown my hefty frame, I wryly recalled the scene from *Joseph and the Amazing Technicolor Dreamcoat*, where Ian McNeice's Potiphar exasperatedly dismisses his fussing staff and welcomes the supporting arms of Donny Osmond's Joseph and Maria Friedman's Narrator. To aggrandise myself thusly, even in jest, had an audacity in whose flippancy I found bravado.

Mam and Dad were unable to follow me into the greyish chamber which preceded the operating theatre.

A bespectacled man gently instructed me to lie back. He applied to my face a transparent conical breathing mask. Cool air blew softly and steadily against my mouth and nose. The anaesthetic would soon set to work, he assured me. I would recall perhaps a further minute or so of consciousness.

And then I remembered nothing at all.

Four Weeks in Hospital

An uncertain amount of time later, I slowly realised that I was lying down, in a numbly familiar greyish room, in which green-gowned doctors bustled. Memories sluggishly began to resurface.

"The operation is over," said the bespectacled anaesthetist. I was glad of this confirmation; I hadn't been quite sure. A hard, thin object ran up my left nostril and into the depths of my throat. I apprehensively considered the tube's eventual removal.

"There's someone here to see you," added the anaesthetist. With aptly dramatic timing, Mam's face swept into view above me.

"Is he gonna die?" she demanded.

"You do wonders for the morale, mother," I croaked.

As my return to the ward was prepared, the anaesthetist recalled, with soothing casualness, his cat, Cleopatra.

Back in my private ward, I lay on my bed in a dreamy state. A nurse attended the various tubes attached to my person and happily noted her imminent departure for home. Mam and Dad explained that she'd been referring to herself rather than us. I realised I'd be here a while yet.

A vertical row of staples burrowed into my middle stomach, much of which was dressed with reinforced patches. From beneath each side of the dressing protruded two transparent tubes, held slightly beneath the skin by stitches.

Long before I'd reached the hospital, my appendix had burst. On realising this, the doctors had performed a major operation to drain my torso of lethal pus. Had they waited any longer, said Dad, I might well have died. My operation, apparently, had been the first of its kind to be performed in this hospital. The tubes in my stomach were to drain residual pus. Another plastic tube, connected to a plastic pouch by the bed, ran into my bladder. The tube in my nose ran into a transparent green plastic sack, which collected bile. Two tubes in my arm respectively provided hydration and, at my press of a switch, morphine.

For the first few days, I was too weak for anything more strenuous than sitting up. A dull, tight ache gripped my mid torso. Once each hour, Mam was allowed to apply to my mouth one of several moistened pink sponges.

In the constant presence of my parents, I felt a sorely tender comfort, a desperate longing for perpetuity of their company.

I dwelled each day on my throat's dragging, stretching plea for moisture. In my catheter-fitted bladder, I eventually felt a mild weight, to which the relevant muscles were still unable to respond. One day, this increased sorely; the catheter seemed to be malfunctioning. Mam and Dad searched the corridor for assistance, but none was yet available. So severe was the pressure that I projected my own frightened, embarrassed voice into the corridor. To my immense relief, the machine was soon repaired.

Mam and Dad showed no desire to go home, for which I was enormously grateful. The Barrowburn dogs were tended to by Uncle Ross, so all was well.

Each day, on waking early, we immediately switched on the telly, which remained on for most of the day. To the loneliness of being virtually immobile in a strange room, constant scenes of people going about their business brought a crucial vitality. All the talk I'd heard growing up about television being somehow unwholesome, a supplier of base gratification and nurturer of idleness, now collapsed before my current desperation for what it offered. Amidst lovingly crafted models, the stop-motion residents of *Postman Pat*'s Greendale showcased a gentler side to humanity which had soothed me in infancy and returned to do so now.

Towards the end of my first week, nurses, on inspecting my dressing, traced seeping pus to several loose stitches. Across the hefty bulge of my lower stomach, the scar had opened to a wide, deep, vertical gash, which I never quite dared to inspect myself.

Henceforth, the dressing was changed daily. Into my lower stomach were eased strands of absorbent material. A barely perceptibly dull pressure hinted their descent beneath inches of my skin.

The assortment of familiar nurses became almost like family.

At the end of the second week, Dad decided to have a walk into town. He asked if I desired any purchases. Since Christmas, John and I had become engrossed in nightly playing of Craig Charles's abridged cassette reading of Doug Naylor's *Red Dwarf* novel *Last Human* (1995), which Aunty Jess had got me for Christmas.

I asked Dad to try to get me a copy of the novel. I'd seen it on the shelves over the years, but my limited concentration had discouraged me from the commitment of purchase.

The removal of my stomach tubes, by this point, had me feeling rather brighter. When Dad successfully returned with a copy of the book, I read and enjoyed the first few chapters, but my lax concentration soon demanded alternative focus. A doctor soon arrived to assess my progress and announced my eligibility for a slightly larger private ward.

"And you'll be glad to get shot of this tube?" he said of the throat-embedded pipe which hung from my left nostril to lie across my chest. I would be indeed but had dreaded the process of removal, not being used to having things pulled out of my throat through my nostril.

The doctor reassured me that it would feel similar to sneezing. As he deftly pulled, the intense stiffness was surreal, but only moderately uncomfortable.

I then moved into a slightly larger ward.

By the ward's bathroom door stood the wheeled drip feeder which had, until recently, supplied my bloodstream with nutrients. I supposed it might well have some electrical components. A few nights into my stay in this new ward, I used the toilet. As I passed the drip feeder, my hands remained moist with tap water.

I considered the fearsome possibility that I may have moistened the equipment, whose next operator was now at risk of electrocution. My fear that a blunder of mine might seriously harm someone overruled my persuasion of the idea's absurdity. I mentioned it to Mam, who, with minimal frustration at my "funny little ways," dismissed my concern.

Each morning, a nurse arrived to change my dressing. One day, as a doctor examined the open wound, my parents saw it. Deep in the chasm of open flesh, they clearly saw what we were informed to be my bowel. Mam, she later said, had nearly fainted. I asked Dad what BBFC certificate might be given a film with such imagery. Dad, who remained his usual cheerily composed self, conceded that it might well get a "15."

To a noticeboard, Mam pinned my mounting supply of "get well" cards, mostly from people who knew me through her and Dad.

An assortment of items arrived from school. A card adorned with the simple image of a sunflower bore a message from Mr Dolan, citing my work in progress to have made his weekend and a bid for my restoration to my "warm self."

A card signed by each of my form class accompanied an encouraging note from Mrs Willis, as well as a nice pen and a copy of Stephen King's *On Writing: A Memoir of the Craft* (2000), which, I noted with satisfying irony, had been written during the author's recovery from a road accident.

Humbled by all this kindness, I wrote a letter of thanks.

Burdy had phoned the hospital to arrange a visit. Days later, his tall frame loomed into the small private ward. Dad accommodated him with jovial ease, as if the two were old friends.

In striking divergence from his usual impudence, Burdy seemed curiously reserved. While Mam and Dad went for a walk, I, irrationally, felt very slightly uneasy in the presence of my schoolmate, reminder as he was of school's unforgiving chaos. Beneath his manic jocularity, however, was someone who diligently cared. He invited requests for items for him to fetch for me. Conscious of my imposition, I mentioned *Storm Harvest* in Appleby's Bookshop.

Days later, my resourceful friend fetched me a copy of the lovely turquoise paperback, as well as a huge stack of old issues of *Doctor Who Magazine*, which for some reason had been on sale in Eldon Square.

Several afternoons saw the arrival of Burdy and Sean, who gave me a small Lego set.

Although I grew used to the nurses' morning changing of my dressing, I remained nervous when ten o'clock neared.

When a nurse arrived with one of the doctors, he donned a rubber glove and explained that he was going to have a feel around inside. I lay back, with a more intense apprehension than usual. The dressing was removed, and I felt a gloved finger ease into the wound.

It then delved deeper than the nurses ever had. It slid past deeper folds of skin to poke at something inches beneath the surface of my belly. The numb, heavy pressure was like that of a stomach ache, but the internal flesh received it with a scarily intense sharpness. The nurse took hold of my right hand. I held on gratefully. Within seconds, the examination was over. I was glad of the assurance that no such further exploration would be necessary.

Dr Gibson, supervisor of my operation, arrived to assess my progress.

"No," he said decisively, of my reclined position on the bed. It was no good, he said, amiably but firmly, my sitting in bed eating chips, although there were no chips present, and seldom were, come to that. My bodily healing, he said, required frequent gentle exercise.

Keen to comply, I asked Dad to accompany me for a lap around the corridor. "That's the stuff!" said Dr Gibson as we passed him on the way back.

During my four weeks in hospital, Dad spent a few nights away to give Uncle Ross a rest from attending Barrowburn.

Aunty Jess, visiting one afternoon, offered to drive Mam home for a night away from the ward. Although Mam agreed, she proved reluctant to go. When the time came, her face crumpled, and her voice broke into sobs. This roused my own heightened emotion, and I struggled to contain my own sobs. Jess remained jovially irreverent.

"He's sick of the sight of you, man," she soothed. With gentle persuasion from Dad and Jess, Mam conceded that a night at home would be for the best. In her distress, she recalled a nurse's recent note of my increased level of white blood cells. I reassured her with a rattling off of my basic knowledge of the immune system gained from several childhood biology books.

"Listen to him!" laughed Mam through her sobs.

Mam returned the next day with a report of the situation at home. Requested by Granda Widdrington to play a certain CD, John had complied and had later retaliated with a playing of his new Eminem album.

I laughingly envisioned our eventual return to a living room strewn with lager cans – on our arrival, John, hunched on the sofa in his underwear, would spring into a seated position, brandish a knife and tell us to get out of his office.

Miss Hammond, on hearing of my brush with death, had made a concerned phone call and wryly asked to be spared the sight of the remains of my appendix. I now asked Mam where it was. The doctors had reported there to be barely anything left of it. It had been ruptured by a hardened mass of digestive waste. I solemnly recalled my childhood years of nervously postponed toilet use.

At the end of the fourth week, the doctors were happy for me to return home. Each day, a district nurse would change my dressing. There would be no school for some considerable time. Finally, I sat in the back of the Frontera as the tape in the stereo reached "Close Every Door to Me."

Back in the living room, rather than a climactic thrill, I felt a rush of deep contentment. Mam and Dad beamed around me, savouring our mutual relief. I forced a stilted cry of "I'm home!" and immediately wished I hadn't.

I went upstairs to see my bedroom after all this time. On the middle shelf, several of my Dapol Daleks and Crash Bandicoot figurines had been moved to make way for several books moved down from the top shelf. Stung by this casual rearrangement, I queried Mam, who explained that Nana had been in to tidy up. I conceded to a few minutes of angry despondence, which happily soon faded.

Within hours, a heavy weariness fell over me, so I went to bed. As I sank towards sleep, Dad lay on John's bed and quietly reflected on the last month's drama.

Wound

For several months, my mobility would be limited to the length of pavement outside the front door. Efficient recovery required gentle exercise, but too much would slow down healing.

Each morning, at eleven o'clock, I lay on the sofa in wait for whichever district nurse was on duty. On weekend mornings, when Mam worked in the kitchens of the Newcastle House, Granda Widdrington, as usual, installed himself in the armchair.

"Morning, nurse," he'd say, with labouredly full pronunciation of the "ing."

Shortly after news of my operation reached the Rothbury surgery, Dr Allan had visited. Dr Kay, over her misdiagnosis, had resigned.

Humbled by the gesture of regret, and with some idea of what a monster guilt could be, I wished her the best.

Going Red There

With Dad at Barrowburn, James in the Co-op, John at school and me on the chair opposite the living room door, Mam briefly went next door, where Dawn, niece to Nana and cousin to Mam, had arrived from London.

Mam soon returned with a familiar-seeming woman who looked around late thirties. Wavy black hair and fine, softly rounded features hinted Nana. A serene jollity implied total innocence of Widdrington gloom.

Over the years, I'd met Aunty Dawn about half a dozen times. With her current visit redirected to look in on the peritonitis veteran, she and Mam continued their generalities. The subject somehow turned to *Doctor Who*, with which Dawn apparently had some familiarity, having shared with her two young sons several Pertwee serials. Encouraged, I happily showcased my acquaintance with the series and even had the front to mention the Silurians.

With a sudden grin, Dawn ventured my familiarity with "the *companions...!*"

I hadn't seriously expected to be challenged with this theme. The show's young, often short-skirted female cast members were renowned for the lust they were apt to rouse in young male fans. The butt of this joke was usually men who had grown up in the sixties, seventies and eighties.

Suddenly forced into the role of teenage boy sexuality, I buckled with shock.

With my bloated torso, and the inordinate timidity and social confusion it had come to represent, any voicing of the idea that I might trespass upon femininity with such coarse predation as lust was apt to choke me with shame. Unable to find a polite means to convey my discomfort, I silently burned with miserable self-disgust.

"Ah," said Dawn with a grin, "you're going *red there*!"

The shared conversation sought further generalities. Minutes later, Dawn's focus returned to me.

"I have a gift for you," she announced. Humbled by the curiously formal announcement of a semi-stranger's pander to my gratification, I received the small sketchpad with thanks.

On the Mend

Mam paid Mrs Hart, a local retired schoolteacher, to guide me through the magnanimously light supply of English and Maths homework sent my way. Mrs Hart eventually opined that my incomprehension of numeracy may indicate dyscalculia, the mathematical equivalent of dyslexia. Under her mildly spoken but challenging guidance, I explored William Golding's *Lord of the Flies* (1954) and produced a numerical chart of recently read books.

Throughout the weeks of healing, I put gradual effort into completion of my coursework but, for prolonged periods of each day, savoured my liberation from school.

One warm afternoon, as I lay on my bed reading *Storm Harvest*, I enjoyed the gleeful detail of an interstellar coastal hotel and the rendition of television heroes in the loving delicacy of prose. While engrossed, I was reminded of what a slow reader I was – when the narration introduced a new setting, my concentration would often sag.

Did something in my upbringing set me apart from James and John; had some discouragement of discipline engorged my appetite and dulled my concentration?

Warmth and brightness crept into the air. With each dressing of my wound, I asked if it looked any smaller. Each week, one of the nurses confirmed that it appeared slightly but undeniably so. It eventually required only several dressings per week. It was decided that small walks around the village would be safe, but I wasn't to go too far just yet.

Dad drove John and me to the Silverlink UCI cinema, where we saw the much-anticipated *Ali G Indahouse.*

Naturally, I returned to SPAR, where Faye now worked. I assumed my position beneath the plastic shelves of VHS and DVD boxes, perusal of which postponed the turmoil of approaching the till. Before I'd stood there for very long, Faye came over with more display boxes.

In thrall to her mousy blond hair and soft, humorous features, I now realised myself to be looking down on her from several inches. She asked if I might pass down the sticker on *The Little Vampire*'s (2000) display box.

The relevant box had two adornments. Attached to its top was a semicircular piece of red cardboard, which read "film on loan." Halfway down, a more permanently attached red label classified the film to be of the "family" genre. Faye's clear request for removal of the label denoting the film's temporary unavailability, for some reason, slipped me by, and I briefly tried to peel off the round sticker. Noticing my misapprehension, Faye fairly easily reached up and removed the cardboard label.

"Are you enjoying your holidays?" she said airily as she shelved more boxes. I explained that I'd be off school for the rest of term, as my appendix had "exploded."

"Did it hurt?" she asked with polite concern.

"Aye, bloody awful," I said, aware of how daft I sounded, but somehow unable to stop myself. What *Red Dwarf*'s Dave Lister had said might be true, I supposed: conversation with a subject of infatuation seemed to shave off twenty IQ points.

Hot blue skies, glazed in humidity, announced summer.

With my wound now much smaller, I was allowed longer walks. Atop the park's arched footbridge, I often stopped to savour the rightward view. Directly below, the River Coquet, a broad, flowing floor of clear deep brown, stretched past laundered grass towards fields, hills, woodland and open sky.

At sunset, over the hills, the sky glowed a deep amber. I recalled the incidental love theme from *Sailor Moon* and cherished my all too brief memories of the show's pastel heroine.

Burdy decided it was time for another visit to Newcastle's Warner Brothers cinema. Dad drove him, Sean, John and me into Newcastle. Across the sun-drenched car park, the four of us approached the multiplex and went to see the gripping, poignant *Spider-Man*.

On the drive back home, I sat in the front seat. In the back, the others conversed with each other and with Dad. I'd brought my trusty cassette Walkman, which held a tape of CD-copied songs. Even without headphones, my conversational contribution would probably have been minimal. Even in the school yards and corridors, when I talked to my friends, the peace and freedom of my own thoughts often dissuaded me from conversation. At the moment, immersed in "We Didn't Start the Fire," I considered my role surplus.

Shortly after our return home, I entered the kitchen to find Mam and Dad at the table. I was surprised to find Dad solemnly preoccupied. Mam recounted his report of my listening to my Walkman while John, Burdy and Sean conversed. My reticence, Dad gently stressed, was inappropriate.

I was taken aback to learn that my instinctive retreat into the comfort of introversion was considered offensive.

Shocked, I was despondent for much of the evening. I wondered what made me this way. Did some ill-bred lack of focus relax my concentration, unfetter my appetite and engorge my selfishness? Or did some mysterious neural quirk tilt my inclinations in unexpected directions? The latter would at least explain my excessive handwashing and obsession with not electrocuting people.

Fifteen

Having long thought fondly of owning a video camera, I used Mam and Dad's offer of an extravagant birthday present as a means to fulfil this pipe dream.

On the morning of my fifteenth birthday, I awoke early. As I looked through my camcorder, thrill mingled with guilt at the extravagance.

I endeavoured to justify my ownership of the small, fresh-smelling device and took it for a walk round Whitton, to film the houses and countryside.

As the day quietly dragged, I read from Professor Stephen Hawking's *The Universe in a Nutshell* (2001), a simplified guide to cosmology with lots of nice pictures, as procured for me by Nana and Granda via Aunty Jess.

Towards the end of the day, Dad drove me up to Lordenshaws. Atop the rounded hill, in the sun-baked evening haze, I recorded the mighty views and gratefully reflected that I'd spent the day well.

A Man Now

"You're a man now," Granda Widdrington said to me one morning.

Near the end of July, Dad asked me if I might help with the Barrowburn Clipping. In years past, the job of fleece-wrapping had fallen to Mam and James, but since both now had external commitments, Dad had finally decided to pass the torch to me. His confidence that I could manage it moved me to face the task to my utmost ability.

The first herd, some hundred and fifty young male sheep, or hogs, were rounded into the Loungies field and into a pen of metal gates by the Hog House's open far doors.

In the middle of the Hog House, Dad and Uncle Ross used two rafter-hung electric shears. Each time a fleece was shorn, I hurried forth, brought it to the uneven wooden table and, with staunch adherence to Dad's tutorial, wrapped it neatly and tightly, thereupon to stuff it into one of the rafter-hung sacks.

Within four hours, the task was done. With hearty but sincere approval, Dad told me I'd performed well. I cherished the achievement of having contributed to my father's workplace.

The following Saturday saw the clipping of about three hundred sheep. This time, John supplied wrapping reinforcement, Granda Widdrington stitched up the fleece sacks, Uncle Ross worked the pens, and Dad was joined by two freelance

New Zealand shearers. The muffled blare of the radio, thunderous bleating of the sheep and infrequent shouts from Dad and Ross underscored the electric shears' grinding rasp.

Against heat and weariness, the thrilling urgency of duty fortified me. As Granda Widdrington stitched up sacks, I solemnly pondered his continued insistence on riding with Ross in their van to various building jobs and how his hands, wearied in their tasks by Parkinson's disease, were today relegated to lighter work.

When the last sheep was finally clipped, the heavy sacks of wool, which had been dragged periodically outside, were now pulled back in. For obvious medical reasons, I wasn't allowed to help with this.

Back in the house, I mentioned in passing that Dad was giving me some money. With a hint of surprise, Granda Widdrington affirmed that my efforts unquestionably required payment.

"Never knew you could work like that," he said. His praise for me usually dwelled on my curly hair, or what a big, strong lad I was. Today, his praise of my diligence and competence unexpectedly and fondly humbled me.

Year Eleven

As well as PE, rendered out of the question by my recently healed stomach wound, Year Eleven would spare me one compulsory subject. "Technology," barely intelligible to me, was the one to go, whereby I would use the free hours, in the library, to catch up on Year Ten coursework.

Within weeks, my supply of last year's worksheets finished. I henceforth used my free sessions for homework and leisurely reading, with fond revisit to HJ Richards' *Philosophy of Religion* (2000) and *The Encyclopaedia of Science Fiction* (1995).

As in Year Ten, Mrs Jennings, on the upper C Floor, taught history. Main focus was on Germany's Weimar Republic, the rise of the Nazi Party and the Vietnam War.

We were often required to arrange ourselves to work in groups. As ever, much of the group discussion went over my head. As my concentration faded, my grasp of the varied themes dissolved into a soup of weary indifference. What, I had to wonder, would be so wrong with just letting us work alone?

To my forward right sat Abbey Charlton. From her serene face and ultra-neat handwriting, I'd suspected a cool reservation. Her finely pale, high-cheeked features alight with mirth, she now shared with friends a humorous memory.

One noon, outside the History classroom, Burdy, apparently acquainted with Abbey, seized on her current proximity for improvisational impudence.

"Will you go out with her?" he asked me.

"No," I said. The idea that I would go out with anyone was distasteful. Unexpectedly, Abbey turned to me with a smirk.

"Have you got a problem with me?" she said in mock gall.

Her high, soft voice, of standard Northumberland diction, rose easily to levity. Thin, straight, light brown shoulder-length hair framed a high, rounded brow, dark blue eyes, a fine pallor, high cheekbones and a slightly pointed nose. As well as History, she took Religious Studies.

In B9, the Religious Studies classroom, tables stood in a joint, room-spanning rectangle.

What little could be seen of the walls, covered as they were in displays, was pale pink. Near the inner door was a postcard cartoon of Moses, who, on having parted the Red Sea, turned indignantly to the Hebrews. "What do you mean, 'it's a bit muddy'?" read the caption. The front wall held a gallery of philosophers, ranging from Plato to Jean Paul Sartre. Beneath them, a second doorway led to the office of Mr Balder, held by James in both eminence and affectionate mirth.

Grey-flecked brown hair and beard framed sober reflectivity, or, more often than not, biting irreverence. A rough North West drawl held hints of County Durham. One breaktime, as I made for the B Floor staircase, Mr Balder's easy drawl drew me into conversation. His voice softened marginally to earnest acknowledgement of my recent ordeal, and that he appreciated its impact on my schooling. He concluded the briefing with a light clap to my shoulder, a humbling gesture from this most unflappable of sages.

I currently sat towards the far end of the room, next to Burdy. Theological and ethical theory, from St Thomas Aquinas to Dr Peter Vardy, was photocopied, distributed and collectively discussed. Mr Balder's lectures might often pursue irreverent tangents, with no shortage of encouragement from the class's more waggish members.

Across the room sat Abbey Charlton and Chloe Todd. Shorter and broader than Abbey, Chloe's deeper skin tone offset straight, loose, richly blond hair. A high brow and soft features framed large eyes. Before and between lessons, the two girls would huddle conspiratorially, with occasional giggles.

Music Videos

Before the living room telly, I often found John attending a music video. He was partial to the channel Kerrang, whose output specialised in frenetic percussion, aggressive imagery and strident vocals.

A stranger so far to the music channels, I was now to become acquainted with Magic. This channel often played music videos of songs from the eighties and nineties, songs of easy cheer and open tenderness, with the occasional liquid shiver or crystal chime of a synthesiser.

Last year, Mam had commissioned Dad to buy the single release of Atomic Kitten's cover of "Eternal Flame." The CD's cover held a close-up of three forward-leaning young women. With their straight, richly blond hair and svelte bare arms, I found each appreciably alluring and curiously similar-looking; each combination of high brow, high cheekbones and straight hair veiled them with a sleek uniformity. I took a liking to the song, with its soft-voiced, confident wistfulness.

On Magic, I encountered the video for Atomic Kitten's cover of "The Tide is High." As each softly lit singer strode towards the camera, I once again pondered their curious similarity to each other. Each head of straight, shoulder-length hair, each high, rounded brow, each set of high cheekbones and long, svelte limbs drew appreciative comparison to Abbey and Chloe.

"Ooh, I remember these lot," said Mam of a recently started music video. Two bespectacled young Scotsmen boomed a lively melody, which climbed to a gloriously rapturous chorus. Having heard this bit of the song on a shoe advert, I'd wondered if this was by the Proclaimers, whose "I'm On My Way" I'd encountered on the *Shrek* (2001) soundtrack. At the end of the video, Magic's curly yellow font confirmed that it was.

Ends

This term was my last under Mrs Willis, who, in the new year, would be leaving for another school. At 12.35, the overhead electronic beep announced the start of the Christmas holidays. Several of the class had conspired to present Mrs Willis with a small parting gift. My disinclination to conversation had, of course, excluded me from contribution to the ceremonial tribute. I regretted this. I cherished the encouragement afforded me by Mrs Willis these last two and a half years.

Resolved to part with some kind of appreciative gesture, I'd signed and sealed a Christmas card. Once the class had dispersed, I re-entered the room with my meek token.

"Miss, card," I said, aiming for droll informality. Mrs Willis accepted the tribute with surprised elation. I fumbled some words of farewell.

On December the 31st, DJs and newscasters, throughout the quiet day, chatted in merry anticipation.

At six o'clock, the rippling clang of the village church bells rang for twenty minutes. As the hours mounted, I savoured the cheery momentum, but was at a loss as to how to properly attend it.

Around ten, I retreated to the upstairs landing for an online browse. On Bianca's Sailor Moon Gallery, I clicked my way to one of my favourite images. On a peach background, Serena, in school uniform, sat with her legs tucked slightly upward. The billowing blue skirt had risen past her knees. Her cherubic face lay on her knee-rested forearms. Above drooping eyelids, a half-smile sweetened her face. While her persona consisted of hand-drawn images and recorded voice acting, I'd always be free to savour such instances thereof as this.

I wandered into the kitchen. James was out on a visit to one or more of the village pubs. Mam and Dad had adjourned to the living room for semi-lit relaxation and wine. John, I supposed, would be upstairs, playing on *Medal of Honor: Allied Assault* (2002). The fridge, in recent service of one of Mam's baking projects, held a small drum of full cream milk. Furthermore, there was a carton of Elmlea pour-on cream.

I resolved, this coming January, to keep going for walks and to eat slightly less. Abstinence from such extravagance as an after dinner bowl of ice cream, or snacking between meals, I supposed, would appease the media's appeal to "eat sensibly." Did I genuinely anticipate that such modulation would make me lose weight?

Probably not.

Although I didn't consciously realise it, I didn't yet know how to lose weight. I had no idea how to precisely limit my food intake. I resolved to evaluate whether a desired amount could be deemed "sensible," and if not, reign in my appetite.

But for now, I poured some cream into what little milk remained in the plastic drum and happily glugged it down.

2003

Exercise and Eat Sensibly

On the floor beneath the shelves opposite my bed lay a set of black plastic weights, indefinitely lent to me by Uncle Ross.

On the middle shelf, in John's silver hi-fi, I installed my new *Best of the Proclaimers* CD. To "Letter from America," I repeatedly thrust up the weights.

Over the next few days, I made a point of lifting the weights again.

After a few more days, I allowed myself a break and, a few days later, resumed weight-lifting.

Loath as I was to admit it, weight-lifting roused minimal interest in me. Its monotonous succession soon drove me to seek inspiration elsewhere.

At breakfast, I didn't suppose my preferred amounts of cereal and milk to be particularly excessive.

Shredded Wheat couldn't be too fattening, could it? Full o' goodness, that stuff. And wasn't milk said to be one of the best things you could put in your mouth? I favoured generous quantities of both. I failed to see the point of filling the bowl to anything less than its full capacity. I might well follow with a toasted marmite sandwich. Mindful of Dr Allan's advice, I forewent butter.

For supper, I would improvise with whatever was in the fridge, perhaps accompanied by what remained of dinner. I gathered and ate a handful of items until I found myself fully nourished.

Hexham Mart

In the town of Hexham, about an hour's drive away, Dad annually submitted sheep for sale. An extra pair of hands to help herd

189

sheep into their pens had been supplied by Mam, but current pub kitchen hours now disallowed this. This year, Dad's casual but genuine request for John and me to provide such aid gave me a rare pride.

Having reached March, the year lay between winter and spring. On Saturday, having risen severely early, I happily anticipated a run in the car. Some paperwork for Dad would follow the auction, so I brought along an issue of *Total Film*. From the car radio, the low synthesisers of Rachel Stevens' new "Sweet Dreams My LA Ex" advanced the young year.

On the outskirts of Hexham, mud-caked concrete bore a vast, open-walled shed, to whose right stood a small complex of offices, toilets and cafeteria.

Across the shed's cool air came the clang of gates, alert voices and the bleating of sheep.

Dad, John and I spent most of the time standing by pens, opening and closing gates, and herding sheep to their subsequent pens.

In the auction ring, raised benches enclosed the floor. Into a microphone, a man ranted with skilful speed.

Dad instructed John and me simply to briskly follow the sheep around the ring, with motivational hand-clapping and general improvised noises. Keen to perform as ably as possible, I moved briskly and decisively.

While Dad attended paperwork, John and I waited in the car.

In *Total Film*, a small article announced an imminent remake of *The Texas Chainsaw Massacre* (1974). The original was said to mark a shocking turning point in filmic carnage. I wondered how gruesome the remake could be.

An inset photo held a blackened hallway, in which stood several young, nicely lit, rather uneasy-looking leads. A larger shot held one of them, Jessica Biel, in close-up. Richly brown shoulder-length hair framed a high, rounded brow. Finely broad cheekbones lent expressive definition. Her proximity to whatever horrors lay in store lent a soft innocence.

I doubted I'd get round to seeing the eventual release any time soon, liable as it was to be an "18."

Cameron Diaz

The next of Magic's music videos to draw my attention was for the Foundations' "Build Me Up, Buttercup." Curiously, in place of any footage of the song's performers was a montage, held mainly across sunlit urban walkways and a spacious living room. Various casually dressed people larked about and danced across the living room floor.

The lively yet heartfelt song, with its rich vocal, engaged me.

In later viewings, I found my attention increasingly drawn to the recurring figure of a young woman. Blond hair framed her head in a rounded, neck-length bob. Below a light blue cardigan, cut off black trousers bared slim, lightly tanned lower legs.

In a sudden nightly backdrop, a well-lit close-up studied her face. Beneath a high brow, her cheekbones lent fine curvature, now stretched in a grin. Her light blue gaze had a welcoming affection.

My reception of this disarmingly cheery figure gave way to the beginnings of infatuation. Her hair, cropped similarly to Faye's, was straighter and not quite as long. In the curvature of the mystery woman's brow and face, I frivolously supposed further similarity.

Online searches for "the foundations" shed no light on what her name might be. I then learned the song "Build Me Up, Buttercup" had been used in the 1998 comedy *There's Something About Mary*, which, I then learned, had starred Cameron Diaz, whom I recognised from *The Mask* (1994) and *Shrek* (2001).

Abbey and Chloe

Throughout Mr Balder's discourses on ethical theory and cosmic conjecture, I stole frequent glances at the two occupants of the leftmost table.

Faye, now absent from the buses, apparently got a lift to school with her boyfriend. Abbey and Chloe now roused in me a similar if milder elation.

Abbey's high-cheeked pallor wove a cool composure, mellowed by her soft, high voice and occasional grin.

Chloe's slightly less overt buoyancy roused similar attraction. Her deep blond hair, high brow, blue eyes and softly rounded face, to me, recalled Cameron Diaz.

Excited murmurings and hushed giggles between the two, more pronounced from Abbey, earned her, from Mr Balder, the nickname of Dopey.

Revision

For this year's exams, teachers encouraged use of the official GCSE revision website. On its brightly coloured screens, small paragraphs eased into my memory traces of historical incident and energy measurement. Some even hinted that they might remain.

From my photocopied history texts, I fumbled to grasp correlations of locations, events, objects and persons, until each sentence merged indistinctly with its fellows. My mind seemed unable to hold more than a few lines of technical information.

"I haven't got the right sort of mind for revision," I theorised.

I guiltily feared some ill-disciplined lack of motivation: the old, hinted charge of laziness. Too lazy to stop being hungry, too lazy to force myself to eat vegetables, too lazy to pay attention, too lazy to use toilets, too lazy not to be frightened of things like getting hit in the face with a ball, too lazy to be patient with the ambiguous approaches of other children. Lazy, lazy, lazy.

In his Physics classroom, Mr Wisher urged the revision technique of repeatedly writing down facts from the textbook. I took heed of this and actually succeeded in retaining some information.

Revision for English was happily straightforward: I mostly just reread bits of *Lord of the Flies*. Mr Dolan assured me that my *Greelashon* opening chapter coursework would be awarded an A*, the highest mark available.

On library computers, I worked on my Religious Studies coursework. In Dr Peter Vardy's *The Puzzle of Ethics* (1999), I read such accounts as C.S. Lewis's unexpected conversion to Christianity. I enjoyed casually revisiting HJ Richards' *Philosophy of Religion* (2000), with its patient, benevolent pursuit of God to the absolute reality of love.

Stepping Stones

As the air warmed, Study Leave began. Should a lesson be cancelled to make way for revision opportunities, Burdy, Sean, I and many others wandered down the hill into town.

On Bridge Street was a newly opened eatery termed The Diner. Modelled on the kind of establishment seen in nostalgic American media, its pale walls held framed monochrome film stills. Burdy, Sean and I made a fond habit of coming here. By now, I was limply persuaded that the way to shrink my torso was to avoid eating between meals, keep exercising (i.e. go for walks) and not to overeat. Since I had no idea of exactly how much less I should eat, I consumed, with more contentment than guilt, some superb vanilla milkshakes.

Beyond the town centre, I hadn't really seen much of Morpeth. In clear, warm air, freedom to walk the quiet streets heralded approaching adulthood.

One day, Sean, Burdy and I wandered beneath a bridge and onto the tree-shaded riverbank. The river, about a foot deep and fifty or so wide, had a row of square stepping stones. In turns, Burdy and Sean stepped onto the first stone and began to cross the rest with ease.

With considerable effort, I focused my nerve and stepped onto the first stone. Above the cold, rippling depths, the possibility of a misplaced step overwhelmed me with cautious fear.

Desperate to resist this absurd inhibition, I forced myself onto the second step, but was overwhelmed with dread at the prospect of being stranded above the middle of the river.

Burdy, now almost at the other side of the river, turned and jovially noted my reservation. His and Sean's mild impatience seemed at being detained rather than at my timidity. I called after them to carry on, as I would only hold them up.

In search of the nerve to overcome my fear, I lingered for twenty minutes, but could only bring myself to mount the first few steps.

Defeated, I ached for an explanation of my susceptibility to such fear.

The answer I dreaded was that I was *spoilt*.

Whereas Granda Widdrington had risen with dawn to build fences and had had to catch rabbits for dinner, we of my generation had been constantly nourished. Had evasion of the educative knocks of a deprived childhood barred my desensitisation to minor obstacles?

As I ruminated, a grey-haired woman arrived. I stood aside to let her past. She nimbly stepped onto the first stepping stone and strode across its successors to the other side of the river.

GCSEs

In the vicinity of progressing exams, silence was sternly urged. Into any exam, no implement besides a pen was to be brought.

I managed to answer some Biology questions and was confident that some of my answers were at least partially accurate.

I answered even more Physics questions.

Since Year Eleven Chemistry had been barely comprehensible, I'd seen little point in revising for its exam.

I found about as much clarity in the Maths exam as one might find in an argument between a hundred voices in a thousand languages.

The Religious Studies exam offered several questions to choose from. I confidently set to work discussing ethical theory and cosmic conjecture.

With some awareness of the texts but minimal grasp of how they interlinked, I faced the History exam with appreciable verve.

I spent much of Study Leave in the school library.

I picked up a recently noticed paperback. Robert Swindells' *Abomination* (1998) explored an authoritarian fundamentalist sect, the liberating joys of such opulence as Kit Kats and coke, and the worldwide community offered by modern technology, here used to stop a sustained practice of horrifying child abuse. I spent most of the day reading it. Next day, I finished it.

No regrets at all.

One heavily wet morning, I sat the English exam. In discussion of *Lord of the Flies*, I found myself scribbling loads. The second, relatively straightforward question concerned poetry.

Having sat all my exams, I seldom had to come into school for the rest of term. While it frankly didn't seem overall likely that I'd earned the five "C"s required for admission to the Sixth Form, time reinforced my natural optimism.

Nerd

Robert Perry and Mike Tucker's second BBC *Doctor Who* novel, *Matrix*, tantalisingly said to be unflinchingly dark, seemed not to be available anywhere.

Burdy seemed to have a certain affection for *Doctor Who*. Knowing as he did of a means to order obscure books, he'd shown a calm determination to get me a copy for my sixteenth birthday. Beneath his whimsical impudence lay a caring generosity.

Several online *Doctor Who* reviews alerted me to *Dust Breeding* (2001), a Big Finish audio play starring Sylvester McCoy, written by Mike Tucker and featuring *Storm Harvest* monsters the Krill.

At the Metrocentre, on the far end of HMV's upper floor, I found *Dust Breeding*. On its cover, the shadowed, superimposed face of the Seventh Doctor brooded over a rocky planet. I decided to indulge my hunger and took the plastic-wrapped CD case to the till.

Back home, the evening remained bright. To the upstairs landing, I took my CD and installed it in the new Windows XP. To listen while at leisure to browse online seemed a promisingly forgiving medium for such concentration as mine.

I clicked the relevant icons, and the twanging, howling strains of Ron Grainer's original theme poured from the speakers. *The Scream* painter Edvard Munch's vision of a sky of blood, while queasily unnerving, was soothed by the concern of his friends and the easy adventurism of Sylvester McCoy's Seventh Doctor and Sophie Aldred's Ace.

Burdened by secrets yet with a jovial curiosity, the Seventh Doctor made for a poignant, reassuring figure.

An evening shopping trip to Kingston Park's Tesco led me to the magazine section.

A DVD magazine reviewed the DVD release of 1964 *Doctor Who* serial *The Dalek Invasion of Earth*. In the 1960s, said the review, while much of the population spent their Saturday evenings in pursuit of booze-fuelled socialising, a certain fringe remained indoors to watch a new BBC science fiction show. This, the review wryly implied, was symptomatic of social ineptitude.

Cartoon sitcoms' equation of devotion to fantasy with weakness was here repackaged.

A DVD release of cartoon topical satire *2DTV* had featured *Geek Wars*, an unaired parody of *Robot Wars*. Several respectively bespectacled, overweight or unkempt robot builders were tasked to win the favour of an exasperated-looking woman. One contestant almost reached his prize, but then withdrew, with the commentator's explanation of having been drawn off by a *Doctor Who* convention featuring Sylvester McCoy.

The function of such terms as "geek," it seemed, was to rib men who, by their absorption in impractical subjects, were ineffectual, unwilling to cultivate the flair and means with which to woo and support women. Such men, in their supposed duty to those who might propagate their genes, were found wanting.

Such terms blamed my inhibitions on my introverted delights.

I railed silently and helplessly against this designation. It charged me with failure at something in which I felt I was too absurd to engage in the first place. The targeting of dear old Sylvester rubbed salt into the wound; I actually wondered if the writer had overheard my discussion in Eldon Square of Dimensions on Tyne.

Sixteen

On my sixteenth birthday, kind, resourceful Burdy had acquired for me a copy of the thrillingly dark, ambitious and heartfelt *Doctor Who: Matrix*.

Mam and Dad's requested present of a digital camera supplied the long-coveted means to capture, instantly review and digitally store images.

Newcastle College

Towards the end of summer arrived a brown envelope.

My only remotely respectable GCSE was a C for English. I'd considered my effort in its exam to be somewhat lacking and was therefore grateful. Dismay at my E for Religious Studies mingled with genuine bafflement; I didn't see what I could have done so wrong there.

The general mood turned to cautious focus on what to do now. Mam hoped for eventual negotiation of my entry to the Sixth Form, completion of which, conventional wisdom held, would help me get a good job.

At an arranged office meeting, Mr Rochdale's gently hushed voice confirmed my ineligibility for the Sixth Form. He phoned Newcastle College with enquiry as to the possibility of my admittance.

My low Religious Studies mark, it transpired, was due not to quality of writing, but to my having attended several questions from one set, as opposed to one from each.

"A pity," the examiner had written, "as he is an able student."

Dad phoned Newcastle College and conversationally lauded my prowess for writing. I was successfully admitted for induction.

I enrolled in English Literature and Philosophy, but for some reason, also had to do Maths.

Apart from actually finding the place, and having to do Maths, my main worry was the severely early rises.

The day before term started, Dad drove me into Newcastle to rehearse navigation. He gave me directions. I naively claimed to understand them. We separated.

I went to where I vaguely understood I was meant to go, failed to recognise its relevance to the directions and kept going. After twenty minutes, Dad phoned me, and we met at the bus stop.

On the first few days, Dad drove me in, for which I was grateful. A mile or so from the city centre, the college stood atop a sloping road.

After lessons, I would wander to the college library, to plough through some more of Iris Murdoch's *The Bell* (1958).

The Corrs

When I had the living room to myself, the thing to do was to tune into Magic, relax and enjoy the possibility, and sometimes arrival, of a favourite song. One week, I caught repeats of the music video of a song which I distantly recalled from the radio.

Soft guitar strings, an electric piano's lilting chimes and a robust undercurrent of drums were led by a soft, high, richly harmonious female voice.

Beneath a blazing blue sky and across a pale grey desert, the video was based mainly around an outdoor stage. The camera deftly shifted to focus on the band members. The source of the voice was a young woman. Straight black hair swept sleekly to her bare shoulders and framed a high-browed, finely rounded face. In contrast to the darkness of her hair and dress, vivid sunshine illuminated her skin's pallor. Dark eyes and an easy smile shone the song's glee.

The singing intermingled with shots of the band taking to the stage.

Two other women, each with fine pallor and straight dark hair, looked strikingly similar to the lead singer. At one point, I was surprised to see one of them playing a violin. Their performance intermingled with shots of a solemn-looking man in sunglasses.

As the video neared its end, Magic's curly yellow script designated the title of the song to be "Breathless," and its performers to be "The Corrs." A curious name for a band, I thought. Perhaps it was meant to imply notions of centrality. Could it be their surname?

Online searches led me to *The Corrs Online*. Its plain white background held a list of links to news updates and discussions from the site's operatives.

Woolworths

On my way home from Newcastle, I sometimes got off the bus at Morpeth to have a look round the shops.

On one visit to Woolworths, I picked up a copy of one of my usual film magazines and brought it to the till, which, I quickly noticed, was staffed by Abbey. One of the things I missed most about school was my daily proximity to her. Since I didn't know her that well, and my attraction was fairly casual, I now approached her easily.

"Heya!" she said with a surprised smile.

She brightly probed my post Year Eleven career. I explained my enrolment at Newcastle College.

"That is mint!" she said of the identity card which dangled across my chest.

She, in turn, was taking several subjects in the Sixth Form, including Religious Studies.

"Do you still get Balders?" I asked, in fumbling mimicry of the sage's gruff voice.

"Yeah, he's mint!"

I privately recalled how dearly I'd love to be doing so alongside her.

Sixth Form

Over the phone, Mam made one last attempt to get me into the Sixth Form.

She replaced the phone and announced success – I'd start tomorrow. My having missed half of Year Ten, explained Mam, had swayed my admission. I just about managed to persuade myself that this may indeed have contributed to my dismal exam results.

At the school office, I received my newly printed timetable of English Literature, English Language and Religious Studies. The timetable was replete with blank spaces for free study.

I gratefully returned to B9 for today's Religious Studies class. On a temporarily arranged row of the plastic blue chairs sat half a dozen of last year's students. As the chattering subsided, I took a seat.

Abbey, seated in front of me, swivelled round with a surprised grin and received me with her signature exclamation of "Oh, my God!"

Mental Shield

At Morpeth's Woolworths, I bought the highly anticipated DVD release of 1989 *Doctor Who* serial *The Curse of Fenric*. The penultimate serial before the show's indefinite postponement, it featured aquatic vampire-type-things.

A 1943 North Yorkshire village, eerily synthesised score, Time Lord strategy, heartfelt revelations and knobbly Haemovore masks, in soft autumnal lighting, had a gothic grandeur. Utilisation of faith as a mental shield to repel telepathic vampires inspirationally fused science and spirit.

One evening, just as the living room television screen showed Sylvester McCoy's Doctor entering the church of Saint Jude, Mam and Dad entered. My distant view of the Panama-hatted figure suddenly recalled Granda Widdrington's playful scorn for televised frivolity.

I found myself compelled to banish the image by pressing "stop." With some surprise, Mam said I could watch *Doctor Who* if I wanted. I humbly disclaimed any wish to obstruct their access to the telly.

Essence

Throughout the year, in online galleries and occasional broadcast films, the aspect of Cameron Diaz had soothed and elated me. I fancifully cast her recorded image as a figure equivalent to the Doctor, an otherworldly visitor, the Essence, to the landscape of my mind. My earlier infatuations, Coco, Faye and Sailor Moon, were the previous incarnations of this spatially transcendent benefactor.

I paid a few visits to *The Corrs Official Website*.

My suspicions had been right; Corr was indeed their surname. I decided to read the most recent interview, which seemed to be with the lead singer. In the "Breathless" video, the camera's prominent focus had set her at the forefront of my attention. Her delicious voice and fine, soft, thoughtful face had roused the beginnings of infatuation.

Her name, I now learned, was Andrea. The interview was written by Barry Egan, of *Ireland's Sunday Independent*. Left of the text was a superimposed photo of Andrea. Framed by a wave of straight black hair, her composed face showed a hint of mirth.

Throughout a daunting twenty minutes, I came to know something of the person behind the voice. Since I misremembered most of the Corrs' songs to have been released around the mid-nineties, I was surprised to learn that Andrea was only twenty-nine.

Barry Egan solemnly narrated the untimely death of the band's mother Jean, who had died, to my curious surprise, in Newcastle's Freeman Hospital, a mere thirty miles from where I now sat.

Tail Chewing

These last few months, my habitual urge to inspect electric sockets for lethal traces of moisture had mercifully lessened.

In the porch, the gas meter and adjacent pipes no longer troubled me.

At school, I still frequently imagined that some small object, such as a battery which may conceivably have slipped into my pocket, may have in turn dropped onto the stairs, endangering the lives of future stair users, thereby obliging me to stop and check. The notional possibility overruled logic and irresistibly persuaded me to linger over the stairs for a few seconds.

This last year, my fretful need for extra reassurance had been channelled most noticeably into excessive handwashing. When washing my hands in any sink, particularly by a toilet, I feared that the taps might bear some trace of dirt from the hands of previous users. Any potential trace of such matter from my own hands had also, of course, to be expunged. I would smear the taps with soap, which, with rinsed hands, I would then wipe, and then rinse my hands again. Not quite reassured, I would repeat the ritual. In my cautious uncertainty, such fears would persist, until I sometimes ended up wiping taps for well over a minute.

Should my hand touch my shoe, or perhaps a surface which may have been touched by the underside of a shoe, I would concede to the dreadful threat, however slight, of having sullied my skin with a trace of dog muck, a substance known for its potential to induce blindness.

One Saturday, Mam, baffled by my inability to desist, beseeched me to find it within myself to do so. Such reiteration of the helpless, frustrated sorrow inflicted on her by my baffling inhibitions would leave me wearily ashamed.

That afternoon, when I got round to watching my recording of Stephen Sommers' gruesome creature feature *Deep Rising* (1998), a slow, heavy crash of the front door announced Granda Widdrington. As the living room door clicked and slid slowly open, I stopped the video and switched off the telly.

He greeted me with his customary query as to what sort of day I'd had today.

Weary of replying to this with "grand, thanks," or "fine, thanks," I chose a more frank reply of "neutral."

His voice rose to mild severity.

"Neutral? Why, what's the *matter* with you?"

His weathered face stared at me in loving urgency. His low voice beseeched me to see that my irrational behaviour of late was simply the product of inactivity. He reiterated his desire for me to more frequently attend Barrowburn to help with such tasks as fencing and sheep-dosing.

"Get away up to Barrowburn and help your dad!" he pleaded. "Learn your trade!"

While glad to help with occasional sheep-rounding and annual fleece-wrapping, I supposed such manual complexity as fencing was beyond me. Dad, with no desire for any of his sons to take over Barrowburn, had never requested our aid in any such task.

Granda Widdrington, having mourned the disuse of his own father's Longhorsley farm, cherished the idea that one of his grandsons would take custody of Barrowburn – specifically, it seemed, me.

"When a dog has nothing to do," he urged, "it chews its tail!"

The League of Gentlemen

On his birthday, Burdy, John, Sean and I gathered in Burdy's bedroom, in preparation for a visit to the Premier, Morpeth's Chinese restaurant.

Before setting out, Burdy showed us the first ten minutes of his DVD of the first series of *The League of Gentlemen*. The dark blue DVD cover showed two men in portrayal of an elderly man and woman, their faces rapt in fearful outrage. In affectation of some curious deformity, the make-up upturned and flattened the tips of their noses.

The first episode started. Beneath a mellow sky, a lush expanse of rolling moorland held a darkly looming detached building – the Local Shop. Tubbs (Steve Pemberton), while clearly played by a man, was garbed sufficiently to invite suspension of disbelief.

She and husband Edward (Reece Shearsmith), played by a similarly youngish man in a grey wig and large spectacles, both rather eerily merged naturalism with grotesquerie.

The One Hundred Greatest Scary Moments

One night, several weeks into October, either John or I happened to switch on my small bedroom telly. On Channel 4, *The One Hundred Greatest Scary Moments* offered commentary on and clips of scary films, television episodes and adverts.

Throughout an atmospherically dim mansion set appeared Jimmy Carr, for humorous narration. Various actors, writers, directors, comedians and critics were shown in respective close-ups as they discussed the filmic curios.

A hooded spectre promoted water safety, a towering gravestone propped John Hurt's thunderous AIDS warning, and, on an episode of *Brookside*, Jimmy Corkhill (Dean Sullivan) found a patio-buried corpse. I found myself increasingly reluctant to switch off the telly.

I decided to press record. As was right and proper, *Doctor Who* was paid tribute with clips from *The Dalek Invasion of Earth* (1964), in which the beloved metal domes glided around a black and white London, and *Genesis of the Daleks* (1975), with the demented ranting of Michael Wisher's Davros.

After Aphex Twin's music video for "Come to Daddy," in which a hairless, grey-skinned man climbs out of a television to scream in the face of an elderly bystander, things got rather more serious.

Against a clear sky, a gigantic, faceless wooden figure loomed over a hillside. The commentating voice of Christopher Lee recalled his role in *The Wicker Man* (1973) to have been specifically written for him. A few clips showed policeman Sergeant Howie (Edward Woodward) amidst sturdy old houses.

Christopher Lee's Lord Summerisle announced a ceremonial sacrifice.

Across a hill, Sergeant Howie was pulled forward.

Back in the studio, Steve Pemberton, a youngish man with a soft, Lancashire-accented voice, recalled the chilling climax.

Another excerpt showed the Wicker Man engulfed in billowing flames as a voice shrieked from within.

Footage from BBC Two comedy *The League of Gentlemen* accompanied input from Reece Shearsmith, a youngish man with a gently twanging Yorkshire voice. Whereas he disclaimed intention to make it overtly horrific, co-writer and co-star Steve Pemberton opined horror to be integral to the show.

Intrigued by the idea of a genuinely scary sitcom, I resolved to ask Burdy if I could borrow his DVD.

The Return of Doctor Who

It was announced, briefly in newsreels and momentously in *Doctor Who Magazine*, that *Doctor Who* was coming back. Well, sort of. A new audio production, set to flash animation by Cosgrove Hall, would be gradually uploaded to the BBC official website, with Richard E Grant as a Ninth Doctor.

One evening, as I sat alone in mine and John's bedroom, Dad popped through the open door and announced a new television series of *Doctor Who* to have been commissioned for BBC One.

In light of the BBC's recent investment, I felt only mild surprise, with a strangely calm elation.

Twenty-six years of fantasy, wrought in wildly ambitious but often technically limited sets and props, having spanned my parents' lifetime, would now be revived with faster pacing and modern visual effects. Television would never have seen anything quite like it.

The Best of the Corrs

One Saturday, I got a bus to Newcastle. Through Northumberland Street's weekend bustle, I waded to Virgin Megastore.

After much wandering around and staring at CD cases, I bought a copy of *The Best of the Corrs*.

That evening, when the living room was empty, I sat in the squashy armchair and put my new CD in my CD Walkman. I raced to track four and savoured the euphoric thrill of having "Breathless" all to myself.

To the chair's wide, rounded sides, I hooked my upper arms and thrust my torso left and right in horizontal flight. My imagination soared. This thrill was only permissible in isolation, preferably when the room was dark. I might often listen to my two Proclaimers CDs, the Abba CDs lent to me by James, and Mam's Kirsty MacColl CD, all of which lay on a small table left of the chair.

My latest CD's cover held four respective shots of each Corr. From the inlay booklet and online, I learned their names: Andrea, Sharon, Caroline and Jim.

2004

Some Kind of Gestalt Entity

In B9, at the far left of several unoccupied tables, sat Abbey and Chloe.

The Sixth Form dress code specified simple black or grey. Such items favoured by the girls included a blouse whose sleeves stopped just beneath the shoulder. Abbey and Chloe wore this garment beautifully; small sleeves gripped the uppermost inches of their respectively svelte and full arms.

Abbey's placid, high-cheeked face often succumbed to abrupt flashes of mirth, typically fuelled by hushed exchanges with her neighbour.

While Chloe's richly blond hair and softly rounded face were lovely as ever, the elation roused in me by Abbey had gendered a mild dependence – while not desperately so, I daily looked forward to seeing her.

The two girls' occasional lateness, absence and hushed exchanges drew Mr Balder's mockery, sometimes to Abbey's half-serious yelps of protest.

I flippantly imagined that Abbey and Chloe, both immersed in each other's attention, embodied some kind of gestalt entity. I'd encountered the term in the introductory biography in each of Rob Grant and Doug Naylor's jointly written *Red Dwarf* novels, which introduced both authors as two separate entities who shared the same body.

The two girls did both seem vaguely similar. While dissimilarly textured, each girl's hair fell long, free and straight about each head. While structurally diverse, each face produced similar expressions.

"Are you going out with the Head Boy?" called someone to Abbey, in amused curiosity. Abbey quietly replied in what sounded like affirmation.

I felt a hollow pang, but stubbornly dismissed my sense of loss. The vulgar exoticism of romance was as foreign to me as ever. I shoved aside my sadness and resolved that Abbey might split up with the Head Boy, anyway.

Before bedtime, at the front door with a mug of Horlicks, I gazed into the night. The fact was, I told myself, that I went to school each day looking forward to seeing Abbey, whereupon I came home and longed to see her some more.

It barely occurred to me that my daily access to Abbey wouldn't last forever.

The Wicker Man

In SPAR, several on-sale DVDs included *The Wicker Man* (1973). On the cover, in a monochrome still, beneath the towering titular totem, Christopher Lee's Lord Summerisle spread his arms in Druid rite.

Since it was only ten pounds, I decided to shoulder the burden of commitment and bought the DVD.

That night, James, John and I watched Disc One's theatrically released cut. In a clear-aired island village, Sergeant Howie (Edward Woodward) arrived in search of young Rowan Morrison (Geraldine Cowper). The Druid villagers' cheerful retreat from convention entailed nightly graveyard copulation. I found myself fretfully aware of the film's "15" certificate – any exposure to the rawness and delicacy of nudity had me queasily uneasy.

"This is a silly billy film!" said John, in imitation of Dad.

While I'd hoped my impressions to have been somehow mistaken, Howie's designation for incineration became increasingly blatant. While Lord Summerisle's tactful endorsement of Howie's Christian martyrdom soothed the cruelty, and Howie met his fate with splendid courage, I shared Steve Pemberton's wish for a timely arrival of police helicopters.

Free Drinks

As the days brightened, I took a bus into Newcastle.

Having last year bought *Sunshine on Leith* for about three quid at Virgin Megastore, I decided to further my relationship with the Proclaimers and bought their new album, *Born Innocent*.

Halfway home, I disembarked for a look around Morpeth and waited for a later bus to Rothbury. In Morpeth bus station, several people slightly younger than me lingered on and around the benches. At the edge of the bus station, I sat in wait for my ride home.

The remaining teenagers, on and around a bench near mine, approached me with impish proffers of conversation.

One girl became increasingly blatantly antagonistic. Holding a blue plastic bottle, she rose and, still talking to her pals, wandered over to stand behind me. Just as I realised what was probably about to happen, a trickle of moisture slid through my hair and spread across my scalp. The girl rejoined her cronies. They set off.

I stood. A curious apathy lulled me. Beneath my dazed dismay lay a muted, monumentally outraged anger. I caught up with the little group on the station yard, just outside the Co-op. I asked the girl why she had poured stuff on me.

"'Cause I don't like fat people," she said and wandered off with her pals.

In this new low of humiliation, I searched for some form of retribution. Before now, phoning the police would have been unfathomable. By now, I was just about too drained to care. I wanted my assailant to face some kind of consequence.

In the Co-op, I asked a woman behind the till if she might have the number for Morpeth police station. She produced a large phone with several labelled buttons, one of which, she showed me, was for the local police station. Still daunted, but recklessly resolved, I made the call.

A man's voice took my report and assured me that some investigation would be made.

All that remained was for me to call home and confess to having missed the last bus.

A passing police officer asked me if I were in any way related to a recent act of vandalism. I supposed this couldn't refer to my recent encounter, so politely disclaimed any such knowledge.

Throughout the evening, Mam's fury simmered.

"If I'd been there," she said, "she'd have been picking teeth out of her arse."

Outsiders

Online, the popular jibe *"Daily Mail* reader" implied said newspaper's readers to be an ungenerously reactionary fringe, who, in their affluent complacency, scorned the plight of outsiders. Since I sometimes read from the paper – I particularly looked forward to Chris Tookey's Friday film column – I found myself rather taken aback by the suggestion that one's entire outlook could be defined by a handful of separately written editorials.

An online interview with JK Rowling saw her playfully chide the American interviewer for having read from the *Daily Mail* – Vernon Dursley's reading of the paper in *Goblet of Fire*, I now realised, denoted his reactionary politics.

Rowling's scorn for obese Dudley had always depressed me.

With talk in the media of eating disorders and funny metabolisms, I clung to the idea that my outsize appetite might have subtler roots than ill-bred gluttony.

A *Daily Mail* opinion piece argued otherwise. Its solemn protest at the strain imposed on park benches mingled with wry aesthetic distaste. The fat, the opinionator said, had chosen to have disorderly bodies, and should be taxed for it. The sinister authoritarianism of taxation for unfashionable flesh was softened, the writer seemed to think, by its target of the flabby fruits of what he assumed was nothing more than bad habit.

Summer Sunshine

My delight in Andrea Corr's rich, light voice had gendered an assured infatuation with its owner. Her jollity, sensitive voice and gentle face soothed and exhilarated me. I cherished the thought of her.

The Corrs Online noted her attendance of the premier for the film *In America* (2002), having sung its Bono-written theme song,

"Time Enough for Tears." In an accompanying photo, a distant Andrea, in a cream gown, met the camera with a small, polite smile.

Increased exposure to her gorgeous voice drew me ever closer. Each evening, I looked forward to an hour or so in my armchair with the music of the Corrs. Going to Barrowburn with Dad at weekends, I listened to a recorded copy on my cassette Walkman.

The Corrs Online announced the imminent release of a new album, *Borrowed Heaven*, whose debut single was to be a song called "Summer Sunshine." I somewhat marvelled at the band's remobilisation so soon after my focus on them.

This week's episode of *Parkinson*, Uncle Ross airily noted, would feature an appearance by the Corrs.

At ten o'clock that Friday night, I had the bedroom to myself. In the small telly, I installed a blank tape. Michael Parkinson faced the camera with a welcoming grin and announced the band's arrival.

Onstage, Jim stood leftward with his guitar, Caroline sat at the back behind her drums, Sharon (now blond) stood rightward with her violin, and at the front, her hair sleekly black above a grey jacket and long pink skirt, stood Andrea. Electric guitar strings opened the song. Rich percussion, keyboard chimes and string shivers wove a lively song whose tender yearnings deepened to gentle melancholy – perfectly apt for Andrea's voice.

Throughout the next week, I listened to my recording of the song at every opportunity.

On Saturday afternoon at the Metrocentre, John and I planned to see *Prisoner of Azkaban*. Beforehand, I stole into HMV, with more in mind than a leisurely browse.

Near the doors, atop a walled display of recent CD releases, I found *Borrowed Heaven*. A white cover framed a greyish living room, in which the Corrs met the outside world with solemn stares. In gleeful awe, I took one of the sealed CD cases to the counter and purchased.

That evening, I had the summer-lit living room to myself. In my earphones, in the pristine incarnation of a studio recording, arrived "Summer Sunshine."

I gorged on the song. I grasped the chair's arms and channelled my euphoria into swift, sideways thrusts. Having listened to the song an undoubted minimum of ten times, I supposed things were getting a bit silly.

The rest of the album merged gentle poignancy with assured, indomitable joyousness.

The next day, the 5th of June, was Sean's seventeenth birthday. As was our recently cultivated custom, Burdy, Sean, John and I observed the occasion with a visit to the Premier, Morpeth's Chinese restaurant.

When we later returned to his house, Burdy lent me his DVD of the first series of *The League of Gentlemen*.

Tickets

The Newcastle Metro Radio Arena, I learned, was to host the Corrs' Borrowed Heaven Tour.

I now had a chance of spatial communion with Andrea, to feed my infatuation with direct, if distant, contact.

Enthusiastic at my mention of a concert, Mam asked who was playing.

"Corrs," I said nervously.

Pleasantly surprised, Mam said I could go and hoped also to attend.

"Would you want your mother tagging along with you?" she asked, somewhat ironically. I affirmed my ease with such an arrangement.

On her way to bed, she half sang the chorus of "What Can I Do?"

Local

Over the next few weeks, I watched the six half-hour episodes of the first series of *The League of Gentlemen*. Charmed by fantastic grotesquerie in a contemporary semi-rural setting, I found increasing mirth in the inhabitants of Royston Vasey. Elderly Tubbs and Edward Tattsyrup, with homicidal paranoia, defended their moor-based Local Shop. Their darkly comic brutality, quaint eloquence and childlike naivety were endearingly outrageous.

Joby Talbot's theme tune playfully crept, shuddered and wailed threats of surreal outrage.

After Tubbs and Edward, my closest point of identification was Harvey Denton. In bald cap, wig, prosthetic ears and warts, Steve Pemberton, familiar from the roles of Tubbs and Pauline, remained recognisable. His deep, sonorous vowels, enforcement of domestic regulation and obsession with toads presented an imposing yet vulnerable misfit. Amidst the morbid machinations of his neighbours, his obsessions had a reassuring honesty.

Seventeen

Mam and Dad asked if I fancied anything in particular for my seventeenth birthday.

Since last year, on the new Windows XP, I'd occasionally typed story ideas. James, now a KEVI teaching assistant and freelance piano teacher, had bought a second-hand laptop. The privacy of my own laptop, I mused, might dissuade the embarrassment which stifled my attempts to write anything more emotionally layered than a basic sketch or concept. Slightly guilty at the extravagance, I asked if I might have a laptop. With Dad's usual excitement at the prospect of new gadgetry, the idea was readily received.

Since the sheep gathering for this year's clipping fell on my birthday, we would have to spend the night before at Barrowburn.

In a dry old bed, I awoke next morning to a windowed view of the looming hills.

Downstairs, in the sparsely furnished sitting room, I opened a lavish book on digital photography from James and a compilation album of nineties pop hits from Uncle Ross.

In the front room, on the ancient table, lay a dark grey plastic square, larger than I'd imagined – my new laptop. Dad eagerly busied himself with setting it up.

The device's expense weighed on my conscience. However, the combination of keyboard and screen, that modern window to innumerable wonders, was now within my private grasp. I reverently echoed Dad's enthusiasm.

The onscreen icon with which to open my user area, installed by Dad, was emblazoned with my name, as well as a small image of a guitar, one of several available graphics. The small image, chosen by Dad, affirmed my creativity and implied a device gifted in esteem. My father's kindness roused a twinge of guilty sorrow at my irrational, inordinate fear of his rarely raised voice.

The onscreen desktop was deep blue. Superimposed into its right, a woman in professional running attire sprinted forth in frozen motion. Guilt dulled by excitement, I went online and visited an *Ed, Edd n Eddy* fan site. Its fond analysis of the madcap cartoon twelve-year-olds made for uplifting reading.

I visited several Corrs sites. A headshot showed Andrea in a purple tank top. I thought about using this shot in a digital shrine of desktop wallpaper, like Smithers (voiced by Harry Shearer) with his photo of Mr Burns (also voiced by Harry Shearer) but decided just to keep it in the My Pictures folder.

Away from the soothing familiarity of home on this lonely day of obligatory enjoyment, I glimpsed yet more frozen moments in Andrea's distant life. Against insurmountable distance, my affection raged. I recalled the last series of *Auf Wiedersehen, Pet*, in which Barry (Timothy Spall) asks if Oz's (Jimmy Nail) love for Ofelia (Josefina Gabrielle), a Cuban ballerina half his age, is stoked by her inaccessibility. While Oz denies such a factor, the bond thrives in defiance of distance. I pondered this.

It was time, I decided, for a bike ride. I tried to prise Dad's old bike from between the others, and they all crashed to the dusty floor. General despondence and humiliating shock spurred me to indulge in a loud expletive.

Later in the afternoon, Mam noticed my gloom. I confided my despondence at having had to spend the day away from home. My frivolous dismay at improper birthday observance was itself humiliating. I made a stilted attempt to articulate some of this.

Dad supposed me to be "in a bad fettle."

Later, Mam heard my lamentation of the burden of birthdays. I took comfort in the ability to retreat into my imagination and in my new window to the media.

Brains

In belated observance of my seventeenth birthday, John, Sean, Burdy and I dined once more at the Premier. Guilt at the extravagance on my behalf, and my collision with a startled waitress on our way out, somewhat paled the occasion.

We later wandered onto the twilit streets of Morpeth. With the doors of Morpeth Leisure Centre still open, I went inside, passed the unattended counter and visited the men's toilets.

Outside, Burdy conversed with a middle-aged man, whose presence at the unattended Leisure Centre might imply, I numbly supposed, some kind of authority. I uneasily asked him if my recent entry to the unmanned facility necessitated payment.

He confirmed any entry for any purpose, including toilet usage, to cost five pounds. While the steep fee implied farce, a dazed submission to authority overruled my scepticism.

As I handed him a five-pound note, he grinned incredulously. Burdy introduced me.

"And do you have the brains that you were born with?" The trickster beamed. I forced myself to laughingly protest my misapprehension to be an innocent mistake.

Vocation

One bright evening, I took my laptop up the riverside and climbed a set of wood-framed earthen steps to a bushy, tree-shaded picnic area.

Microsoft Notepad, with its wide typing space, somewhat eased my self-consciousness. I attempted the unthinkable. I typed stage directions to imply some inner chamber of the TARDIS. I typed dialogue for Ace and then for the Seventh Doctor. I wrote dialogue to imply their friendship and lifestyle. Through a barrier of shame, I forced each word onto the screen.

Why was this so hard? My attempt to type my recognition of the emotions of broadcast personalities recalled the playful sneers and pious scorn with which Granda Widdrington had bemoaned "that bloody telly." Trying to type others' emotions stoked my self-shame at imposition on others of my inhibitions.

I gave up and wandered home.

Obsessive-Compulsive Disorder

One warm Friday afternoon, my excessive handwashing once more vexed Mam. This time, however, she ventured that my urges might be worth discussing with a doctor. An appointment was arranged.

To Dr Anne Redmile, a dark-haired woman with a patient, Standard-English-leaning voice, I explained my desperation for repeated reassurance of cleanliness and to ensure that, when walking, I hadn't kicked stones into an arrangement which might trip some future pedestrian headfirst into the road.

Arrangement was made for my consultation with a St George's-employed psychiatric nurse.

What I'd suspected for years was confirmed. My years of irrational worrying did indeed have root in something other than ill-governed fussiness – apparently, I had something called obsessive-compulsive disorder.

Year Thirteen

Back at school, I was now casually but assuredly infatuated with Abbey Charlton. Her reserved voice, with its occasional buoyancy, entranced me.

As well as his role of kitchen assistant to Mam, James, in addition to his studies with the Open University, now worked at his beloved old school as a teaching assistant. With me in my final year, John nearing his GCSEs and James in his job, eight o'clock each morning (or more likely, several minutes later) saw the three of us board his blue Fiesta.

With more time in the mornings, I could now afford a shower. It made sense, I supposed, to wash away the sweat of slumber more thoroughly than at the bathroom sink.

Carry On As Normal

One late afternoon brought the arrival of psychiatric nurse Mr Dale Hartley. A deep North West drawl lent his easy geniality a sober thoughtfulness.

I confided my fancifully exaggerated fears of contamination of my prized possessions and of the contamination I might impose on the world beyond my own body.

Obsessive fears, Dale explained, were typically an irrational exaggeration and could be dissuaded by deliberately ignoring them.

"Worrying thought – the importance we give them – carry on as normal," he prescribed.

Calories

At the newsagent's, Mam bought an illustrated book. With note of the calorific values of a comprehensive list of foodstuffs, it advised the recommended daily calorie allowance for men and women and, in accordance with current weight and desired weight loss, how greatly to reduce it.

In order to get down from twenty stone to eighteen stone, I was allotted a daily limit of 2,400 calories. I could eat as I pleased, as long as I kept within the calorie count. Wonderfully, within a few weeks, I'd slightly but noticeably lost weight; my mountainous torso seemed faintly but noticeably diminished. My movements were marginally less constrained. Astoundingly, we seemed to have found a weight loss method which might actually work.

Within a few weeks, I resolved, instead of counting calories, simply to eat what didn't seem too likely to exceed my advised calorie limit.

The weight loss promptly stopped.

Borrowed Heaven

The 1st of November neared foreseeable reality. Anticipated for much of the year, the concert now loomed across weeks, then days, and then, at last, hours.

While glad of Mam's share in my delight in the Corrs, I guiltily held a slight frustration at her refusal to take payment for purchase of my ticket.

I would wear, Mam decided, James's old denim jacket. In a stylish expanse of blue, it enfolded my broad frame and rotund bulk. Mam then smeared some gel across my hair. I felt curiously grand.

In the darkened evening, as I boarded Dad's Suzuki jeep, elated apprehension flavoured my usual thrill of travel.

An hour later, we arrived in the car park of the Metro Radio Arena.

While Dad sat in the car with a book, Mam and I followed several people through wide, windowed doors into a cavernous, well-lit lobby. A huge, wall-mounted poster frame held a towering version of *Borrowed Heaven*'s sombre album cover.

On submission of our tickets, we each received a small leaflet, on which a gold-tinted shot of the band accompanied an address by which to order concert photos.

The vast arena, familiar from a recent school trip, was rowed with plastic blue chairs, as were distant, towering, stair-mounted aisles. Fairly near the leftward stage, Mam and I climbed to a row near the top.

The concert was set for seven. This might, I supposed, be for a support act.

In the leftward distance below loomed the stage, a hall-sized alcove whose extended floor stood several feet above the seats. It was distant enough to be somewhat dwarfed, but near enough for us to clearly see its quarry of drums and guitars.

My giddy thrill of anticipation began to succumb to a barely tolerable dread. Might Andrea's emotional return to this city stay her patience with the appetites of its public? I barely dared to comprehend my share in such disgrace.

At seven, the lights dimmed. The displayed instruments were for support band Myslovitz, who played some nice songs which, under different circumstances, might well have stayed with me.

When Myslovitz bowed out, the lights came back on. My fear churned ever furiously. It was absurd, I realised, how nervous I was. Another hour passed.

Eventually, nine o'clock neared. My fear mounted to a stifling panic. The air was promptly filled with a thunderous rendition of the instrumental introduction to "Baby Be Brave." The imminence of climax somewhat soothed my dread.

My resolve to fortitude was suddenly interrupted.

"*Good evening, Newcastle!*"

The female voice, light and joyous, was thunderously amplified throughout the arena.

Simultaneously, into a pale spotlight which suddenly shone within the darkened stage, there swept a small figure, discernible by a flash of creamy pallor, long black hair and a flowing, shin-length black dress.

This figure, whose presence laughed away my fear, was exultantly, jovially and undoubtedly Andrea Corr. And never mind any need to be brave; she now launched into "Humdrum," *Borrowed Heaven*'s bouncy seventh track. Her arrival, and the glee with which she blessed us, had me in a dazed euphoria.

Across the stage, Andrea skipped and bounded in time to her song. The hem of her black skirt rose and fell to reveal, above sturdy black boots, glimpses of her pale shins. On either side of the stage, a huge screen each cast a closer view of the singer. Instantly familiar from photos and music videos, her sleek black hair and high, rounded brow framed thoughtful dark eyes and a happy, finely rounded face. Her cheeks were blotched rosy pink.

Throughout the following two songs, "Only When I Sleep" and "Forgiven, Not Forgotten," I took in the presence of Sharon, Jim and one or two others in the darkened recess. To Andrea's right stood Sharon, rapt with her violin. To Andrea's left, on lead guitar, stood Jim. At the back of the stage, a wall-covering screen glared a dancing succession of blue, white and purple lights.

After the first few songs, Andrea spoke.

"It is, of course, wonderful to be back in Newcastle," her Irish vowels reverberated across the distant air. "We always hold this place as very, very special…"

The Toon, it seemed, as promised by Jim's online pledge of gratitude to the Freeman Hospital, was cherished as a source of care for their mother.

"I'm sure you've noticed – I hope you've noticed – Caroline is not with us," said Andrea. "She just had a baby girl, Georgina!" Applause rose at the announcement. I fretted a tad at having fallen short of Andrea's approval in my failure to detect Caroline's absence but reasoned that I hadn't been able to see the back of the stage, where a replacement drummer was now revealed to humbly sit.

"And if you ever want to join in," Andrea reassured us, "don't feel… restrained. We love a…"

In my small plastic seat, surrounded by distance and darkness, I bathed in the presence of this cherished figure from afar.

At one point, Andrea paused from singing and aimed her microphone at those seated on the floor. No audible voices arose. I winced. I couldn't escape the idea that I'd somehow telepathically infected the audience with my introversion. Andrea took it in her stride.

The band struck up the faster "Angel."

"*Come on, Newcastle, let me see your hands in the air!*" cried Andrea. I would usually have shied away from such flair, but for Andrea, I didn't mind.

"You heard the lady," an imaginary operator of my neural workings grunted to his colleague, who pulled an imaginary lever. I raised my hands.

Halfway through "Runaway," Andrea again asked us to sing along. A murmur of the wistful melody shivered through the stalls. My reserved voice felt a ridiculous intrusion on such splendour, but for Andrea, I uttered a low warble.

The band struck up "Summer Sunshine," one of my absolute favourites. As Andrea jogged and twirled, I meekly savoured a full view of her bare back. More than once, she punctuated her song by raising her arms high above her head, as in the video for "Breathless."

For a while, Sharon's violin dominated with an instrumental. Before the blaring lights, Andrea, on the spot, leapt in high, rhythmic manoeuvres, jigging away like a human firework. Humbled by the panache of a distant land proffered by its fair daughter, I didn't quite dare behold her at this point.

About halfway through, Andrea introduced the title track, "Borrowed Heaven," as based on "the idea that we've got this life on loan from God." To religiousness, this most joyous of voices lent a touching sincerity.

On the jollification raged. One of the huge screens showed a brief view of the thriving audience. Saturated in tender glee, I savoured tonight's brief but mighty union. After the rawly poignant "Goodbye," the stage darkened, and the band vanished.

"They'll come back on, you know," said Mam.

The lights glared once more, and the band roared into "Breathless," the song which, nearly two years ago, had drawn me to the Corrs. Around halfway through, people throughout the arena rose to their feet. Once the grey-haired woman to my right had done so, I bit the bullet and joined her. Looking across the happy crowd to my onstage beloved, I exalted.

As the others played on, Andrea concluded her song with announcement of each band member.

"And on the lead vocals," roared Jim, "Andrea!" To the thunderous crowd, the band grinned, gave their traditional joint-hands bow and waved.

"Thank you very much. You've been *great!*" cried Andrea. For a while, they stood before the dazzling backdrop of lights, beaming and waving. I steeled myself to send a little wave in return.

Finally, the stage darkened, the arena's dim lights returned, and the crowd began to amble through the stalls. On the screens, credits rolled. The instrumental "Silver Strand" played on speakers. My instinct was to attend this final touch of artistry, but Mam urged me on. It was now about half past eleven. Around us, the merrily murmuring crowd huddled slowly through the double doors.

"By, *she's* fit, that Andrea!" appraised Mam. With the dwindling crowd, we stepped into the night. "By, *she can play the violin,* her! Sharon!" said Mam. I'd seldom seen her so relaxed and elated.

In the car park ahead, a woman sold programme guides. I went over to buy one.

Above a thin layer of cloud, a full moon, small and faint, bathed the night in a weak glow. As Dad drove us home, my euphoria rather numbed the thrill of travel. I felt a tender sense of satiated accomplishment.

We got home at about one in the morning. I took the programme guide to my bedroom, propped it against the wardrobe by my bed and retired.

Andrea

I awoke tired, but tolerably so.

Downstairs by the telephone lay one of the small leaflets, emblazoned with an invitation to order concert photos. Last night was confined to memory, never to be lived again. Andrea, framed here in glossy, gold-tinted photography, could only be seen from afar.

As I rode to school with James and John, a weary yearning mellowed last night's euphoria.

In Mr Lloyd's dingy form classroom, I realised I'd come as close to Andrea as circumstance could ever possibly allow. My yearning succumbed to a giddied sorrow. As always, I could savour traces of Andrea's aspect in the media, but direct, sustained share in her presence was ludicrously implausible. Against its futility, my desire raged.

Loneliness anchored my mood to a numb ache in my upper chest.

While B9 seemed already to be occupied, several of the small class continued to wait in the gloomy corridor. As I made to enter, Abbey bobbed into the doorway with a slightly manic smile.

"I wouldn't go in there, if I were you!" she said. Her unprovoked address of me was a momentous boon, all the more so in its playfulness. What would normally have been a delicious thrill was now mild elation.

Inside, one of the tables held photocopies of today's text. As Abbey and I reached for a copy, I came within inches of brushing against the bare skin of one of her arms. This couldn't fail to thrill me to some extent.

"Sorry," I muttered.

"It's alright!" she said, with a touch of residual mirth.

I indulged a notion that she somehow sensed my desperation for Andrea and was giving me attention as a kindness.

Irrevocable separation from Andrea stoked my longing for her into a sorrow which raged, with alarming desperation, throughout the week. Just a few hundred miles away, she was getting on with her life. At thirteen years my senior, her birth was as close to mine as those of my parents. For a time short enough to register, but long enough to alienate, she'd known the eminence of adulthood.

Anyway, I lamented wryly, even barring all this, she was hardly likely to find me desirable.

In James's car, at school, and in the evenings at home, the inevitability of a lifetime without Andrea weighed on me.

In foreword to *Are You Afraid of the Dark?* episode *The Tale of the Dream Girl* (1994), a both chilling and poignant tale of a love which transcends the grave, Midnight Society member Sam (JoAnna Garcia) notes the pain of love to be a genuinely frightening notion. The empathy offered a slight balm.

One morning, in English Literature, a hot, tremulous weight behind my nose unmistakably threatened a sob. Determined to evade the humiliation of breaking down in class, I forced myself to suppress it.

In B9, in between stealing leftward glances at Abbey and Chloe, I fantasised that Abbey and Andrea might be allowed to swap places, so I could more aptly feed my casual attraction to one and my desperate attraction to the other.

I recalled my old fantasy that Abbey and Chloe were separate projections of the same multifaceted being, that each girl, independently of ancestry, was genetically related. The interpretable similarities of each girl's appearance might also, I supposed, be traced to the Corr sisters.

In my near-panicked longing, I hoped that such a surreal revelation might present itself.

On the bus home, my Walkman played the soundtrack of the 1999 production of *Joseph and the Amazing Technicolor Dreamcoat*. In "Close Every Door to Me," Donny Osmond's Joseph laments his exile and wrongful imprisonment, but trusts in a purpose beyond the foreseeable, by whose grace he will yet find peace.

In "A Pharaoh Story," Maria Friedman's Narrator announces the astonishing revelations set to save Joseph. I clung to the notion that my life might yet glimpse the otherworldly. Was such a glimpse revealed to my mother, back in 1989, when she was astounded to see an angelic figure which appeared to be my two-year-old self crawling across the bedroom wall? In my sorrow, I hoped.

Amidst the bustle of the Lower School B Floor, I resisted another pang of futile longing.

James was himself soon to visit the Metro Radio Arena, for an Elton John concert.

However remotely, spectator and performer nurtured each other, independently of distance. Even without direct contact, the devotion was real.

Did seeing and hearing visual and audible recordings of the Corrs somehow reach some kind of immaterial union? Did my perception reach beyond mechanically preserved light and sound and, on some unconscious level, telepathically convey my devotion? I was desperate enough to trust in this wondrous notion.

Anyway, I still had that voucher for concert photos.

Back home, I put the voucher in an envelope, took it into the cold November evening and dropped it into the letter box opposite our house.

Friends

By December, my despair had numbed to a forlorn resignation to make do with what I could see and hear of Andrea through the media.

Burdy's DVD of series one of *The League of Gentlemen*, which John and I had long-since thoroughly watched, offered, in its outrageous yet vulnerable characters, a certain fellowship. The comic grotesques were drawn with affection as well as absurdity. In maniacal defence of their Local Shop, Tubbs and Edward shared a loving ideal.

The show saw eccentricity through a lens of empathy: desire, however bizarre, was universal, its variety both comical and sympathetic.

My meetings with Dale Hartley were now held on Fridays, during the school lunch hour, in nearby St George's.

One day, just before Dale arrived, I sat alone in our consultation room. From a speaker near the ceiling, a radio station aired "There She Goes," by the La's (it might've been Sixpence None the Richer's version; I loved both).

My sorrow, never far these days, twinged at its eulogising by the lovely old song.

Memory

The Corrs Online announced Andrea's appearance on Channel 4's evening chat show *Richard and Judy*. I prepared a blank tape and, with the living room to myself, sprang into action.

Fifteen minutes into the show, a brief montage of music video footage was followed by announcement of the latest guest.

The band had broken up for Christmas, so Andrea (she laughed) got lumbered with the final job.

A black dress emphasised her soft pallor, black hair and dark eyes.

A clip played from the music video of the newly released "Long Night." In atmospheric gloom, the Corrs played before the staircase of a stately hall. Andrea's singing mingled with separate footage of her silent argument with a tall, suited man, who later carried her in a marital embrace.

In *Red Dwarf* episode *Thanks for the Memory* (1988), Rimmer's (Chris Barrie) drunken regret of his near-lifelong celibacy spurs Lister (Craig Charles) to use the ship's Dream Recorder to transfer memory of his affair with Lise Yates (Sabra Williams) to Rimmer, who, initially euphoric, is later distraught to learn of the memory's artifice.

Lister urges Rimmer to see that however painful the loss, an encounter with love imparts a newfound splendour. Although she never knew him, Rimmer loved her, and nothing can change this. Cherishing another person is his burden, his privilege, and his triumph.

My perception of Andrea, I decreed to myself, was mine alone. My love, even if she didn't sense it, was a nurtured, nurturing and irrevocable part of my own existence, and nothing could ever take it away.

Neighbours

Mam and James had always watched *Neighbours*. Throughout the nineties, Mam had also followed *Home and Away*, *Emmerdale*, *EastEnders* and *Coronation Street*, but these days, her pub kitchen work allowed only for *Neighbours*. I'd often half-watched and even partly followed storylines of all five but had been generally distanced by the adult convolutions.

Now, as *Neighbours* aired on BBC One, I found an increasingly soothing consistency in the discussions, consternations and machinations of its easy-going sunlit cast.

Flirtation

In the last week of term, Mr Balder ended a lesson early. As he and several lingering students happily nattered, I filed today's photocopied text.

With Chloe having left, Abbey remained in the corner of the room. In a beige fleece jumper, her head and arms rested on the table. As the moment of our parting neared, I kept a fleeting hope that she might talk to me. To my mild amazement, she did.

"Andrew," she murmured.

I seized this opportunity to look directly at her.

She gazed at me, her face sleepily alight.

"Will you carry us home?"

Aware that she probably wasn't serious, I wondered why she'd chosen me for such banter. Dared I imagine that she might be flirting with me?

"I can't, sorry. I'm getting a lift," I said.

"Well, will you carry us out of the classroom?"

Nervous, but dazedly thrilled by her request for a service which would require me to touch the backs of her knees, I finished stowing my file.

"Are you serious?" I blurted, but she was already standing up.

Souls

On New Year's Eve, James's keyboard-playing services were required at the Newcastle House pub. I took this opportunity to inspect from the inside this annual outlet of midnight whoops and yells.

Going out on New Year's Eve, it turned out, involved a lot of noise and bustle.

I joined James at a table with several of his bandmates, the tall one with the glasses, and Paul Walker, lyricist and avowed atheist. Amidst the drunken din, we engaged in cosmic musing. A *Daily Mail* piece about near death experience had mentioned a claim of all things, including blades of grass, to have souls. The idea, in its sanctification and immortalising of all forms of existence, appealed to me.

The four of us rambled vaguely on through the noisy build-up to midnight.

2005

How to Lose Weight

For the stomach indentation and hernia induced by my 2002 operation, I'd been offered corrective surgery.

In January, Dad drove me to the RVI for consultation with Mr Haldenby. Smooth black hair and small glasses framed a rounded face, whose gentle urgency emerged in a sober, North-West-accented voice.

The more weight I managed to lose, he said, the easier the operation would be.

I mentioned my nightly performance of two hundred stomach crunches.

Such exercise, he explained, would only burn off the calorific equivalent of a piece of toast: weight loss required significant food reduction.

Daunting a proposition as this was, I now knew how to actually go about it. Last autumn, the Calorie Count had had undeniable results: I'd lost some weight. In favour of a fatally vague resolve not to overeat, I'd stopped counting calories – as had the weight loss. I now knew what I had to do.

Irishry

In various unexpected circumstances, I kept finding unrelated mentions of the country of Ireland. In an English Language classroom, a small poster by the door listed several Irish authors. Did circumstances deliberately conspire to imply my connection to Andrea by cosmically premeditated mentions of her homeland? Or was I showing the human tendency to find order in randomness?

I was due for an eye test, so Dad took me to Specsavers. Still conscious of my over-reliance on my parents, I told Dad I could manage the reception interview alone.

I couldn't.

A young woman asked when my last appointment had been. I couldn't remember if it had been last year or the year before. It didn't seem that long ago, so I recklessly submitted an estimate of eight months. With politely subdued perplexity, she pondered the clumsy estimation. I waited for Dad, who arrived to explain the required details. Minutes later, a youngish woman called me into the small, dark examination room.

Light brown neck-length hair framed a fine, bespectacled face. Her calm, polite voice was unmistakably Irish. Irrational dread of my imposition on her refined person mingled with intrigue at her accent which, for me, had such tender connotations.

Dad and I then had a look round Northumberland Street. At the far end of the first floor of HMV, I perused a display of Corrs CDs. My wallet held a few ten-pound notes, so I decided to splash out on *The Corrs Unplugged*.

At the front of the shop, the serving cashier was a girl around my age, probably a few years older. Her face, framed with curly black hair, held one or two metal studs. On reception of my purchase, her face lit up in recognition. With conspiratorial glee, she asked something I didn't quite catch. Wonderfully, her accent seemed to be Northern Irish. Touched by her endorsement of my devotion, I blurted a grinning confirmation.

Real?

Could Andrea really somehow be related, independently of genetic ties, to Abbey? Might their respective beings, by some inscrutable force, be jointly shaped?

Expectation of worldwide genealogies to pander to my desires was, surely, a farcical pursuit of wish-fulfilment. Might the cosmos, in its mystery, yet show such beneficence? I couldn't reasonably expect it, but I desired it anyway.

On one of my evening visits to *The Corrs Online*, I peered at a small headshot of Andrea. The angle lent height to her cheekbones. In straight, loose tresses, black hair framed a high, rounded brow. The distinction was lucid enough to persuade me that this face might yet have some supernatural, genetically transcendent parallel to Abbey's. Fanciful contrivance? Or a genuine possibility?

With Mam and James, I now attentively followed *Neighbours*.

Jarrod "Toadfish" Rebecchi, better known as Toadie (Ryan Moloney), having arrived on Ramsay Street in the mid-nineties as a teenage prankster, was now a lawyer. His anarchic jollity now found outlet in pizzas, PlayStation and shared occupation with several other young men of the House of Trouser. Beneath neat brown hair and a high brow, his features had a patient openness, which I traced, involuntarily, to my brother James.

Endearingly fussy patriarch Harold Bishop (Ian Smith) now lived with newly returned son David (Kevin Harrington), whose ambition for reputable excellence would often fog his pursuit thereof. James and I found him hilarious.

Businessman Paul Robinson (Stefan Dennis) now eyed David's wife Liljana (Marcella Russo), or Lil for short, whose relaxed, affectionate amiability I found endearing. In pursuit of my fanciful theory, I studied her face. Its structure and expressions wove a signature comparable to Abbey's.

One evening, in an instant, a glance at a shot of Lil's face announced to me that what I hoped for was real. A high, rounded brow framed a thin face. High cheekbones lent urgency. The eyes focused in such a way as to both laugh and entreat. With dark eyes and high cheekbones, the face arranged an expression which insistently recalled the face of Abbey and drew swift comparison to the Corr sisters. The familiarity of Lil's face seemed practically to nag me into recognition of having seen its like elsewhere.

With ease inversely parallel to its spectacle, a miracle had announced itself. I now lived with something I unquestioningly believed to be supernatural. In genetically unrelated faces lay, imperceptible to most, similarity which transcended distance and matter. It seemed only fitting that I term such persons Essences.

The subject of the supernatural had always delighted me. Vague yet irresistible indications of it had occasionally manifested to several of my family.

Mam had been perplexed and astounded to see a white-robed, angelically glowing figure, which resembled my two-year-old self, crawl across a bedroom wall.

James had awoken one night to find the string-operated electric light above his bed unaccountably switched on.

In the kitchen one afternoon, Mam and John had heard the front door open, followed by a rapid ascent upstairs, with no visible sign of intrusion.

On a separate occasion, Mam had heard, from across the stairs, a young boy's cheery call of "hello, there!"

The glimpse of the supernatural with which I was now presented was both subtle and monumental. Worldwide genetically unrelated faces seemed to hold elements of each other, and only I, seemingly, could see it. Absurd as it was undeniable, ubiquitous as it was grand, and perplexing as it was astounding.

Stephanie McIntosh, who played Sky Mangel, soon emerged as an Essence. Straight blond hair curved around a high, rounded brow. Dark eyes led this face to insistently vivid familiarity.

The character, with her self-righteousness and high-minded quirks, sometimes rather annoyed me. For a short while, I insisted to myself that the shape of her brow had driven me to imagine the miraculous similarity. But I couldn't deny what I saw. Her brow, mouth and eyes aligned in expression which lucidly reflected Andrea. The parallel arrived in my perception with immediate familiarity.

I learned to differentiate Sky's occasional pugnacity from the wonderfully illuminated face behind the role.

The Trip of a Lifetime

In the Morpeth WHSmith's magazine rack, a low-angle shot of Christopher Eccleston as seen in ITV's *The Second Coming* (2003) announced *Doctor Who Magazine*'s embrace of the *Doctor Who* renaissance.

The magazine was now a far jollier affair than once it had been. Essays on old serials and announcements of BBC books and Big Finish releases were now stoked with the furious glee with which arrived every scrap of news of the imminent new series. The cataclysmic news thereof had been announced with a quote from executive producer and head writer Russell T Davies.

Each issue now concluded with a word from Russell, whose television prowess had pulled *Doctor Who* from the mire. Throughout the months, a few unashamedly excited paragraphs from this man, with hints of on-set goings-on, whetted my appetite.

Fizzlin'

The Calorie Count was working. My mountainously bulging torso became slightly but definitely easier to manoeuvre. At its now visible recession, everyone marvelled. I could only just see it myself but received the revelation with momentous glee.

Milk Roll was a great help. These cylindrical loaves were sliced into discs of bread, each only forty-six calories. Mam's Taiwanese colleague "Golf" had introduced us to Nam Prik Pao, a thick, sweetly spicy spread to which I took a liking.

As had always been the case when I'd finished eating, a residual dragging sensation in my throat sought more of the sensuous joys of tasting and swallowing. Having lunched in the Sixth Form Centre, I placated these urges with a small cup of tomato soup from the hot drinks machine. Sweet, fizzy diet cola also helped persuade my appetite of satiation.

By evening, I'd sometimes used up most or all of my daily calorie allowance. My longing to be soothed by the sensations of taste and swallowing soon succumbed to a tight, burning hunger, to which I refused to concede. If people in the Third World could live on a few grains of rice, I crassly declared, I could go without supper. I'm not sure how safe this really was, but I never found myself dangerously hungry. Weight loss was possible; it was happening, and it would continue. For the first time since the age of four, my torso would be free of its cumbersome shell of flab.

"Whoa, Andy!" said Dale Hartley on arrival one evening. "You're fizzlin'!"

The Ninth Doctor

Near seven, with BBC One on the telly, I prepared to press record on the Video Gadget. It was time!

A wheelchair ensemble of basketball players, arranged in circular affectation of the BBC One logo, accompanied a merrily understated continuity announcement.

The screen was then filled by a swirling tunnel of CGI lighting, which streaked at breakneck speed through a dark blue void.

With a blast of Murray Gold's pacy rendition of Ron Grainer's famous theme tune, the Time Vortex sped forth. Through it, three-dimensional block capitals flew in announcement of the names "CHRISTOPHER ECCLESTON" and "BILLIE PIPER," followed by the sleek new amber *Doctor Who* logo, which, in a pleasing echo of the McCoy era and TV Movie, briefly spun.

An orbital shot of the planet Earth zoomed down to contemporary London, where a working day in the life of Billie Piper's Rose Tyler was covered at high speed.

Christopher Eccleston's Ninth Doctor, by leather jacket; jeans, boots and North West accent, fit easily into a recognisably modern BBC drama. This intense yet buoyant stranger knew of wonders now to be shown in modern special effects. This was the Doctor, in contemporary form.

For me, one of the most exciting bits was Rose's consultation of Doctor expert Clive (Mark Benton), whose friendliness and competence portrayed Whovians touchingly favourably. His Teesside-sounding voice pleasingly acknowledged the further North. With his scant but undeniable account of a man mentioned in otherworldly encounters, disasters, and who seemed to transcend time, Clive portrays the Doctor in candid awe.

After the credits, I tuned into channel 115, for BBC Three's *Doctor Who Confidential*. Narrated by Simon Pegg, a succession of input from cast and crew accompanied a montage of Regeneration scenes, set to the Kinks' "Dedicated Follower of Fashion."

The central interviewee was executive producer and head writer Russell T Davies, whom I recalled from his *Doctor Who Magazine* column. Gingery brown hair topped a high-browed, faintly rounded, easily jolly face. A storyteller's glee offset the officialdom of his neat haircut, bookish glasses and semi-formal attire. A deep, soft Welsh voice boomed enthusiasm for the fusion of laborious creativity of which he was in charge. This was the man who had written tonight's episode and was most centrally responsible for bringing back *Doctor Who*. I felt a tender sense of esteem for the man by whose design this had come about.

A New Day

The Calorie Count had noticeably reduced my weight. My torso still bulged in the same directions, but less heftily or expansively, and was now easily concealed beneath a shirt.

From the age of four, I'd wondered what it must be like not to be fat, to inhabit a torso which didn't pursue all directions. I'd always been told that I needed to eat less, but until recently, had never known how much less, how to measure my intake in a way which indicated said lessening.

My impending operation and unprecedented success motivated and encouraged me.

Decent Society

On the second floor of the Sixth Form Centre, a small room held several computers. Before morning registration, I started coming here, for warmth and websites.

One free period, I had the room all to myself. I didn't see much point in the door being left open. For a bit of extra privacy, I closed it.

In a small office next door, Audrey, surname unknown, did some kind of facilitation job. Around mid-fifties, with shortened, greyish mousy hair, she held with Sixth Formers a slightly more relaxed rapport than that of a teacher.

As I stepped away from the closed door, it was shoved back open. With a mild glare and a voice of hushed urgency, Audrey explained the need for the door to be left open, to ease the heat generated by the computers. Her virtuous outrage reiterated a tendency of my naivety to rouse the wrath of the innocent.

For the next few minutes, my banishment from decency crushed my chest. Audrey's muted ire politely challenged my destructiveness. Her mild, virtuous aggression shocked me with frightened shame.

I sought to convince myself of Audrey's unenlightened vindictiveness. I recalled an opening line of Monty Python's "The Galaxy Song," but couldn't sincerely apply its jibes.

A Good Job

As I neared adulthood, I couldn't see what job my cognitive abilities might allow me.

My irrational shame at the prospect of writing emotionally layered stories, I hoped, might eventually wear off. Supposedly, studying English at university might help me along, or at least steer me in the direction of employability.

A poster in the school library urged university's importance.

Under the patient guidance of Mr Rochdale, I applied for nearby universities which might accept someone of my predicted grades.

Having first sipped cider at the age of twelve, I'd been allowed, these last few years, the odd can of Strongbow.

At weekend evenings, Mam and Dad shared a few glasses of wine or cans of Strongbow; after an evening in the pub kitchens, Mam found cider especially relaxing.

Having made a more frequent habit of my occasional sips, I now looked forward to Saturday evenings around the kitchen table, where alcohol supplied a relaxing, invigorating release. A measure of Diet-Pepsi-diluted rum, I soon found, did so with a deep, soothing glow.

Dan Aykroyd

One afternoon, I found James watching the Biography Channel. Today's episode was devoted to the career of Dan Aykroyd.

Having devised the concept of and co-written and starred in *Ghostbusters I* and *II*, Dan Aykroyd was a pivotal influence on the introduction of my brothers and me to cinema. I'd picked up somewhere that he was originally from Canada, ancestral home of James's old friend Ted.

I arrived too late to catch much of the documentary, but it closed with a note from Dan himself. With a polite, sober intensity strikingly akin to that of Uncle Ross, he mused British comedians to be a cherished influence on the comedic pursuits of his countrymen – a touching gesture.

One Friday night, as the drinking was just getting under way, I went into the living room to briefly inspect the telly and found a broadcast of Richard Attenborough's *Chaplin* (1992). It featured Dan Aykroyd, who was now on-screen.

While I'd watched *Ghostbusters I* and *II* countless times, I couldn't remember seeing him in much else, apart from his cameo in *Casper* (1995) and the trailer for *Dragnet* (1987). His appearance in anything recalled the intense yet jolly erudition at which I'd awed in infancy. I now took a moment to see what else Dr Stantz had got up too.

These last months, I'd scanned various broadcast faces for the miraculous similarity which, seemingly, only I could see. I'd been increasingly persuaded that Dan Aykroyd was such a person, an Essence. His smooth black hair and broad brow shone a distinction as strong as memory – of my having seen its like in other people. To Andrea Corr, I traced the combination of dark hair and high brow. In the broad brow, high cheekbones and thoughtful intensity shone a faint but insistent hint of *Neighbours'* Toadie (Ryan Moloney).

In the current scene of *Chaplin*, Dan's character was getting cross. His weary face suddenly rapt with ire, he shouted in solemn fury. The outburst was strikingly similar to rare *Neighbours* scenes of Toadie's wrath.

I now saw an obligation to stay and attend the face of Dan, whose secret aspect had miraculously appeared to me. However, the film would run well into the night, and I'd anticipated the giddying release of a few shots of rum with Mam and Dad.

My current impression of Dan's face, I lamely reasoned, might not necessarily perceive a miraculous parallel; the similarity, faint as it currently was, might be imaginary.

My conscience tolerably pacified, I turned off the telly and headed for the kitchen. This abandonment of my post later became one of my greatest regrets.

Visual Appeal

Each Saturday evening brought a new episode of *Doctor Who*.

In Russell T Davies' *The End of the World*, on space station Platform One, Christopher Eccleston's Ninth Doctor, to Soft Cell's "Tainted Love," rhythmically swayed his shoulders. Crinkled eyes, small, suddenly widened mouth and steep cheekbones cast a grin strikingly similar in shape and movement to Abbey's. Suggestible as I was to metaphysically shared likeness, the familiarity seemed strong.

As Billie Piper's Rose sank fearfully beneath a lowering sheet of lethally unfiltered sunshine, I found myself oddly daunted by my suspicion that Billie Piper, with her reputation for partying, might be an Essence.

The following week, in Mark Gatiss's *The Unquiet Dead*, Billie's high brow and cheekbones tilted her expressions to a distinction to which I traced shadows of the Corr sisters and Abbey.

I emphasise that while I was in no doubt of this metaphysical phenomenon, it excited me to receptive credulity. It seems that in some cases, I wilfully traced certain arrangements of facial structure and expression to appealing sources. While in some faces, the uncanny vividness irresistibly announced its like elsewhere, others, while not quite so obvious, offered the same uncanny sense of recognition – whose like, I, at least to some extent, interpreted.

In Robert Shearman's *Dalek*, the new series' emotional realism wove to true monstrousness the ideas behind the Daleks. Etched in charred, hefty bronze, the cherished image of the stalk-eyed dome looked every inch a lethal machine built on some distant war-torn planet. Shamed and frightened by the human desires born of its absorption of Rose's DNA, the creature opens its shell to reveal an exquisitely detailed mutant occupant. Murray Gold's choral score poignantly evokes the tragic waste to which this genetically engineered creature has been conditioned.

On the following episode of *Doctor Who Confidential*, a Dalek montage played along to "O Fortuna." Sylvester McCoy mused how on their 1960s appearance, the Daleks evoked fearful wartime memories of battle tanks.

Having been struck two years previously by an inscrutable familiarity in the face of Cameron Diaz, I now triumphantly supposed her to have been an Essence all along. Her rounded brow, blue eyes and finely high cheekbones, while entirely distinct, drew recognition from elsewhere; some of their expressions seemed so close to those of the Corr sisters or Abbey as to announce genetic link.

The face of Jessica Biel, having that same year drawn my eye, now shone with a distinction which I traced to Abbey and the Corr sisters. Calm eyes, straight hair, high brow and finely broad cheekbones cast expressions which, to me, paralleled the aforementioned as closely as would genes.

Visual appeal, it seemed, might herald something other than aesthetic appreciation.

For now, I endorsed any supposed possibility of who might be an Essence. Undeniable to me as my insight was, my trust in it was blithely credulous.

Late one weekend night, as I rose from my chair, my gaze fell on my stack of CD cases, atop which lay the soundtrack of semi-animated *Doctor Who* webcast *Death Comes to Time* (2001). In Lee Sullivan's (I think) cover painting, the dark, wavy hair of Sylvester McCoy's Seventh Doctor was slightly longer. The brow's height, breadth and curvature, I now supposed, might well hint the lineage of an Essence.

Neighbours Essences

Among the *Neighbours* cast emerged several more Essences. Brows, expressions and facial structures wove a familiarity as elusive as a faded dream yet as keen as luminescence.

In adulterous Izzy Hoyland (Natalie Bassingthwaighte), straight, dark blond hair, finely high cheekbones and dauntless dark blue eyes wove expressions to which I instinctively recalled Abbey.

Precious Things

At the Metrocentre, with a few ten-pound notes in my wallet, I browsed HMV. *The League of Gentlemen* DVD box set was well within my budget. I decided to try life on the edge and buy it.

At the till, I considered the ease with which I might take from the counter an unguarded ten-pound note, put it in my wallet and leave the shop an illicitly rich man. In my guilt-ridden fear of the possibility, I persuaded myself that I may indeed have snatched the unguarded cash. Elation at my purchase lent logic an upper hand, and I managed to just about quash the fear.

I, too, am local, I thought as I proudly held the carrier bag.

Down to the Ground

This last year, my emerging wisps of facial hair had grown into a fuzzy stubble. While it was a bit ungainly, I decided to savour a while longer this marvel of adulthood. At the end of one Religious Studies lesson, I fell into conversation with Mr Balder. He noted my facial acquisition.

"It's for the exams," I said. "It makes us feel wise!"

To my delight, he laughed.

Much of my preparation for the A2 Level exams involved going to the library after the final bell, sinking onto one of the plush seats in its entrance foyer and further familiarising myself with *Othello*, before at half past four getting a lift home with James and John.

For English Language, I looked through the sheets of photocopied text which cluttered my file, most of which my mind refused to absorb – I'd see a linguistic term, try to grasp its description, how this in turn referred to another linguistic term, and so on.

To plough my mind through endless such terminology was like trying to swim in treacle. I fell back on my old conclusion that I just didn't have the right sort of mind for revision. Beneath this resolve, the word "lazy" reasserted its claim to my every inhibition.

Religious Studies lessons, often held in the afternoon, would draw to an agreeably prolonged close, with Mr Balder's reflection on ethics, theology and various subjects to which either notion might remotely lead.

I'd lost so much weight, he one day noted, that my trousers were in danger of falling down.

"These philosophers and people," said Bruce Duggan, "just... talk *shite.*"

"Well, it should suit you down to the ground, then," said Mr Balder, to hoots of laughter.

There came a point when Abbey would gather her things into her handbag, stand and, with Chloe, approach the door. I ached for Abbey to stay a bit longer, for her to mutter some more with Chloe or share some more banter with Mr Balder, but inevitably, all too soon, she was gone for another day.

My daily thrill to Abbey's soft vibrancy had gendered earnest infatuation. If ever I were to go out with someone, I mused to myself, it would be her. But that sort of thing was beyond me. To taint our scant but happy relationship with the vulgarity of romance would be obscene. Instinct demanded I remain in the peace of my own head and not impose on the world my confused self.

One afternoon, when the Sixth Form Centre was particularly noisy, I retreated upstairs to the plush chairs outside the computer room. To my improbable fortune, Abbey and Chloe arrived nearby. They leaned over in inspection of a wall-mounted photograph of last year's Year Thirteen. Abbey, mere inches to my right, leaned even closer. I felt something soft and firm press briefly against my upper arm. This was a taste of something of which I barely dared to dream. Might it, I hoped deliriously, have been deliberate?

That evening, with Mam at work in the pub kitchens, and Dad, James and John upstairs, I lounged in the sunlit living room and, on Fox Kids, watched an episode of *Martin Mystery*. Its anime-influenced animation staged supernatural scares in such sumptuously detailed settings as *Return of the Dark Druid*'s (2004) depiction of Nova Scotia.

By now, I fecklessly interpreted any familiar-looking brow as another instance of my witness to identity's transcendence of space and matter.

The cartoon aspect of Diana Lombard (voiced by Kelly Sheridan) was now deemed such a figure. Straight brown hair, parted around a high brow, framed a fine, thoughtful face, given easily to excitement, fear or annoyance with her impudent stepbrother Martin (voiced by Samuel Vincent). Her agitated yelps put me in mind of Abbey, as did her lithe build and proportion of face and hair. To a delicious day, half an hour of animated Essentiality brought a sweet aftertaste.

Card

With Study Leave near, lessons became less formal. In Religious Studies, Abbey blurted out the date of her imminent birthday. Naturally, I took mental note.

During Study Leave, I spent many an hour traipsing the quiet, sunlit streets of Morpeth. I passed rushing cars, midday shoppers and, occasionally, fellow Sixth Formers taking a well-earned break in a pub or café. All I wanted was a glimpse of Abbey. If I just saw her, from across a street, the trip would not have been in vain. Lessons proper had all but ended, and my Abbey supply was drying up. As time put further distance between me and happy, bubbly, graceful Abbey, our every parting left me hungry for more.

After much deliberation in WHSmith, I chose one of those cards with humorously captioned black and white photos of quaintly attired actors. A suited man, noted by the caption to have rang someone's doorbell, broke into a run.

On Monday, with the enveloped card in my bag, I wandered halfway down the school bank to one of the exam huts, for a resit of last year's Religious Studies exam.

Beneath sunlit trees, in warm, clear air, I waited. Dare I approach Abbey with my presumptuous trinket? Would it give her the idea that I fancied her? Did I want it to?

Someone walked down into the clearing and casually called out to me. In a fraction of a second, I realised my absurd good fortune. After weeks of waiting, Abbey was talking to me like it was the most natural thing in the world. In a black tee shirt whose sleeves, while not as sexily short as usual, showed an appreciable length of arm, she sought confirmation of the resit's location, which I promptly supplied.

Alright, it was now or never.

"Um, was it your birthday yesterday?" I said.

"Yeah," said Abbey blankly. Amused surprise lit her face. "Ah, how did you *remember*?"

I mumbled something about having got her a little something and reached into my bag.

Her face spread into a sweetly gormless grin.

"That is *so* nice of you!"

I handed her the slightly scuffed envelope.

"Erm, there you gan," I said, trying to keep things informal.

"I'm just gonna..." She smiled, with a gesture to those gathered outside the hut's door. I smiled an understanding farewell and prepared to savour the aftermath of the moment.

Phantom

Further trails around Morpeth yielded no further Abbey sightings. When my bus time neared, I looked around the quiet, sunlit streets.

Having seen little of the high street beyond WHSmith and Woolworths, I decided to visit the small Oxfam charity shop.

It had a good selection of second-hand books, DVDs, CDs and even cassette tapes. *Highlights from the Phantom of the Opera* was available for eighty pence. I liked the two songs I'd heard from this musical and had a consistently high regard for stuff by Andrew Lloyd Webber. I bought the tape.

That night in the armchair, before my usual diet of nineties pop hits, Proclaimers and Corrs, I put the tape in my cassette Walkman and fast-forwarded in search of the title song.

With a blast of organ keys, the famous song began. The mighty orchestra was a gothic delight. The voice of the Phantom seemed familiar. Soft and light, with thunderous steel, something in its fine lilt drew faint recollection. The inlay booklet listed it to be that of Michael Crawford.

Something called "Asperger's Syndrome"

In respect to my 2002 operation, the offer of reconstructive surgery had included optional counselling sessions, which I, in search of answers, had accepted. A letter invited me along to the Rothbury Practice.

In the waiting room, I, to a consultation room, was led by a slightly stout woman with shortened ginger hair and a Standard English accent.

We discussed my childhood tendency to solitary playground wanders.

The final session closed with her tentative, almost apologetic suggestion that I might have something called Asperger's syndrome. This, she stressed, was far from certain. The possibility encouraged me to consider that my inhibitions weren't, as I'd feared, due to ill-discipline, but were, to some extent, innate.

I decided not to continue the sessions. Perhaps I just wanted to finish my adolescence and pursue some kind of place in the world.

The Federation Brewery

The Year Thirteen Leavers' Dinner was to be held at Gateshead's Federation Brewery. James fondly recalled his own "Leavers' Do." Now being a member of staff, he planned to attend mine, of which I was glad.

I was to wear a white shirt of James's, his old bow tie and dinner jacket, and a pair of Dad's suit trousers. James had rented himself a suit.

Around six, Mam smeared gel across my hair.

Dad drove James and me into Morpeth. By the leisure centre stood two hired coaches.

In warm sunshine and gently cool air lingered several teachers and an increasing number of Year Thirteens, all dressed in suits and softly bright gowns.

Eventually, several teachers directed us onto the coaches, through one of whose windows I caught my first glimpse of Abbey.

The coaches chugged into life and rolled us into the waiting summer night.

We eventually pulled into the Federation Brewery's car park.

Year Thirteen filed into the building's foyer. In the slow bustle, my old friend Mr Dolan greeted me warmly.

At the far end of the dim, smooth-floored, balloon-decked hall, James and I found our table, where, amidst the roaring babble, we discussed *Revenge of the Sith*.

"Bit of a sad film, really," said James.

The plates were cleared away, and the diners stood to mingle.

I moved to stand near the bar. My top priority was to ease myself towards wherever Abbey might be.

But first, a drink wouldn't go amiss.

My hover around this vicinity was rewarded with several Abbey sightings. A purplish blue floor-length gown, topped by a looped collar above her bare shoulders, enfolded her lithe frame. Iridescent sparkles gaily offset the garment's soft flow and lush hue. On sight of my sweetly daft classmate in such tender finery, I almost ached with longing.

Throughout the darkened air loudly played a song from *Team America: World Police*. Unable to enjoy music at such volume, I made my way through the foyer and outside to the back of the building, to stare in dignified melancholy at the overcast black sky. After a few minutes, I got bored and went back in.

Back in the hall, I sank several pints of Strongbow, goodness knew how many pints of Diet Coke and wearily hovered. Several people approached to ask if I was having a good time. I forced myself to enthuse in the affirmative and wondered why people kept asking this.

Always happy to give me a brief word, why couldn't Abbey approach me now? I recalled Henry van Statten's (Corey Johnson) furious plea for the captured Dalek to recognise him. But it seemed Abbey wasn't going to.

I returned several times to the cool peace of the men's washroom. Amidst pockets of conversation, I re-encountered Mr Dolan. Smartly suited and bright with cheer, my old friend seemed genuinely keen for a jolly old natter.

"Now, I don't want you to be offended," he said with delicate candour, "but I think maybe you're someone who doesn't always... fit in?"

I readily agreed.

"That's... not a weakness," he said with a small smile.

Back in the hall, the gowned and suited crowd jumped and writhed with renewed zest. The disco struck up "The Road to Amarillo." It slightly lifted my mood, but overall reminded me of what I was missing. Through the darkness, I scanned the dim, gaudy, wildly darting spotlights. To my distant right, in the wildly twitching crowd, Abbey grinned and rhythmically thrust her frame. The motion cast her in a brash grandeur I was too embarrassed to behold, much less approach.

Eventually, the music stopped with no resumption, and the crowd began to disperse. Back to reality. No more Abbey.

By Morpeth Leisure Centre, the gowned and suited revellers disembarked onto the concrete to make ceremonious farewells and board pre-booked taxis. Among the dwindling huddle, I savoured one last glimpse of a beaming Abbey among similarly grinning friends, around one of whom she slipped her arms.

James and I arrived home around three. I supposed it was high time I was in bed. Lying there, I tried hitting the wall with the back of my left hand. A sickly, desperate weight constricted my chest. I wondered why I couldn't seem to let some of it out in a sob.

Sleep, for the time being, wanted nothing to do with me. Oh, it was no good. I got up, washed my face, went downstairs and, after twenty minutes of listening to Abba, felt ready for bed.

Abbey

I awoke around six, not feeling very tired. With everyone else in bed, I went downstairs and opened the back door. In mild, strong sunshine, the small concrete yard, the foliage of the terrace lawn and the distant fields and hills positively glowed.

I returned to stand by my bed. To my relief, the intensity of my woe was fading. Cheered, I recalled the bit in *Red Dwarf* episode *Quarantine* (1992), when Lister's bodily defences are anticipated to resist the effects of the Luck Virus. My own natural defences must be on the march.

Throughout the next hour, I nurtured an exciting resolve. I didn't have to surrender to the supposed inevitable. I would get a bus and have a wander around Morpeth. My spirit soared at the possibilities.

Eighteenth Birthday

The day of my coming of age would see a pre-arranged consultation at the RVI. This suited me fine; birthdays went better when I didn't languish in guilty fear of failing to sufficiently enjoy myself.

That bright noon, I arrived in the kitchen to a display of presents. For Mam and Dad's present I'd requested cash and was humbled to find in their card five twenty-pound notes, some of which I'd spend later today in Newcastle's Forbidden Planet.

Aunty Jess had got me, on behalf of Nana and Granda, a double CD, *Pop Art*, being a compilation of the greatest hits of the Pet Shop Boys. Having often watched their videos on Magic, I'd never lost my love of their music.

In the Royal Victoria Infirmary, Dad and I made our way through cool, stern-smelling corridors to the relevant waiting area. Mr Haldenby noted my pointedly reduced weight. How much had I lost?

"Five stone," I said hesitantly, not entirely sure of the strict accuracy of this.

"Absolutely su-perb!" said Mr Haldenby, a sincere esteem in his smart tones.

A2 Level Results

In the final week of August, around midday, James drove me into Morpeth to collect my A2 Level results. Across the lawns and paving of the school grounds, several ex-Year Thirteens, now in casual clothes, lingered in conversation.

I didn't honestly expect my exams to have gone all that well.

In the hall, in the milling procession ahead of me, I caught a glimpse of Abbey. On one of the rowed tables, I found the brown envelope with my name on it.

Back outside, I opened it.

Just as I'd expected, I'd done as poorly as last time. An E for Religious Studies, a D for English Language and, only slightly humiliatingly, a C for English Literature.

A fretful shame simmered in my chest. I'd been admitted to the Sixth Form on the technicality of the supposed impairment of having missed much of Year Ten.

My inability to grasp technical data or instruction once again disgraced me. Could I have forced myself to revise harder? Other people had revised for hours. Here it was again, that lifelong accusation: lazy. From my scant restraint of my appetite to my supposed refusal to force myself to listen to teachers, I seemed to lack focus. Might neural formation have sown such impediment? What syndrome had that NHS counsellor ventured I might have?

Naturally, James was comfortingly calm and stoic about it. Before going home, he decided to visit the gym at Morpeth's leisure centre. I tended to prefer a nice walk, but I craved a distraction.

In the gym's sweet, cool air, my head full of Abbey Charlton and my inability to do normal things, I mounted a treadmill. At one point, the radio played Talk Talk's "It's My Life." Or it might have been No Doubt's version – I loved both. The song's doomed yet principled defiance lent me front to assert that, despite everything, I had some kind of place in the world.

As soon as we got home, Mam, before hearing my results, hastened to reassure me that it didn't matter too much.

The envelope included several mind-boggling forms in aid to university application, which Dad, at the kitchen table, masterfully perused. The forms occasionally required input from me, such as some number allocated to me by UCAS. The complexity slackened my focus. I didn't know anything about any such numbers.

"Andy, what are we doing, man?" said Dad with a rare sigh. I couldn't always rely on my parents to sort things out for me, he stressed.

In need of relief, I went for a walk up the river.

I returned to find James, fretfully attended by Mam, on the phone to Northumbria University. I'd applied here to study English Literature, because it might nurture my writing aspirations, it might increase my employability, and because I didn't know what else to do with myself.

James eventually put down the phone to confirm that Northumbria would be willing to accept me to its course of Film and Television Studies. The idea of writing essays about films and telly sounded both exciting and dispiritingly frivolous. Taking this course would be a culmination of my academic ineptitude and hopeless need for my elders to arrange things for me. Downcast, I supposed there was time to decide.

"I would be grabbing this with both hands," said James with a rare urgency. His endorsement was decisively encouraging. Back in 1999, the prospect of studying music away from home had overwhelmed James with anxiety, so he currently walked the slow path of studying it via the Open University.

"Will you please just try it?" said Mam.

It would be an adjustment, but I was starting to accept the idea.

Days later, I managed a trip to Morpeth, to find Abbey at her post behind the Woolworths till nearest the shop's door. From the open fridge, I took a can of Diet Coke. In the queue, my nervousness mounted almost unbearably. From the face which brought me such joy, I dreaded the slightest look of weariness or impatience.

I braced myself, glanced at Abbey's passive face, passed the can onto the counter and awaited a calm request for eighty pence. Instead, Abbey looked straight at me and grinned.

"How'd you do?" she demanded.

Dazed, I savoured what I'd ached for throughout the Leavers' Dinner.

"Or do you not wanna tell me?" she wryly added.

Only slightly ashamedly, I reported my results. Barely able to believe my luck, I joined her in conversation, with regard as to what we were both now up to.

"Ah, cool, that sounds really interesting!" she said. "I wanna get a proper job," she added with a self-deprecating smirk, "and... not work here!"

Transaction completed, we shared a fond if casual farewell, and I resumed my Morpeth wanderings. For hours, glee swelled palpably in my chest.

Northumbria University

I was still undecided about devoting my next three years to Film and Television Studies. I pondered the daily hour-long bus rides to a secondarily chosen course whose studies might prove to be beyond me. But I'd agreed to give it a try.

In cool air, beneath an overcast sky, I stepped into the mounting morning bustle of central Newcastle.

Past St Mary's Place, the colossal university library overlooked a broad, building-flanked yard. Across it swarmed people in their late teens and early twenties. Past the central building of the Squires Annex, along a length of pavement, stood the Lipman Building.

My first port of call was a lecture theatre which, at the very back of the building, lay on the basement floor. A grey-toned hall, its stair-mounted seats faced a broad, high wall. A bustle of people around my age gradually sat.

A middle-aged woman took to the floor. She asked us to turn to our neighbours and present a carefully considered answer to her question: "Why... are you... *here?*"

This was exactly the sort of thing I'd hoped to avoid, a command to relinquish the peace of my own head for the dauntingly innocent gaze of strangers, and to enthuse about an endeavour about which I was far from sure. I forced myself to turn to my neighbour, an amiable floppy-haired lad, and improvise some worthy-sounding reason for my presence.

It was then off to the library to get our student identity cards. On its bright, expansive basement floor, we queued to pose for a passport-sized photograph, which was quickly printed on a card with our name and registration number. Visibly thinner than it had been this time last year, and swathed with fuzz, my face looked about as confident and excited as I felt.

In a smaller, classroom-sized room at the front of the Lipman Building, a bald man discussed the Arts and Social Sciences wing. The course, he seemed to be saying, would nurture joint effort from students. Again, a demand to join in, to overcome my supposed bad habit of preferring to work in solitary contemplation.

I spent much of the rest of the afternoon in a melancholy funk. When I got home, I'd now all but fully decided, I'd tell Mam I'd given it a try, as she'd asked, but this course was not for me. I'd rather do an English Literature course with the Open University and get a part-time job.

At the end of the day, back in the basement lecture theatre, it was time for the first screening. In the cool gloom, amidst the babble, I waited for things to get started. A square white projection screen now adorned the front wall. Beneath it, a man took to the floor.

His appearance and voice instantly held my attention. Smooth black hair topped a broad brow, which framed a rounded face. From behind round glasses, his eyes shone with friendly enthusiasm. A blue jumper neatly enfolded his short, portly frame. With an East-London-sounding twang, he introduced himself as course leader Peter Hutchings and asked us not to address him as "sir," as this would make him feel old. A jovial smile punctuated much of his speech. The following screening, he announced, would be of *Stranger on the Third Floor* (1940), an hour-long film noir.

This man exuded a rapt delight in the subject of film. I was put in mind not of lofty essays, but of such gleeful fascination as which beamed from Russell T Davies and Steve Pemberton. Peter's thin, straight hair, high brow and rounded face recalled Russell.

With its higher, fuller cheeks, the face similarly evoked Steve. Beneath smooth black hair, the features also evoked Dan Aykroyd. In Peter, I was warmly assured of a kindred spirit. If I choose to stay, I decided, it would be for him.

After the long bus ride home, I remained largely persuaded that the course wasn't for me. Mam entreated me to give it a bit longer.

Having briefly read about Nigel Kneale's controversially scary trilogy of 1950s science fiction serials, I enjoyed a screening of the soberly intense first episode of *The Quatermass Experiment* (1953), with its surprisingly convincing props.

The following seminar, hosted by Peter, discussed 1950s television. He described Professor Quatermass (Reginald Tate) as "a kind of fifties Doctor Who, trying to sort everything out..." and the amorphous, tendril-waving monster as "a kind of slimy, yucky... there's gonna be thousands of these things!"

Even if I couldn't manage the reading, bits of this course might yet prove fun.

By my waist, a leather satchel held a pen, notebook, library books and the occasional magazine. For classes and screenings held at nine, I'd force myself out of bed on four or five hours' sleep, get a bus to Morpeth and wait there for a Newcastle bus. With a lonely sense of futility, I faced the morning chill and bustle.

Following another half hour's ride to Newcastle, a ten-minute walk led me to the Lipman Building. On the way, I often stopped in the Oxfam charity shop, enticed by mildly priced books. Terrance Dicks' 1994 *Doctor Who Virgin New Adventures* novel *Blood Harvest* pitted the Seventh Doctor against 1920s gang warfare and N-Space Vampires.

Waiting for classes to start, I often dipped into *Blood Harvest*. Alternatively, I might visit the library, on whose sixth floor I sometimes made a principled yet foolhardy effort to grasp technical, psychological, economical and ideological film-related discussion. Bare white walls, a strong smell of toilet disinfectant and dizzying views of the distant cityscape lent the hall-sized room both sterility and vibrancy.

By Dr Peter Hutchings, this floor held anthologised articles and his own book, *Hammer and Beyond: The British Horror Film* (1993). His thematic analysis of *X: The Unknown*'s (1956) radioactive blob, *The Quatermass Xperiment*'s (1955) carnivorous plant hybrid and *Quatermass II*'s (1957) giant Saturnian jellyfish all had me entranced.

Hi, Andrew!

Out of the top floor classroom, my class filed into the dim corridor. I slipped through the swinging double doors into the quiet, echoing stairwell, where I prepared to savour a relaxing few minutes of staring into space. On this occasion, Dr Peter Hutchings happened to follow me through the doors.

"Ah, Andrew," he said, the smile never quite leaving his face, "I'm missing an essay from you."

I lived in dread of such oversights. Peter's affability eased my shock. "You've been getting good marks," he replied to my fretful stuttering. "We want you to do well!" He led me to his office and supplied me with a familiar-looking essay sheet, something to do with a recent screening of John Ford's *The Searchers* (1956).

Thereon, whenever the course leader and I passed in a corridor, he'd throw me a jolly "Hi, Andrew!"

When this published author of one of my favourite subjects bid me genial greetings, elation and fretful shame giddied me. I feared to defile a society whose kindly bid to include me had fallen on the rocks of my confusion and introversion. Distant memories of my confused social offences ached in forlorn dread.

Elation and guilt conspired to garble my attempt at a casual reply of "heya!" I could never quite get into "hi," but I didn't want to sound too formal.

Michael Crawford

One afternoon, my timetable allowed for an early return home. Mid-journey, I stopped for a wander around Morpeth.

Oxfam had a second-hand copy of Michael Crawford album *With Love*. From nighttime listenings to *The Phantom of the Opera*, esteemed familiarity with the soft, strong voice called for further attendance.

In a dark blue background, an evening-wear-clad Michael gazed calmly forth. Neatly cropped curly brown hair framed a broad brow. A mild, high-cheeked face held pensively downcast eyes. The face might flippantly be imagined to parallel mine or Uncle Ross's. It didn't yet speak to me of what I would later term transgenic kinship, but I'd sensed in Michael's voice a pronounced similarity to that of Sylvester McCoy; in both voices, flattened vowels were sometimes similarly drawn out in a high, strong pitch.

Online extracts of Michael's autobiography, *Parcel Arrived Safely: Tied With String* (1999), hinted a strikingly similar background to that of Sylvester; born halfway through the Second World War within a year of each other, both had Irish backgrounds through their mothers, and both had a flair for stunt work.

While most of the album's brassy musical numbers weren't instinctively my taste, I learned to savour them through the mighty yet tender voice.

Fixed

I decided to email the course leader an explanation of the possibility that I might miss a few classes early next term, as I might not yet be entirely recovered from my operation. On emailed summons to Peter's office, I blurted a summary of my email. With his usual easy jollity, Peter noted his recent reception of it, that I happened to be last of today's interviewees, and that my attendance record was "...*excellent*..."

"And... have a good Christmas," he concluded as we made our farewells.

Cheered by this man's affability, I left for the streets. From Eldon Square car park, Dad drove me to the RVI.

The three surgeons, all of them supportive and reassuring, fixed my hernia and the indentation beneath my navel. Among boundlessly caring nursing staff, I spent five nights. My torso initially felt a bit taut, and there were a few tubes, but thankfully, none went up my nose.

2006

Avril Lavigne

The army, who no longer used the Barrowburn Deer Hut, let it to my parents for use as a small accommodation business. One of its regular visitors, Northern Irish soldier Seamus, fell into closer acquaintance with Dad and became a regular visitor to the Barrowburn farmhouse.

One night, several weeks into January, as the wind howled across the darkened hills, Seamus, Mam, Dad and I huddled, with drinks, in the glow of a mellowing fire.

When Seamus, Mam and Dad went to bed, I, as usual, stayed up to spend some time with my CD Walkman. Invited to browse Seamus's CD wallet, my eye was drawn, with a sense of duty, to Avril Lavigne's 2002 debut album *Let Go*.

Encounters on the music channels with some of her videos had assured me that Avril was an Essence. The video for "Complicated" sees Avril and her band linger in a sports park, before relocating to a nearby mall, where, in between instantaneous returns to the sports park for performance of the song, they cavort through the shops.

The mellow song mingled exasperation and yearning. Avril's voice had an uplifting clarity, high and smooth, with rich emotion.

As with Abbey Charlton; the Corr sisters, several of the *Neighbours* cast and Billie Piper, the breadth and curvature of Avril's brow stoked an instant familiarity. Her high cheekbones dark blue eyes, slightly pointed nose and impudent smile shaped expression which I, irresistibly, recalled from one or more of the aforementioned. Structurally, her face most obviously resembled that of Sharon Corr and Abbey Charlton.

Now, with her debut album free for my inspection, I supposed I'd better get more closely acquainted.

Electric and acoustic instruments carried the high, rich voice through both rousing and soothing melodies of loneliness, vexation, resignation, dismay and desire. I happily resolved to see about getting my own copy of this album.

Timothy Spall

Each weekday morning, or if I was lucky, afternoon, I left the Haymarket bus station to stroll up St Mary's Place.

A high shop window held a poster. Against a shaded backdrop, various heads and shoulders were superimposed to form a triangular huddle. At the top of the poster, one face seemed familiar. Beneath floppy, dark blond hair and strong eyebrows, a high brow framed high cheeks, whose slight fullness lent the face curvature. Dark eyes crinkled in benevolent mirth. I believed this face to be that of Timothy Spall. In the poster, he raised a glass to anyone who cared to look.

On *Auf Wiedersehen, Pet*, the casual eloquence and nervous outbursts of his Barry Taylor were both endearing and hilarious. In his broad-browed, high-cheeked face, a mild joviality matched, with the uncanny clarity to which I'd grown accustomed, the faces of Dan Aykroyd, Dr Peter Hutchings and Russell T Davies.

Buffy

One day, alone in the living room, I idly tuned into Sky One's current broadcast, and found myself watching a few seconds of a repeat of *Buffy the Vampire Slayer*.

Six years previously, John and I, following many a double bill of *The Simpsons* on my bedroom telly, had sometimes caught the first few minutes of an episode of this new supernatural teenage drama. Its young cast had a put-upon early adult sternness; all a bit above and beyond my twelve-and-a-half-year-old self. Even so, the CGI melding of human faces into those of bulky-browed, rat-eyed vampires was inventively lurid. Buffy and friends were advised by a bespectacled, middle-aged man, whose Standard English accent sounded genuine. At one point, I'd been almost persuaded to give this brash new show a chance. John, however, couldn't be bothered, and I was easily swayed.

I'd never thought I'd get around to properly watching *Buffy*, but, having tuned into Sky One, circumstances quickly obliged me. My eyes fell on the face and brow of Alyson Hannigan. A loose bob of neck-length ginger hair emphasised her brow's height and curvature: the first hint of an Essence. Dark eyes and a soft smile wove a gaiety which I suddenly found quite engaging. My newfound appreciation of her face longed for the realisation of a newfound Essence.

Persistence rewarded me: her high, rounded brow and soft gaze combined shape and expression which I involuntarily traced, with irresistible recognition, to such as seen on the face of Andrea Corr.

Another afternoon, I flicked through the channels to find myself poised once more over a *Buffy* repeat. I tuned to Sky One, and checked to see if Alyson was around. She wasn't, so I supposed myself to be free to move on to the music channels. I then glanced at Sarah Michelle Gellar, and something rather strange happened.

The height and curvature of her brow urgently drew my focus. The feeling came with a faint but definite twinge of recognition, like the sudden return of a subsidiary memory. Having seen the face many times in the media, it now offered me a veiled yet irresistible familiarity, which I traced to the Corr sisters; Alyson Hannigan, and several *Neighbours* personnel. The distinction with which Sarah's face hit me evoked the urgency of a verbal command. *Get over here and watch me*! her face seemed to say. I was proud to oblige.

JK Rowling

JK Rowling now had a website. I now enjoyed her brief biography, with its added fun of minor revelations.

Soon after I'd found it, the website made the papers. Fascination endured with the single mother who, on struggle with poverty and depression, had gone on to earn millions with her colossus of kids' books, her sober, unassuming face an emblem of hard-earned triumph.

Aged twelve, engrossed in *Harry Potter*, I'd found myself encouraged by its aspiration, in a world beset by grief and violence, to the prevalence of kindness. With my anticipation of each book, however, had lingered a suspicion that I wasn't really wanted here.

For an author to mention a bad character's excess weight wasn't uncommon. While suggestions that my torso was apt to offend might leave me a tad dismayed, I clung to the possibility that should the author happen to clap eyes on me, they might not find my own bulk quite so offensive.

The weight of JK Rowling's Dudley Dursley implicitly stems from the same ill-bred bad habit as his love of punching people: he's spoilt. Hagrid's spite towards Dudley's weight is staged as a wholesomely gruff reappraisal of a sheltered little slob. At a smack round the head from his panicked father, Dudley snivels. Such feebleness recalled my fear of things like getting hit in the face with a football or being shouted at.

In *Goblet of Fire* (2000), Dudley's weight outgrows his school uniform. Irrepressible prankster Fred Weasley slips Dudley a toffee which grows his tongue to a size which chokes him and sends his parents hysterical with fear.

Aged twelve, I'd tried to reassure myself that I probably wasn't as fat as Dudley, and that Rowling didn't necessarily mean her depiction of Dudley as a diagnosis of all such torsos as mine. Mightn't Mrs Weasley, Neville Longbottom and cheerful ghost the Fat Friar indicate that Rowling didn't hate all forms of excess weight? However, these characters' excesses of weight are excusably lesser: Mrs Weasley has had seven kids, Neville Longbottom is only slightly fat, and the outright fatness of the Fat Friar is cosily veiled by his folkloric lineage and scant appearances. None of these characters affront normalcy like spoilt, greedy little boys.

Aged sixteen, I'd learned the jibe *"Daily Mail* reader" to scorn said paper's readers as a fringe of petty, unimaginative bigots. Little Whinging firm director Vernon Dursley, a brutish, bigoted authoritarian, is noted, in *Goblet of Fire*, to be reading the *Daily Mail*.

Scorn for such heathens, softened by the flippancy of the jibe "*Daily Mail*-reader," seems to hold bigotry to be a defect of the unfashionably secluded.

In *Harry Potter*, bigotry mainly takes the form of racism – the affluent Dursleys loathe wizards, the rich Malfoys revile wizards of Muggle parentage – a stigma nurtured by Slytherin House – and the Gaunts, descended from Salazar Slytherin, sire mass-murdering pureblood supremacist Lord Voldemort.

Unlike some forms of social discrimination, fat-bashing doesn't fear others' ancestry or unapproved romantic desires. The brutality to which these fears may lead has seen momentous challenge - by the time of Harry Potter, they were socially unacceptable.

Fear of excess weight deems it a minor deviation from bodily convention, whose affront to normalcy, it's assumed, may be amended with better habits. With this in mind, calling it a perverse imposition on society is deemed fair game.

And so, one bright evening, I clicked my way over to JK Rowling's website, which had a new headline.

Rowling had recently read an article about an underweight female celebrity. One of the young male *Harry Potter* actors had then revealed a female friend of his, despite her blatant lack of fatness, to have been called fat.

Following the publication of her sixth novel and birth of her third child, an old acquaintance had praised Rowling's apparent weight loss. On her website, Rowling now bemoaned society's obsession with fashionable weight, and the readiness with which a breach of this standard was used to belittle girls and women. Fatness, Rowling implied, was wrongly maligned.

A dumbfounded gall numbed me.

"Well, *you've* changed your tune," was all I could murmur.

Her grievance seemed to be with the preoccupation of thinness as a fashionable standard, as girls shouldn't be burdened with such shallow nonsense.

The implication is that Dudley, a boy, supposedly evades such burdens, so ridicule of his appetite and size is fair game: Rowling is free to openly dehumanise him.

She had done great good in the world. I would read and enjoy the final *Harry Potter*. But to her preaching, I now shed my deference.

So increasing indication that she was an Essence unduly disturbed me. Immature, mean-spirited and dogmatic as it may have been of me, I couldn't abide invasion of my secret miracle by such piety. But whether I wanted it or not, it was staring me in the face. Her long, straight fair hair, high brow and high cheekbones most obviously evoked Sharon Corr, Avril Lavigne and Abbey Charlton. Rowling's face shone a distinction all its own, yet to the aforementioned shone a near-luminescent similarity, a new lens to host a similar ray of light.

I shied away from the revelation. I fogged it in the supposed possibility of my over-imaginative misinterpretation. It would be a few years before I could accept what I saw.

Kindred Spirits

After a screening, lecture or seminar, I often got an early bus for a walk around Morpeth. My wanders through its cool, quiet air gained a soothing familiarity, sweetened by the chance of a glimpse in Woolworths of Abbey. Over small hills to a wooden footbridge beneath the trees, I often brought a magazine – usually of the *Doctor Who* variety.

My comparison of Russell T Davies to Dr Peter Hutchings was no longer mere whim. The familiarity I saw in Peter seemed clearly to be of the kind to which I'd been in thrall this last year. A broad brow, full cheeks, gentle smirk and a wry, flighty gaze subtly but directly recalled Russell.

Peter's facial structure recalled the higher-cheeked faces of Dan Aykroyd, Timothy Spall and Steve Pemberton. While smooth black hair recalled that of Dan, Peter's stout frame recalled those of Timothy and Steve. Aesthetic taste seemed also to traverse this genetic transcendence; film lecturer Peter specialised in, and clearly loved, horror. Steve Pemberton, along with the rest of the League of Gentlemen, was famous for his love of horror. Scriptwriter and actor Dan Aykroyd was fascinated by the supernatural.

Russell T Davies had restored to television *Doctor Who*, famous for its scares and fancies. I wasn't sure how Timothy Spall might feel about horror or supernaturalism, but, as with Dan, Peter and Russell, the back of his head had an occasionally visible bald spot.

Buffy and Friends

While sustained attendance of any show was something I tended to shy away from, my perception of transgenic kinship roused a sense of duty. Alone in the living room, if *Buffy* appeared in the listings, I'd watch, even if I'd already seen it that day. Should the living room door open, I'd immediately banish the brash, emotive fancies. The threat of such material's revelation to my elders, and of my exposed consumption of it, panicked me with irrational shame.

As well as in the recurring central heroines, I perceived transgenic kinship to shine in Anthony Head's Giles. Short, curly brown hair and a high brow impressed a familiarity whose clarity announced an Essence. A dark, sober gaze, honed by brow and cheekbones, shaped expression which promptly recalled that of my brother James. Set with the hair, it even rather reminded me of myself.

In *Buffy*'s intrigue, thrills, emotion and wit, I got quite absorbed. But something stifled my engagement. Its dry mockery of its own fantastic spectacle, reverence of its heroine's burdens, and scorn for people who irked or hindered Buffy and friends, had, at least to my inordinate sensitivity, a caustic aloofness.

YouTube

One hot Saturday evening, *Doctor Who* episode *The Impossible Planet*, by suggestion of devilish menace to lie on a desolate planet, stirred primal scares.

On Outpost Gallifrey, to Rowan Atkinson's anticipation of *The Impossible Planet*'s depiction of the Devil as a man named Toby, someone posted a link. I clicked and found myself on a site I didn't recognise. On a white background, a rectangular red and black logo read "YouTube: Broadcast Yourself."

Towards the page's left, a smaller digital screen quickly began to play an old Rowan Atkinson stand-up sketch. In a little pair of plastic horns, he bid newcomers to Hell a genial welcome and introduced himself as Toby. Here I was, watching an online video, and it took barely two seconds to load! With sincere marvel at this sudden extravagance, I wondered what else might be on here.

All sorts, it seemed. What ancient broadcast to retrieve first? *Are You Afraid of the Dark* came to mind. As far as I knew, the series hadn't been released on video in the UK. To my incredulous delight, I found myself once again watching *The Tale of the Crimson Clown* (1994) – a relatively simple episode, but definitely among the most frightening.

Next Saturday, following broadcast of *The Satan Pit*, *Outpost Gallifrey* discussion compared the eponymous cavern and entombed gigantic horned beast to CITV's 1990 cartoon *The Dreamstone*.

Having glimpsed some of it around the age of four, I recalled a pastel mix of sweetness and dark fantasy. On a gigantic throne, the towering, dragon-like sorcerer Zordrak commanded the hapless, humanoid, lizard-tailed Urpneys. The music had a rich tenderness, of which I was now reminded by a YouTube upload of the show's "outro." "Better Than a Dream," written and sung by Mike Batt, with rich, light voice and awed melody, wove a wistful euphoria.

One bright early evening, as I reached the top of the Bilberry hills, I found myself registering various details of the landscape with a clarity which seemed new. Beneath the mellowing glare of a deep blue sky, purplish brown heather, boulders, grassy slopes and dry soil reached my gaze with distinction whose urgency seemed deliberate.

I enjoyed the vague notion that whatever insight I had into the physical transcendence of human facial features might extend, however slightly, to other structures. In the blaze of summer, as the land shone hints of cosmic secret, I took a moment for reflection.

Lovely

At the Metrocentre, I browsed. As Abbey's birthday was the day after tomorrow, I nurtured an audacious resolve to buy her some kind of present. My dread of such presumptuousness was overruled by desire to know her more closely. I didn't have much idea of what she was into, but I'd seen her wearing earrings.

On the upstairs aisle, opposite HMV, I perused a jewellery shop. After much deliberation, I chose a small pair of several tautly joined gold and pink cubes, which had been reduced to twenty quid. Both nervous and excited, I took them to the till.

I couldn't make it to Morpeth on the day of Abbey's birthday, having offered to help Dad and Uncle Ross with lamb dosing. The night before, I had the fascinating new experience of failing to get literally any sleep at all.

In the pens at the foot of the Loungies hills, it was my job to busk, that is, apply keel, a kind of glutinous paint, to the lamb's middle or hip, depending on its sex. In blazing sunshine, knee-deep in agitated lambs, I busked alertly, but with a heavy sense of drainage.

Next day, I slept into the late afternoon and caught a late bus to Morpeth. In an envelope, with a humorous card about a small child having hidden the family gin, I'd stored the pouch which held the earrings. In the humid bustle of Woolworths, a few minutes before closing time, I forced myself to approach the till. Only this time, my cargo wasn't a purchase.

"Erm, I got you a small present for yesterday," I said and passed the envelope across the till.

"Oh, my God, you remembered!" squeaked Abbey.

I thought it best to stay away from Woolworths for a while. In a way, I supposed, what I'd done was outrageous. As nice as Abbey would undoubtedly be about it, she might well feel some gall at my extravagance.

A week later, when I next approached the till, Abbey gave me a bright "Hi, Andrew!" Having processed my purchase, she kept her gaze and with a coy grin, added, "And can I just say, thanks..." She grinned. "They're *lovely*!"

In a euphoric daze, I mumbled my acceptance of her gratitude.

She beamed. "Really made my day."

Sweet

Granda Tait, in his early eighties, now lived in Morpeth's old folks' home. His voice, now noticeably lower, was lucid enough. He retained some recognition of me, but, as Dad assessed, his mind, while intact, was focused on several decades ago.

As presenting myself to others for conversation felt forced and intrusive, and as Granda Tait himself had never been much of a one for visits, I'd seen little of him for years. Now, with Dad to manage primary conversation, I accompanied him on each visit to Morpeth.

While Granda Tait had always passed a tenner onto Dad to put in birthday cards addressed to my brothers and me, I, somewhat regrettably, had never given him any object.

One Friday, James decided to have an afternoon in Morpeth, mainly to visit the gym. I came along for indiscriminate wanders and an eventual visit to Woolworths. With hours to spare, I bought, at the newsagent's, a large bar of Cadbury's Dairy Milk and paid a lone visit to Granda Tait, who was currently in the dayroom.

"Thank you, son," he said of his bar of chocolate. "Pleased w' that..." I stayed for a while and tried to offer some conversation which might relate to his misplaced memory. I eventually bade him farewell and took to the streets.

For over a year now, I'd got by on drip feedings of contact with Abbey. I wanted more. I didn't know quite what this might entail, or what arrangements I'd have to make for it, but I yearned for contact deeper and longer than shyly blurted greetings across the counter. I wanted something more from her than "I'll get you a bag." I wanted to hear her voice constantly. I desperately pondered the mystery of her skin.

I'd made a decision. I was going to ask her, as it were, out. This sort of thing was still perversely strange to me. The thought of obligation to daily devotion was overwhelming. The thought of imposition of myself on womankind was obscene. In my desperation for Abbey, I managed, at least for now, to dismiss all this. Closer proximity to Abbey, an Essence, could only be right.

A mighty downpour suddenly cleared the humid June air. Through heavy raindrops, I walked the splattered pavement to Woolworths. As usual, I lingered along its aisles, in faux fascination with their trinkets. I forced myself closer to the vicinity of the till. Between till and door, I hovered at the wall of CDs, edging infinitesimally closer to the till. My solemn procrastination was abruptly disrupted by Abbey herself.

"I hope you've got a coat!" she laughed.

"Erm, when do you get a day off?" I asked, my fear numbed by urgency.

A tad thrown, she explained that such arrangements were still undetermined.

"'Cause," I said, "I was thinking of going to the pictures sometime. Would you fancy going with us?"

The obsceneness of my presumption to such grandeur would hit me later, to twinge throughout the coming years, but for now, the ease of my utterance amazed me.

"Oh, cool!" She grinned. "I'll see what I'm doing!"

I wandered happily into the rain.

On Sunday, I got a late bus into Morpeth. I hovered through the aisles of Woolworths, more nervous than ever. I inched towards the DVD shelves near the till.

I then saw Abbey approach me.

"Andrew," she said with confidentiality that seemed almost nervous, "about what you said before... I think you're lovely and everything, but I'm... kind of seeing someone at the minute, so... maybe not a good idea?"

I blurted polite dismissal of any concern she might have. She began to say something else, but I blurted more apologetic reassurance and took my leave.

In the scorching afternoon, I wandered the streets in search of a place to relax. I'd still see her, but no more frequently or closely than in Woolworths. Abbey now knew how wonderful she was to me. This eased the loneliness, but only briefly.

The bright, warm streets, with their intermittent flow of pedestrians, had lost their lure. The scene now seemed harshly different: its joy seemed to exclude me. Any of these people might know Abbey, but I would never have the extent of access I so sorely craved.

My loneliness swelled into a sorrow whose desperation neared panic. I had to do something, just to be with her a little longer.

In the slowly mellowing heat, by Woolworths' huge leftward window, I stood on the pavement. Four o'clock passed, and the shop closed. Resolved to seek a last word with Abbey, I lingered. For an hour or so, the staff continued to bustle inside. At one point, Abbey looked straight at me, her expression blank. I was going to miss the bus and suffer the ignominy of calling for a lift home. Today, I was almost proud not to care.

The double doors finally opened, and the staff emerged. In place of Abbey's uniform red smock was a yellow, frilly, short-sleeved blouse. Having bid farewell to her colleagues, she crossed the road to the square tunnel which passed several shops to the bus station. I pelted after her. In the tunnel's cool gloom, she heard my approach and turned.

"Sorry, could I just have a word?" I panted. "Sorry if this sounds like a bit of a callous question, but if it ever didn't work out, would you give us a chance?" Perverse as it was to offer such submission, desperation overruled principle.

"Okay, Andrew," said Abbey, a grin spreading across her face, "I think it's really flattering that you feel that way about us." With reassurance that my infatuation was harmless and welcome, her grin broadened. "I think it is *really*, really sweet."

From behind us, on the benches outside Woolworths, came a wolf-whistle.

"Boys!" laughed Abbey.

Her endorsement of my devotion gave me a strange, deep comfort. For her smile and voice to know me in such a context was a dream come true.

"You were standing out there a long time," she said.

"Well," I said breathlessly, "I really, really, really, really, really, really, *really* like you."

With nothing to lose, I added, "You've got lovely arms."

"Arms?" She chuckled. "Well... never heard that one before."

I was too feverishly elated to be forlorn. "So, if it ever didn't work out...?"

"See what happens," she said with a final smile.

Later, Mam and I talked long into the night.

"I'm sorry for you, Andy," she said, as I blubbered on her shoulder.

For my nineteenth birthday, I got from Mam and Dad the DVD releases of *Tomb of the Cybermen* (1967) and *Ghostbusters 1 and 2* (1984, 1989), a small hat from John, and from James, two books: *The Day I Died: Remarkable True Stories of Near-Death Experience* (2006) and *Will Storr vs the Supernatural* (2006). The former opened with a casual yet eloquent account of a dying young man's entry into a place of rejuvenating clarity and feeling of absolute acceptance.

Will Storr vs the Supernatural, whose author I'd seen interviewed on *Richard and Judy*, opened with a pleasing reference to *Ghostbusters II*. It offered a fascinating glimpse of spectral investigation.

A few days later, Barrowburn saw two sheep-shearing sessions. For my fleece-wrapping, Dad gave me fifty pounds. On Saturday, in Morpeth's Oxfam charity shop, I finally got round to buying a copy of Avril Lavigne's *Let Go*.

Martians

Many an evening saw John and I, on UK Gold, re-watch *The League of Gentlemen*. In the innocently anonymous union of spectator and performer, I held these comic fantasists in a kind of silent, impudent fellowship. By now, I perceived the three on-screen Gentlemen to be Essences.

Reece, to me, looked like my younger brother. Amidst the height of his cheekbones and breadth of his brow, the eyes' hesitant yet sharp focus and loose manoeuvre of the mouth recalled John.

Mark's closely cropped hair, wide brow and high cheekbones steered his pensive expressions to smooth resemblance of my uncle Ross and older brother James. The sharp face's occasional twinkles of glee evoked Sharon Corr and Abbey Charlton. The slightly pointed nose recalled those of Avril Lavigne and Abbey Charlton.

Reflected in Steve Pemberton, however, I saw myself. The broad curvature of his brow, the height of his full cheeks and his softly bright gaze combined structure and expression to, irresistibly aptly, evoke my own face.

One day, as John and I climbed the steep bank to the Bilberry hills, John noted his identification with the performance flair of Reece Shearsmith.

"You kind of look like him," I said.

John, in turn, happily noted my vague resemblance to Steve Pemberton.

I recalled a 1999 afternoon at the Metrocentre, when James, on seeing the cover of my recently purchased copy of Patricia Wrede's junior novelisation of *The Phantom Menace*, half-seriously pondered his resemblance to Ewan McGregor. By my uncanny insight, I now earnestly endorsed this. Whatever this gift was, I wondered if my brothers had some trace of it.

Doctor Who Magazine commemorated this year's series with a special issue, packed with production history and commentary. In *Love and Monsters*, the Abzorbaloff, as designed by nine-year-old *Blue Peter* contest winner William Grantham, had been played by Peter Kay.

In Russell T Davies' *Love and Monsters*, he first appears as the Abzorbaloff's human avatar of Victor Kennedy.

As I browsed the magazine, my gaze lay on a full-colour still of Peter Kay's Victor Kennedy, sat at his desk. The more I looked, the more irresistibly blatant it was: Peter Kay looked like me. Or rather, I looked like him, as he was older. The similarity lay not in one or two interpretable parallels, but in an inextricable distinction which shone in his expressions and the facial structuring thereof. His hair, whether a dye job or a wig, was light grey, but the cropped curls, broad brow, high, full cheeks, soft mouth and temperate eyes lay in such a way as to directly parallel my own facial formation, like a similar combination of notes played on a different instrument.

Peter's smooth black hair recalled that of both Dan Aykroyd and Dr Peter Hutchings. The two Peters shared similar physique and facial structure with Steve Pemberton.

While I was quite happy to share transgenic kinship with Mr Kay, his role of Victor Kennedy rather unfavourably recalled traits of my own person. With the London Investigation 'N' Detective Agency, *Love and Monsters* affectionately parodies *Doctor Who* fandom: an assortment of innocent bystanders who, having glimpsed the Doctor's travels, meet to pursue their shared interest with such wholesome socialising as impromptu band formation.

Victor Kennedy, who turns up to boss LINDA around, is noted by the magazine special to parody overbearingly controlling fans. He refuses to be touched, which he claims is because of eczema, and prefers private endeavour to cooperation. This reflected my aversion to group submission. While my contribution to *Outpost Gallifrey* was at best meek, and I had no desire to boss folk around, I worried that Davies, an Essence, had unconsciously parodied my introversion. I put this down to paranoid fancy.

In my rapt perusal of Dr Peter Hutchings' *Quatermass* essays, I'd read a synopsis of Nigel Kneale's 1957 serial *Quatermass and the Pit*, wherein discovery beneath London of a Martian spaceship reveals that 5 million years previously, Martians fled their dying world to augment in their own image Earth primates, which led to the emergence of homo sapiens. The mantis-like Martians' life-cycle included periodical elimination of large numbers of each other; this resurfaced in human tendency to xenophobic violence.

I'd whimsically paralleled the arrival of Essences in my perception to *The War of the Worlds*, with each Essence likened to

268

an advanced civilisation which, by wondrous technology, invaded the backwater planet that was my mind. It now seemed that I not only perceived their genetic transcendence but shared in it.

Deeply Selfish

To raised or sharpened voices, I still reacted inordinately. In the media, should someone enact anger, their urgent expressions, abrasive volume and harsh emphasis might grip my chest in fearful, sorrowful humiliation.

The frank ferocity of a man's ire might shock me with the shame of my past imposition on others.

However, a meek glare, fine features, soft hair, slightness of frame and lightness of voice sanctified a woman's snarl or shout. Not only did her fury frighten with its violence; it dwelt a tender grievance whose wrath, I irrationally felt, could only be completely deserved. It overwhelmed me with a sense of my obsceneness, that I earned obliteration by the innocent. Ashamed of my feebleness, I'd sulk for a moment in mournful self-disgust.

The first term of the second year of Film and Television Studies held, each Monday morning, a lecture in the basement theatre with Dr Peter Hutchings, who prepared us to write an essay on Alfred Hitchcock's *The Birds* (1963).

"It's one of the greatest films of all time... in my opinion," he said with a small smile. He discussed filmed depiction of terror and societal collapse, in view of such influence as Hitchcock's fear of the police. To share in Peter's fascination was a privilege.

Several books were prescribed to help us with the essay. With my lax concentration, I thought it might be conscientious to borrow one of the books for a prolonged while and keep it in my bag for easy access.

Two Mondays later, I arrived in the basement theatre for my favourite part of the course. Peter prefaced today's lecture with an announcement. It had been brought to staff attention, he said, that some people had been borrowing library books "...and sitting on them."

"Now," he said wryly, "this is deeply selfish..."

He gently urged us to the path of cooperative consideration, and to "...be a good citizen!"

Jovial as it was, the criticism of "deeply selfish" noted a fresh misdeed of my confused inattentiveness, which furiously expelled my intrusion on Peter's kindness and excellence.

I promptly returned the book. *People can sting you*, I thought heavily. I railed against the shame that weighed almost palpably in my chest.

Perceiving

I took a walk down Northumberland Street to Virgin Megastore, where I bought Avril Lavigne's second album, *Under My Skin*. Its cover held a monochrome shot of a seated Avril, looking slightly more sombre than on the cover of *Let Go*.

Several videos on Avril's website showed her going about her business whilst on tour. In contrast with the irreverence and moody indignation hinted in some of her music videos, I was struck by how jolly she seemed. Her easy smile strongly evoked Abbey's.

Halfway through a degree with no obvious goal, and unsure how I would ever overcome the irrational shame which stifled my lifelong ambition to write stories, I was assured of my metaphysical insight, and of my obligation to observe it.

2007

UFO?

I'd always longed to see a UFO. While I loved the subject, I'd never seen any aircraft that seemed unattributable to earthly origin.

One January evening, I took my usual walk. Out of the village, up the steep cemetery bank, past the pine-shaded farming estate, left again, and the road flattened.

The leftward field overlooked the village. The rightward field bordered the moors, crowned on the rightward horizon by the ancient tower of Sharpe's Folly and the distant Simonside hills.

Of course, tonight, I hadn't a very clear view of all this, as the sky was black and largely overcast. Leftward, from the village below, a dull orange glow seeped from numerous lamp posts and windows. In the distant rightward sky, dark clouds were bleached pinkish orange by the light of neighbouring towns. Before an occasional breeze, the clouds sometimes parted to show glimpses of the clear sky beyond. As I peered casually at a star, I saw, coursing slowly below it, what I took to be a plane. A tiny white gleam enveloped a silhouetted, elongated body. In its middle, another light, also white, pulsed in a constant flicker. Yep, it was a plane, alright.

Was it just me, or was the movement of this plane a tad... odd? It didn't seem to be streaking at a constant, directional pace. It drifted with slow, occasionally tumbling thrusts. As I watched, it seemed to have drifted into a region of the sky impertinent to its course. It seemed to be acting as much like a balloon as a plane. Undeniably perplexed, I classified the incident as mildly but definitely odd.

A Nice Bloke

One day in February, my timetable having finished early, I took a bus back into Morpeth to while away the afternoon until getting a lift home with James.

As the hour neared three, I went for a browse in the Oxfam charity shop. In its soft gloom, the sight of shelved books and DVDs had a soothing intrigue. Several regions of the brief floor were occupied by various elderly folk. An elderly man asked a fellow browser if they might direct him to the nearest public toilet. Alas, they weren't sure.

I was suddenly visited by an uncharacteristic urge. The allure of cooperation overrode my instinct to avoid the shame of imposing myself on others. I interjected with an explanation of a nearby public toilet to be found in Burnt Orange, beside Woolworths.

The enquirer's age was hard to tell. Beneath smooth grey hair, a broad brow framed a full face, which peered with gentle intent from behind small glasses. Several inches shorter than me, his stout frame, supported by a single crutch, encompassed a paunch.

"But I'd have to buy a drink first, wouldn't I?" mused the old boy. I assured him that Burnt Orange had never sought monetary retribution for my use of its toilets.

We talked for what might have been over an hour. With dreamy intrigue, his mild, Standard English voice pondered the benefit of charity shops and revisited several of his favourite printed titles. I, buoyed by his invitation, aimed to respond in kind.

On the way home, about a mile past Morpeth, I, in the front seat of James's car, peered through the windscreen at the clear, darkening blue sky. A few stars had emerged.

In the sky directly above me, I looked at a star which shone noticeably more brightly. And then, without the slightest hint that I might have blinked and misinterpreted, the tiny, silvery white orb blurred, contracted and faded from view. The clear sky held no barrier to obscure the star, if as such it might still be described. An inch to the right of where it had been, or so it appeared from my earthly perspective, it reappeared. In a soft bloom of light, the thing which looked like a star spread itself back into visibility. It vanished and reappeared several times.

If I needed proof that my supposed glimpse of the metaphysical lay beyond fanciful misinterpretation, here it was. My good fortune weighed on me in serene awe. Unless I was somehow hallucinating, something very strange was clearly going on. In the genetically transcendent likeness of various faces, and in this mercurial star, I'd glimpsed the mastery of mind over the supposed confines of matter.

Whatever lay ahead, I was not alone.

Self, Self, Self

One Saturday afternoon, Mam, Dad and I went to the Metrocentre. I planned to see *The Number 23*; starring Jim Carrey, an Essence, it was essential viewing.

On the way, we stopped at Kingston Park for some shopping at Tesco's. I hovered at the magazine aisle. Naive aspiration had me pick up a displayed copy of *New Scientist*.

I turned a page to find a picture of a beach, across which stood several ethereal silhouettes. The interview was with Douglas Hofstadter. From what I could make of the interview, he maintained the concept of self to be some kind of illusion, as indicated by his study of the brain.

The article sowed in me the seeds of a very special kind of worry. That which encompassed all I'd ever been or known wasn't really there. The supreme peace of wilful awareness was illusory, a chemical quirk allowed, and eventually to be destroyed, by blind chance. All joys only seemed joyous; the supreme, rejuvenating nurture of love had no real will to give and receive itself but was mere shadow of blind chance. The prospect, to me, offered only insurmountable misery. Getting round this would take some work.

That evening, I trawled the web for hours in fruitless search of some indication that Hofstadter's claim was mere theory.

For weeks, the revelation weighed on me. I'd never felt something of this magnitude: existence itself, with its chance that life's joys might always endure, was suddenly proclaimed never to have been there.

To the ethereal being who, resembling my two-year-old self, had appeared to Mam on the bedroom wall in 1989, I made a mental plea. If this being was indeed my guardian angel, I beseeched of him the possibility of deliverance from my newfound strife. If consciousness really did transcend matter, then surely Hofstadter's claim was suspect.

In WHSmith, I bought a science magazine, whose skull-illustrated cover offered discussion of the mystery of consciousness. While science could explain how sensations were processed, said the article, science had failed to explain consciousness: how a combination of light absorption and neurons resulted in purple.

Relief – for now.

The Best Damn Thing

Last year, the release of Avril Lavigne's third album had been announced online. Delighted, I once again pondered that my attendance of an Essence was often followed by their return to the spotlight: the Corrs, with their *Borrowed Heaven* album and tour, The League of Gentlemen, with their theatrically released film and live show, and now, Avril Lavigne, with her third album, *The Best Damn Thing*.

One spring morning, tired from a typically brief night's sleep, I sat in the back of James's car as we pulled into Morpeth. The lively chat of Chris Moyles and co paused for the airing of a new record. At breakneck pace, drums and electric guitars wove a song of uplifting, impudent bravado. The high, rich, lively female voice sounded familiar.

Chris Moyles announced a return from Avril Lavigne with "Girlfriend."

From HMV, I bought the single. Its cover featured a shot of Avril looking stern. Her hair was now blond and streaked with pink.

At home in my chair, I happily listened many times to the disc's two tracks, "Girlfriend" and "Alone." Drums, keyboard and electric guitar strings wove a balance of exuberance and heartfelt defiance, stoked and soothed by Avril's high, rich voice. Engrossed, I hungered for the full album.

A heavy warmth reached the days' mild air.

In Newcastle's HMV, I bought the deluxe edition of *The Best Damn Thing*, which included an interview DVD.

Avril, filmed riding her skateboard by the recording studio, came across as disarmingly innocent. Bright sunshine accentuated the lightness of her hair and the lushness of her pallor, from which her smile shone easily. I was rather wonderfully reminded of Abbey.

In the early hours of many a morning, I grasped the arms of my beloved chair and, fuelled by *The Best Damn Thing*, launched myself in sideways thrusts. The solemnity and vexation of *Under My Skin* had given way to impudence, raw tenderness and exuberant celebration of the joys of life. The closing track, "Keep Holding On," closed the album with a violin-orchestrated plea for perseverance.

I probably wasn't quite mindful enough of my fears that I should lower the volume a bit.

Synchronicity

Hallmark, a channel several pages down on the Sky Digital TV guide, started showing episodes of American family drama *Seventh Heaven*. Since I'd read of it to host the rise to prominence of Essence Jessica Biel, I, when alone in the room, dutifully tuned in. I found myself increasingly engaged.

While I couldn't find Jessica, I keenly registered the features of her former co-star Beverley Mitchell: straight, dark blond hair framed a high brow, large blue eyes and high cheekbones. The face's structural and expressive distinction seemed almost luminous. As well as its own oblique familiarity, it insistently recalled the features of persons genetically unrelated; here, I was particularly reminded of Abbey.

Elsewhere, I saw a trailer for quirky crime drama *Dexter* to feature *Buffyverse* Essence Julie Benz. Throughout the weeks, as I secretly watched episodes on FX, I began to appreciate, in the hair, brow and expressions of lead Michael C Hall, distinctions which recalled those of Anthony Head, my uncle Ross, and Jim Corr. Sometime later, co-star Jennifer Carpenter drew previously unnoticed but now blatant parallel to Avril Lavigne and Abbey Charlton.

Not for the first time, it occurred to me that Essences, people whose features seemed to parallel those of persons genetically unrelated, seemed unwittingly drawn to work together.

James Herbert

At several points in the last few years, my older brother James had mentioned his encounters with some of the novels of James Herbert. The name evoked the last few decades' increased allowance for graphic depictions of carnage and depravity.

With a sober smirk, my brother pronounced *The Fog* (1975) to be the most disturbing thing he'd ever read. A tale of homicidal mass insanity induced by insidious gas, it staged a lecherous teacher's restraint and castration. On James's bedside cabinet lay an old copy of the book. Its creased black cover held a close-up of a blond woman's messily severed head – not the sort of book to approach lightly, I supposed.

My brother's conversation occasionally returned to this author, whose stories visited not only the brutally morbid, but the metaphysical. Emotion, *The Magic Cottage* (1986) had apparently ventured, was what had ultimately created the universe. I found myself reassured and inspired by this suggestion that sentience was no mere by-product, but, on the contrary, shaped and transcended all matter.

In Morpeth's Oxfam charity shop, on a shelf by the window, I found a James Herbert title: *Others*. Published in 1999, its cover looked far more recent: a bluish white void held a svelte, ethereal silhouette, whose half-formed arms stretched outward. The blurb was a brief, first person narration. It spoke of Hell, redemption and widely varied realisations of the human form.

I paid about a quid for the paperback and stored it in my leather bag – I'd have plenty of time to read it between lectures. While I'd find quite a bit to distract me this year, I'd get around to reading it fully in 2009. Not encountering Herbert's books earlier would become one of my main regrets.

UFO!!!

Since the undeniably perplexing aeroplane seen back in February, I'd seen several such objects. By July, I was in no doubt that they surpassed conventional understanding.

On many a darkening evening, when I strode out of the village and up the cemetery bank, the newly emerged stars were frequently joined by a tiny, elongated silhouette enfolded by a faint, silvery white glow, within which constantly flashed a smaller light, either white or red.

Of course, each object clearly resembled a plane. But these last few months, I'd observed the way they moved, and had reached the unavoidable supposition that planes didn't normally behave like this. These things, unlike conventional planes, didn't course continuously across the sky: they *drifted*, in a delicately tumbling, meandering trail, from one side of the sky to another, over the horizon and out of sight.

Having been offered a glimpse of something beyond earthly understanding, I stopped, with obsessive diligence, to watch the objects.

Whereas an aeroplane impresses a sense of solidity tempered by distance, these things seemed not to reflect light in any way as to affect this. Their size, and precise location in the sky, were unclear. They looked as big as a plane seen from the ground might be expected to look, but, going by their lack of obvious mass, they might well have been holograms, floating fairly low in the sky.

Often, one or two others joined the first, whereupon they drifted indiscriminately around the sky for several minutes, before departing over the trees atop the Bilberry hills. These objects didn't seem to be extraterrestrial craft as discussed in ufology; they most obviously resembled an ethereal approximation of a terrestrial aeroplane. Well, we've heard of ghost trains – what about ghost planes?

Around ten in the evening on the 19th of July, the night after my twentieth birthday, I opened the back door.

Beneath a black horizon, atop the sloping fields, silhouetted trees shaded a huddle of houses and farm buildings, some of whose windows shone strong yellow light. For the lower tree branches, it was hard to tell whether these lights came from the same building – which was why I didn't think it necessarily odd to see a concentration of such light – a soft-edged breadth of strong yellow, as one would expect a nightly window to exude – glowing just above one of the buildings.

Perhaps this wayward sibling was from one of the buildings on the other side of the field. Still, it was unexpected enough to warrant further observation. Within seconds, with no apparent movement, the light seemed to shine beneath a different region of the branches, as if I now saw it from a different angle.

After several minutes, I was convinced that this wasn't some elusively positioned house light. Instantaneously, without perceptible movement, it had shifted to several different positions between the branches above the houses.

With giddy excitement, I summoned from the kitchen Mam, Dad and John. Dad, tired and slightly tipsy, supposed it to be a house light and went to bed. John was unsure. For about an hour, Mam and I stayed at the back door.

Through binoculars, I saw, at the centre of the rounded yellow glow, two dense orbs of a more deeply yellow radiance. These seemed to orbit each other, having apparently rotated on subsequent inspections.

As was I, Mam was calmly, elatedly convinced of our having seen evidence of intelligence beyond human understanding.

"I think that was a genuine UFO you witnessed, Andy," she said fondly.

Excitingly, my apparent view into the metaphysical had now been shared in.

Eternity

I continued to read *Will Storr vs the Supernatural*. His scepticism having been challenged by a discarnate voice and a chill touch to the back of his neck, Storr conducted several supernaturally themed interviews.

About halfway through, someone apparently debunked Storr's assortment of supernatural evidence and pronounced emotions to be illusory.

I once again buckled with sorrowful fear that scholarly authority might yet confine existence to blind oblivion.

One Saturday, as the air began to cool, I rose unusually early and decided to get a bus to Newcastle.

At the bus stop, I saw that I'd mistaken the time; the bus wouldn't arrive for another hour. I needed the distraction of a day out: worries were mounting up. Existence was under attack. The prospect that self might be illusory, that all I loved had never really been and was doomed to oblivion, was devastating. In science's failure to determine exactly what consciousness was, I had some refuge: there remained a chance that existence might yet be immutable.

I was starting to consider what might be the alternative to oblivion. In the other book James had given me for my nineteenth birthday, *The Day I Died*, a man, near death, had found himself in an ethereal realm and had felt a sense of supreme acceptance.

That account in the *Mail* had claimed even blades of grass to have souls; the idea that Soul formed matter, and not vice-versa, was profoundly liberating.

It was definitely preferable to never even having existed in the first place.

I pictured a realm beyond the blackness of space. The zenith of existence, an infinite firmament of goldish white, where all discarnate souls, having completed their earthly trials, stood, or floated, in absolute fellowship. They might pursue further endeavours whose awesomeness lay beyond the grasp of earthly awareness, but, following the trials of this mortal coil, here was the end. It was supremely benevolent. It soothed all earthly woes. But, so it seemed, it was still an end.

Was it *the* end? Aside from oblivion, was this all there ever could be? I imagined finding out just what eternity felt like. I would exist. That was good. I couldn't do without that. Such a state of being could never conceivably end. Beneath me, back in the material cosmos, the mind-boggling enormity of time would drag on and on. I, and everyone I knew, would be suspended in perpetual preservation.

But would there be anything beyond this supreme state? No comforting notion of something transcendent and immutable? Was eternity just seclusion, stretched across the mind-boggling inevitability of infinity, as the cosmos below outlived and dwarfed all that had ever defined us?

I was nearing panic. I needed this to stop.

I pictured my arrival in the infinite radiance of ultimate acceptance. My anxiety flared into panicked misery.

I eventually calmed. Maybe the afterlife wouldn't be as simple as that. Maybe what actually happened was beyond mortal comprehension.

Halfway back from Newcastle, Morpeth wanders remained second nature.

One afternoon, as I browsed WHSmith, a shelf of books aimed at ages nine and up held several copies of a new hardback. The cover illustration, etched in stylish black and white, showed the head and upper body of a gloved, fedora-hatted skeleton, who loomed over a separate view of an urban street. The art style implied both playful eccentricity and a touch of the macabre. Along with the title, *Skulduggery Pleasant*, the cover, with droll edginess, etched the quaint image of a living skeleton. I would have to take a closer look sometime.

The Sound of Drums, penultimate episode of this year's *Doctor Who*, had included a few seconds of the song "Voodoo Child" as performed by the Rogue Traders. Having learned their singer to be none other than Essence Natalie Bassingthwaighte, who'd played Izzy on *Neighbours*, I bought from HMV a copy of their album *Here Come the Drums*. While slightly more percussive than my usual tastes, the songs quickly engaged; Nathalie's versatile, slightly smoky voice aided a playful whimsy.

I looked up the Wikipedia entry for "love." One theory seemed to hold that monogamous relationships lasted because of bodily allowance for tolerance of the same partner, presumably, I supposed, for harmonious breeding purposes.

A supreme joy – satiation, inspiration and nurture by the unique existence of another being – was reduced to a reproductive aid.

That black, overcast night, I wondered whether existence really was such a happy place to be after all. I was now twenty, and my parents were in their late forties. The vastness of adulthood loomed before me. As surely as life itself, the years would advance to destroy everything I knew.

"By, it's *hellish* when you get old," was Granda Widdrington's mournful catchphrase.

I furiously resisted this threat to the faces of the Essences, whose splendour, I insisted, lay in the gleam of individuality, which, despite the erosion of its earthly vessel, was eternal. Although wear had structurally altered some of his skin, Sylvester McCoy's face, lit by an affectionate, impudent grin, instantly impressed the same signature as it had twenty years ago.

"Love," so tender yet so fundamental, both eased the burdens of, and inspired, existence. Could it be a hormonal construct, bred as a survival aid?

The Thought War

Throughout several weeks of June and December of 1998, I'd sobbed frequently over prolonged bouts of irrational guilt and the despair to which this drove my mother. I'd described my condition as depression. I'd later supposed this wasn't actual clinical depression – rather than misery, depression, I'd gathered, was a kind of emotional disconnection from life. I'd known my brother James, in his late teens, to have had some form of it. I'd wondered if I would ever learn how it felt to be clinically depressed.

By the October of 2007, aged twenty years and three months, I was in no doubt that I'd been allowed such a glimpse.

Over nine months of desperate rumination, I'd concluded that consciousness was, in fact, a scientific mystery, and that evidence for ghosts and out of body experience was strong. I could now suppose that the body channelled rather than created the mind. Now, however, this fortress of ideas was besieged by a threat to match that of oblivion.

As unfathomably beautiful as the afterlife might be, I still feared what it might hold. If the soul really was eternal, would we all have to remain in the same state forever? I pictured a white void, peopled by the souls of all who had died, to be joined ad infinitum by their juniors. I would end up here, united with those close to me, and we'd exist forever. All things must end up in this ultimate receptacle of existence. Such suspension could never conceivably end. With no existence beyond eternity, this void was all there could ever be.

By now, the concept of eternity staggered me.

While it made existence bearable, could love thrive forever? Would eternity numb such attachments? Would affection, in perpetuity, seek new homes? Might instead earthly attachment burn forever, a hormonal arrangement stretched across the mind-crushing anonymity of infinity? The thought of such loneliness was devastating.

Immature as some might think me, I couldn't want these fundamental drives to end. But the idea of hoarding them against eternity staggered me with mind-splitting loneliness. The idea of immortality, and its reduction of all love to meaningless spasm, combined to bring a terrifying new sensation: recognition of woe without end. It revoked any chance of comfort. The life-driving possibility that all might after all be well, was now kaput.

JK Rowling had identified depression as, distinct from misery, a conviction that one could never be happy again. I felt sure that I was now in such a state.

My frightened misery churned with a desperation which was, I suppose, an emotional equivalent to burning or choking, a suffocation of the soul.

The Last Great Time War, final battle between the Time Lords and the Daleks, had gripped the universe in unprecedented, torturously protracted destruction. The private universe of my mind, I assessed, was now engaged in such a war.

One afternoon, as I sat on the top floor of the university library in an attempt to retain some of the required reading, a pang of depression hit me square in the existence. Without any gastric nausea, I longed to run into the nearby men's toilets, stick my head down a bowl and vomit out the horror inside me.

Throughout October, I woke up dreading it. On coming downstairs, I had to force myself to take a few bites of breakfast. Despair left little room for hunger, I realised.

A pang of depression might hit me on the bus, or halfway through a seminar.

From the 2005 *Doctor Who* episode *Aliens of London*, I recalled the pig, augmented by the Slitheen with the cerebral capacity to pilot a spaceship into Big Ben. I supposed I was like that hapless pig, forced to face concepts I was unequipped to grasp.

For some reason, I hadn't seen, on the list of Third Year options, the offer of Dr Peter Hutchings' horror module. Instead, I'd chosen Contemporary European Cinema.

Not a lot of what we watched was what one might call jolly. Listening to a man bemoan the futility of bodily gratification didn't rouse me to panic, but I briefly worried that it might.

How I wished I could have listened to dear old Peter talk about horror films!

Throughout that dreadful month, life went on as normal. I told no one of what was happening to me. The immutability of what I faced staggered me with fear. I couldn't see what any counsellor could possibly do.

One Thursday evening, I went in the car with Mam and Dad to Tesco's, where I bought this month's issue of *Doctor Who Magazine*. The closing footnote from Russell T Davies discussed spin-off material. Lately, the Cruciform, as mentioned in this year's *The Sound of Drums*, had been listed, in Gary Russell's *Who* encyclopaedia, as a planet. Russell now explained that the Cruciform was not a planet, but something whose description would be quite inappropriate for pre-watershed broadcast. The Time War, he said, was a hellish perversion of Time itself.

I found solidarity in Davies' mention of an unimaginably horrible perversion of reality. This depression, or whatever it was, was my Time War. It was the Thought War. The Doctor had got through his, so perhaps, I dared to imagine, I might get through mine.

Russell went on to discuss the uniqueness of each fan's interpretation of an episode, all of which spawned spin-off material exclusive to one's own imagination, to be kept forever.

His jollity and unashamed sentiment was itself an encouraging hint that life might after all be worthwhile. His persuasion of the joys of life seemed absolute. Even if by "forever," he meant as long as one's neurons remained functional, his very suggestion of a beloved image to remain with one "forever" suggested a state which irrevocably retained the joy of its genesis.

Sanctuary

On Sunday morning, alone in the living room, I slipped on my DVD of *Ghostbusters II* and skipped ahead to the scene where Dana, alone in the Manhattan Museum of Art restoration lab, glances behind her at the towering self-portrait of Vigo the Carpathian. The face of the haunted portrait briefly twitches in a sinister leer.

The scene cuts to the arrival of Dr Peter Venkman. He playfully jokes with Dana and goes on to mock the fearsome painting. Randy Edelman's incidental score, with its merry bounce of soft, fluting chimes, hints Peter's disarming levity and protective affection. In desperate pursuit of the possibility that its benevolence could never cease to matter, I clung to this music.

Later that day, Mam, Dad, James, John and I went in the car for a walk along the beach. On the deserted, windswept dunes, I gazed at the sea. The idea that something would always be bigger than everyone soothed the apparent loneliness of eternal consciousness.

We then went for fish and chips.

One cool October noon, weary from constant anticipation of existential terror, I arrived from Northumbria University at the

Haymarket bus station. I decided to walk down to the Gate multiplex to see the newly released *I Now Pronounce You Chuck and Larry*. It didn't sound like my sort of thing, but Essence Jessica Biel made it required viewing.

In the near-empty auditorium, I sat with only a large Pepsi Max, my appetite all but crushed out of existence. With fear and misery currently slight enough to allow moderate contentment, I settled down to watch.

To my pleasant surprise, Chuck (Adam Sandler) and Larry's (Kevin James) boss was played by Dan Aykroyd. Having long recognised him as an Essence, I saw his smooth black hair to recall that of Dr Peter Hutchings and Peter Kay, as did the breadth and height of his brow, likened also to Steve Pemberton, Andrea Corr and myself.

The last three Dan's hair and brow recalled with slight, near-luminously clear parallel. Their adjacency to gently intense eyes drew just as irresistible parallel to my uncle Ross.

Dan, having been born in 1952, was well into his fifties, older than my parents. The age he'd reached held a lore of constant loneliness and ruination as time slowly destroyed all.

At the climax, Dan Aykroyd's New York fire chief stormed into the courtroom with a decisive solution to the plight of the titular fraudulently gay couple. While visibly aged, Dan looked very much his old self. His face, although more drawn and somewhat lined, instantly beamed the same signature. The smooth black hair, while lesser in quantity, retained its shape. Age had happened, but the Essence was still there. While flesh might fade, the signature it wrote remained. If the body was a word, I supposed, then the soul was its meaning: if the word was erased, its meaning continued to exist beyond the boundaries of pen and paper.

Here was an inevitability to counter those I feared: identity was, by its very nature, immutable.

On YouTube, someone had uploaded a scene from this year's *Doctor Who* finale, *Last of the Time Lords*.

In the previous episode, John Simm's the Master had, via genetic manipulator, forced David Tennant's Doctor into a state of immobilising old age. The Master had then had his hordes of Toclafane, sadistically giggling floating metal spheres, destroy a tenth of humanity.

In *Last of the Time Lords*, captioned to take place one year later, Freema Agyeman's Martha Jones wanders the ravaged world on a covert mission to bring an end to the rule of the Master. (*Spoiler alert!*) Brought back aboard the flying fortress *Valiant*, Martha explains her having told the depleted populace of the Doctor's frequent intervention to save Earth. The Archangel Network of telepathic satellites, previously used by the Master for hypnosis, now projects humanity's knowledge of the Doctor.

As the countdown nears the launch of the Master's Black Hole Converters, people across the world join in a Doctor-themed chant. The ancient Doctor exudes a burst of bluish white light.

The scene is scored by Murray Gold. A softly orchestrated choral wail wistfully falls, then rises like a sob of relief. Within the bluish white halo, the Doctor reverts to bodily youth. Partly made of light, his features shine as if age has never worn them, as if they are as immutable as the light itself. The identity to be found in an aged face, I supposed, was an assertion of something from beyond matter.

Each night, I returned to this scene. Its music, in the face of devastation, announced stunned relief. Its images implied that, in the face of destruction, there remained a constant chance that life might reassert its joys. Decay, a by-product of physical development, might obscure identity, but could never erase it. Existence, I mused, didn't need to outsit the relentless loneliness of eternity; existence, in some currently inconceivable way, *was* eternity.

Last year, I'd unearthed from the living room bookcase James's second-hand copy of Terry Pratchett's *Johnny and the Dead* (1993). Twelve-year-old Johnny Maxwell learns of his unique ability to see and hear the occupants of a local cemetery. The Dead visit the town canal, where two of their number, Addison Fletcher and Solomon Einstein, enable a broken television to receive newly broadcast signals, whereupon the Dead become addicted to

Australian soap opera *Cobbers*. Since the television doesn't have a screen, much less a power source, Johnny realises it to channel the respective ghosts of electricity, components and signals. But surely machines don't have ghosts?

Solomon explains it's simply a matter of finding a moment of their physical existence.

Johnny realises all things, living and inert, to be eternal.

The *Daily Mail* account I'd read a few years ago about life after death seemed to concur with this. All things, it had implied, following earthly degeneration, remained eternally in a state of being beyond the reach of matter. Even blades of grass, apparently, had souls. Every facet and instant of the universe, I supposed, existed immutably and eternally.

The daily pangs of despair continued to scream their threats of existential torment. In search of an image of stubborn tenacity in the face of overwhelming odds, I flippantly aspired to Churchillian defiance of the Blitz. Andrew can take it, I said to myself.

Throughout Christmas, I retained a numb, weary sorrow, eased by cautious optimism. The pangs of existential despair, or whatever they were, had stopped after October and hadn't returned since.

2008

Facial Contact

One mid-morning, along St Mary's Place, I strode to Northumbria University. The wide path which bridged the courtyard was, today, attended by several girls in red tops, trainers and short black skirts. They approached passers-by with offers of leaflets, which apparently held the chance to win something.

The girls' sporty attire evoked a brash pageantry, the thought of my intrusion upon which shamed me.

I reached the path, mounted the short wall which bordered the adjacent car park and kept my stride with relative ease. I gazed ahead, trying to look as unapproachable as possible. In seconds, I reached the dreaded throng.

"Do you wanna be in with a chance of...?" said a bright female voice.

I quickened pace and kept my face blank.

"Fine," called the voice, "it doesn't want to be with you either!"

My younger brother John, having settled into his first year of studying Philosophy at Newcastle University, now lived with several others in a converted convent.

He had the idea of inviting me along, one spring afternoon, for a relaxed urban adventure, perhaps to culminate in our taking a seat on the grass before Northumbria.

We patronised a newly opened restaurant. These last two years, for me to pursue such extravagance alone would have been unthinkable; I dared not invade an innocent outlet with my awkward person, to burden its staff with my dependence. Now that I had someone to go with, it would be okay.

As the young waitress addressed us, something overwhelmed me with a need to keep my gaze away from hers: her femininity and courtesy evoked an innocence and refinement on which

I dared not intrude. It roused old shames of my discourtesy, inordinate timidity and social confusion.

As she later saw us out, I, to her surprised-sounding thanks, shoved a pound coin into the tip box.

On telling Mam of the outing, John noted my conspicuous reluctance to make eye contact with the waitress. Mam had also noticed, in shops, my habitual avoidance of eye contact with cashiers. To my surprise, she one evening asked if I might like to seek some form of counselling.

An online directory for counselling in the North East of England drew my attention to the profile of Cara McGrath. In a small headshot, wavy brown ringlets framed a young face set in a sober smile.

I made an appointment over the phone. Her polite voice was accented with Standard English, with a hint of what sounded like Durham or Teesside.

On the spring evening of our drive to Kingston Park, Mam warned that should anyone from next door ask where we'd been, I should say we'd been to Tesco's. Granda Widdrington, apparently, didn't approve of psychotherapy.

"Bloody quacks," quoted Mam.

A short way from Tesco's, Dad drove us to the online-specified district.

In a palpable grip of shame and dread, I forced myself to approach the detached house and to knock on the small door. It soon opened. Cara, her hair now straightened, calmly welcomed me. Despite her assurance that it wasn't necessary, I left my shoes in the porch. She led me upstairs to a small, brown-toned room, set with two small, facing armchairs.

Throughout the interview, I veered my gaze sideways: imposition on her fine, scholarly face choked me with shame.

Throughout the next few weeks, as the weather warmed, I, with nervously hasty precision, summarised to her the fear which stifled any attempt to write any story more emotionally layered than a basic sketch or concept, and my similar fear of the shame of being caught attending any broadcast or recorded media with which others were unfamiliar. It was tolerable, I explained, if I didn't know much about the production in question, or if those around me were familiar with it.

"What about relationships?" she asked.

I fumblingly explained that I'd never "felt ready" for such a social engagement.

After several weeks, Cara delicately suggested that I might have Asperger's syndrome. I recalled a similar venture from the NHS counsellor back in 2005. Asperger's syndrome, explained Cara, was on the autistic spectrum. It had similar tendencies to autism, such as introversion or social confusion.

For monetary reasons, she advised me to seek, through the NHS, counsel from someone who specialised in Asperger's. It was thus arranged for my referral by the Rothbury Practice to Alnwick's Hawkhill community mental health service.

A Celestial View

One night, with the option of a lie-in the following morning, I lingered in the living room to listen to CDs on my Walkman for much longer than usual. As the hour neared four, I lumbered into mine and John's darkened bedroom, which these days I had to myself.

My gaze lingered on the drawn curtains. I suddenly felt a mild urge to draw the curtains for a quick view of the clear night sky. This urge encompassed a sudden persuasion that tonight's sky might hold a surprise.

In semi-darkness, lit partly through the open door by the landing light, I drew back the curtains. Above the net curtain, the tall window's upper pane held a clear, dark blue sky. The road, the grassy slope and the row of stone buildings above were dwarfed from behind by the Bilberry hills, a horizon-spanning slope whose looming crest of pine trees were in turn dwarfed by the sky.

The dark blue sky held a few stars. Just above the leftward trees, one star in particular drew my gaze. What was it about this star? I was no astronomer, but its presence above the trees looked somehow unfamiliar. Its structure seemed distinct from what one expected of a star; its density evoked an airborne spark of fire. Its silver glow held several peripheral shimmers of purple and, further in, yellow. The yellow seemed slowly to shift, as if in rotation. I understood atmospheric distortion to change stars' apparent shape and colour, but this process seemed slower.

And then, in the clear sky, before my now-alert eyes, without the slightest allowance for fanciful misinterpretation, the star, if that was what it was, promptly contracted and faded from view, so the clear sky behind where it had been now appeared empty.

Immediately, in the sky, several (from my perspective) centimetres to the (my) right of where the star had been, a yellow spark, slightly larger than the star, pulsed into being, spread into a soft flare and then flickered, shimmered and dimmed to a pinprick silver orb, laced with purple and yellow.

This process repeated several times, as the celestial body, if indeed each appearance was of the same object, hovered in several positions above the trees atop the Bilberry hills.

Delighted and mildly astounded, I reverently savoured this new glimpse of intent beyond the known limits of matter.

Manchester

I'd ventured to Mam my desire to attend Avril Lavigne's "The Best Damn Tour" concert in Manchester. Mam wasn't entirely comfortable with the idea of my going alone, so directed me to use her card to buy three tickets, just in case.

On his Myspace, mine and John's old friend Alan had posted the music video for "Girlfriend." I messaged him with the offer of a spare ticket, and he seemed keen.

With such little notice before departure, train ticket prices had gone up, so it was arranged for Alan and me to go to Manchester by bus. It would be, joked James, like the Harry Enfield sketch "The Scousers Go to That London."

On the bright day of departure, I took my old leather bag down to the bus stop.

Today's bus driver was a youngish, wiry man with short black hair and a silver stud in one earlobe. I had him down as an amiable sort. Surprisingly, he didn't have change for a tenner. I asked if I could just collect my change at Newcastle, as I'd done from other drivers. He pressed the point with surprising fervour and sent me across the road to the newsagent's for change.

"You should know better," he said as I disembarked.

"I beg ya pardon?" I said, giddy with panicked outrage, but numb enough for composure.

He repeated his reprimand.

Throughout the journey to Newcastle, I sorrowed at my inability to meet the requirements of society and at my feeble, dazed abasement before the more aggressive of its members. Despite this, I resolved to assert myself.

At the Haymarket bus station, I waited for the other passengers to leave and stole myself to approach the driver.

"'Scuse me," I said, in the courteous hush with which I usually addressed strangers, "I'd just like you to know that on the rare occasion change's been a problem, nobody's ever been rude about it."

As I turned to search for Alan, the driver called me back.

"I've got two minutes," he said. He launched into a protest at his unfair burdens and my unwarranted impositions. My attempts at interjection fell limply against his robust ire.

"*Stupid!*" he fumed. With the fortitude of those who took hard knocks and toiled, he crushed my childish naivety. "Piss off!" he huffed, with an offer of his middle finger.

I habitually raised a hand in farewell and soon found Alan.

"Hello, Alan, nice to see you!" I said, shaking his offered hand. While genuine, my esteem was anchored by hefty, burning regret.

In the Manchester Evening News Arena, Alan and I sat facing the stage from about halfway up.

Far below, the distant, towering stage eventually darkened to show a screened animation in which the name of our songstress was spray-painted onto a wall.

Into the darkness bounded a spotlit Avril, dressed in fetchingly casual tee shirt and jeans. In a newer, rawer intonation, her high, rich voice happily belted out "Girlfriend." As I'd fondly hoped, Avril's heartfelt vitality banished, for now, my residual ache of humiliation.

Lazy?

I'd always suspected that a course in Film and Television Studies was unlikely to earn me such eminence as to seduce prospective employers. It now looked very much as if I'd been right.

A flair for writing had earned me an average pass.

At school, attempts to grasp technical information had quickly dulled my concentration. I'd therefore shunned attempts at serious revision, for which I'd resigned myself not to have "the right sort of mind." All those times I'd given up reading a photocopied textbook page in favour of a film review or novel, I hadn't been able to entirely dismiss the old, shaming suggestion that I was *lazy*.

The term seemed to have defined me from the age of four, hinted by teachers' vexation at my baffling ineptitude.

My cumbersome torso had seemed to wear it well.

I ate too much. I lacked the discipline to stop. I must be lazy.

I seldom knew what I was supposed to be doing, as I couldn't concentrate on what teachers were saying. I must be too lazy to listen.

I was scared of going to the toilet, being shouted at and hit in the face with a football, presumably because I was too lazy to muster greater resolve.

Granda Widdrington had warned us to enjoy our health, the implication being that time, if not some horror of the wider world, would inevitably take it away. Whereas he'd spent his childhood toiling in abject poverty, I was consistently nourished.

However, I now found myself engrossed by the possibility that my inhibitions hadn't really been entirely my fault.

A science editorial in the *Daily Mail* had suggested that some brains didn't process pleasurable sensation as closely as those of others, so felt a need to seek more of the pleasurable sensation.

Couldn't even a slight calorific excess gain weight? What seemed an innocuously sized portion to some might unexpectedly gain them weight. Not because of ill-bred, self-entitled hedonism, but because that was what seemed natural to them.

And now, there was this Asperger's syndrome thing. Could I accredit my inordinate timidity and lack of focus to some neurological heritage? I would soon find out.

Meanwhile, to break into my life savings, I filled in some forms. Mam and James persuaded me to apply for jobseeker's allowance.

At Morpeth's Jobcentre, a playfully smirking middle-aged woman recalled to me her career, a period, she twinkled, which had probably lasted "longer than you've been *alive...*!" in which she'd never found anyone apt for the role of, for example, brain surgeon.

Local jobs supposedly within my ability tended to include cleaning or administration. Naturally, all my applications were unsuccessful. I cancelled my jobseeker's allowance.

As Christmas neared, I took a bus to Newcastle.

Metro reported someone in the public eye to have suggested that whereas promotion of anorexia by underweight celebrities should be challenged, so should such overweight celebrities as James Corden, the sight of whom might supposedly lull viewers to lapse into supposedly dangerous weight gain.

I had some difficulty in articulating my outrage at this. Since I held my outsized appetite to be innate, blaming it on carelessness which might be caused by *the mere sight* of an overweight person, seemed fecklessly patronising.

On Christmas morning, I opened my presents to see that Uncle Ross had got me the DVD of Alan Parker's 1996 version of *Evita*. Its starring of suspect Essence Madonna made it required viewing. Composition by Andrew Lloyd Webber assured agreeability.

2009

Future Essences

The cool evenings began to brighten.

In the kitchen, Mam prepared homemade fish and chips. The frying pan sizzled, and Radio 2 blared.

As I ate, I passively listened to an interview with a newly emerged young songstress by the name of Taylor Swift. Last year, on Magic and Bliss, I'd watched some of her music videos. With soft percussion, smooth strings and a brightly clear, richly emotive voice, Taylor's songs somewhat recalled Avril's.

In this age, seeing a young female songstress hold a guitar seemed something of a throwback.

With a curiously touched surprise, it occurred to me that Taylor might turn out to be an Essence.

Last year, "Bright Eyes" and *Dreamstone* composer Mike Batt had released a compilation album. While I'd heard relatively little of it, I loved his music, with its sober, open tenderness and unashamed fun.

On his blog, in search of a hint of transgenic kinship, I peered at several recent profile shots. By way of a broad brow, his gaze seemed memorable enough to offer such uncanny familiarity, but I couldn't be sure whether this was simply receptiveness on my part. Most obviously, the mild, thoughtful face drew comparison to my brother James.

I allowed myself a minor extravagance and bought *A Songwriter's Tale*.

With Mam and Dad at Barrowburn, Uncle Ross called in. I took the opportunity to acquaint myself with the DVD of *Evita*.

The DVD cover stirred memories of, in 1996, the momentous arrival of a film version of a musical by the respective composer and lyricist of *Jesus Christ Superstar*. On a dazzlingly backlit poster, a weary Antonio Banderas and a sorrowful Madonna hinted heartfelt solemnity. Her slightly exotic-sounding name and proudly brazen flair held monumental mystique, which this film had channelled into theatrical eminence. Ross had long stressed the critics' surprised concession to this.

"I think she's a talented lass," he'd said.

We now settled down to watch. Sultry lighting, expansive cinematography and the surreal candour of diegetic music staged a solemn yet whimsical view of thirties/forties Argentina.

Antonio Banderas's Che, in song and flashback, dryly narrated. The excitedly vexed "Oh, What a Circus," set to a funeral procession and a montage of flashbacks, offered an impassioned glimpse of history.

Familiar from the music channels, Madonna's high voice, softened by a fluting depth, sang "Buenos Aires" with instant lovability. Surprised to feel a glow of fondness, I realised I was starting to see what Ross saw in this creature.

By now enamoured by the heartfelt, lushly symphonic music encountered in the DVD of *Evita*, I took a step further and bought the soundtrack album.

On nightly listens, the clear, proud-yet-poignant voice of Madonna stoked a deeper affection for those of her songs I knew.

On catching one of her eighties videos on a music channel, her fine, soft face, with its buoyantly styled curls, now cheered and touched me. While I'd always quite liked some of her songs, I hadn't expected to yearn so earnestly to attend her face and voice. I still couldn't be sure if I saw transgenic kinship.

I decided to designate her an honorary Essence and bought the album *Like a Prayer*. On a few weeks of audible and visual attendance, I was delighted to sense, in the correlation of her brow, eyes and cheeks, irresistible recollection of such Essences as Avril Lavigne.

Asperger's Syndrome

In February came my first appointment with Adrian Bishop.

A tall, broad man with full, dark grey hair, his calm, amicable voice had a North West accent.

The initial focus of our meetings was for me to find a daily occupation.

I eased into a fairly comfortable pattern of going with my parents and Uncle Ross to Barrowburn, where I would wash dishes for Mam's newly opened tearoom and help Ross prepare the Camping Barn and Deer Hut.

The pleasantly orderly task of making the dishes squeaky clean had me quite content. To Ross's preparation of the old school house and adjacent wooden bungalow, I, with a peaceful sense of purpose, lent my dusting, bed-making and floor-sweeping skills.

While I now knew the joy of full, productive days, fulfilment of my ambition to write stories still seemed a long way off.

Throughout Adrian Bishop's monthly visits, we arranged for me to type and print off daily experiences.

As spring began to dawn, I wrote, in addition to a daily account, of things which had, over the years, confused or inordinately intimidated me.

I wrote of how Granda Widdrington's playful sneers and solemn scorn for what John and I watched on telly had gradually steered me to ashamedly hide privately indulged broadcast or recorded material.

I wrote of how since the age of four, I'd preferred the quiet adventures of my own imagination and had scant interest in communal activity.

I wrote of my overwhelming fear of getting hit in the face whenever someone in my vicinity kicked or threw a ball.

I wrote of my inability to grasp teachers' instruction.

I wrote of my need, until age ten, to lie in bed with my mother in order to fall asleep.

I wrote of my habitual aversion, until age twelve, to toilets.

I wrote of my decision, aged ten, to, despite vague notions of the barbarous outrage thereof, expose myself as a means of retaliation to playground derision.

I wrote of my miserable self-disgust at Aunty Dawn's playful suggestion that I might be capable of sexual attraction to women.

I wrote of my aversion to such private body parts as breasts.

I wrote of my immobilising fear of walking across stepping stones.

I wrote of the frightened shame with which a slightly raised or sharpened voice burned away any desire for me to even think of myself.

Adrian Bishop, on finishing my lengthy account, gently offered his considered opinion that I was "acutely sensitive," that I was missing a metaphorical layer of skin. He definitively debunked old fears that my inhibitions were born of ill-bred selfishness.

Asperger's syndrome, he explained, might impair desensitisation to the uncomfortable or unfamiliar, such as getting hit in the face with a ball or to the sight of private body parts. Asperger's syndrome seemed to account for my reclusiveness, inordinate timidity, inordinate sensitivity, lax concentration, limited navigational ability, incomprehension of numeracy, or "dyscalculia," as Mrs Hart had identified it, and our old friend, obsessive-compulsive disorder.

While not hugely surprising, Adrian Bishop's debunking of old shames stoked an esteemed sense of relief. The shame in which I'd grown up would continue to curtail my engagement with society, but confirmation that my inhibitions lay partly in neurological arrangement gently fortified my new adulthood.

After our meeting, I sat alone in the living room, in fond anticipation of the day ahead. Dad took a phone call. With gentle solemnity, he then told me that Granda Tait had died.

I observed my paternal grandfather's passing with solemn momentum, but ultimately, I felt happy for him: free from the impositions of age, his memory was now immortalised in the eternal dignity of death.

New Essences

Since I'd started properly following *Neighbours*, many of the regular cast had been replaced. I now caught traces of Essentiality in Ashleigh Brewer's Kate Ramsay. On introduction, sudden bereavement of her mother and the constant demand of self-sufficiency had a gentle pathos.

Kate's aspect put me at ease. Her sorrowful expressions invited easy appreciation of her face. Long, straight dark hair framed a high brow, light blue eyes, a faintly pointed nose and high cheekbones.

The high facial structure and softly pointed nose paralleled respective features of Avril Lavigne and my old infatuation, Abbey Charlton. Ashleigh's features, in turn, channelled expressions irresistibly similar to those of the aforementioned.

This year's *Doctor Who* was reduced to a trilogy of hour-long specials.

The first, Russell T Davies' and Gareth Roberts' *Planet of the Dead*, aired at Easter. The episode co-starred Michelle Ryan, whom I now quickly supposed to be an Essence. Her long, straight dark hair and high cheekbones vividly paralleled Ashleigh Brewer. The structure of Michelle's face, faintly but insistently, tilted its expressions to evoke those of Avril Lavigne, Abbey Charlton and Ashleigh Brewer.

In the last year or so, bookshop displays of *The Gospel According to Chris Moyles* (2006) had increasingly impressed me with indication of the Radio 1 presenter to be an Essence. On the cover, his broad brow, high, full cheeks and easy mouth aligned in open joviality. This combination of facial structure and expression irresistibly recalled Dan Aykroyd, Steve Pemberton, Peter Kay, Ryan Moloney and me.

In due appreciation of his amiability and charisma, I'd long found Chris Moyles' exuberance somewhat overwhelming. Daunted by his inclusion among those with whom I believed myself to share transgenic kinship, I feebly tried to write it off as misinterpretation. The more I glanced at the face, the clearer its familiarity became. I now saw Chris Moyles to be an Essence.

To see my withdrawn self paralleled in a national emblem of impudence was almost comical. I committed myself to watching his new Channel 4 panel show.

Perhaps this desensitisation helped me to finally acknowledge JK Rowling to be an Essence.

As well as Chris Moyles, peripheral media observation had drawn my gaze closer to the faces of Ian Holm, Anthony Hopkins and Ian McDiarmid. In each, a rounded brow and eyes apt both to geniality and solemnity shaped expression which drew insistent comparison to each other and to Sylvester McCoy. In the eminence, geniality and steel of each, I happily acknowledged their Essential credentials.

Years of a rumoured return to television by *Red Dwarf* had, last year, found confirmation. A ten-year gap couldn't dull my affection for the exceptional sitcom.

I was now almost entirely persuaded that Craig Charles, who played Lister, was an Essence. A broad brow, high, faintly full cheeks and gently jovial eyes shaped expression which I traced, increasingly irresistibly, to Dan Aykroyd, Peter Kay, Chris Moyles and myself.

At Morpeth Library, I finally got round to reading Derek Landy's *Skulduggery Pleasant*.

I became engrossed. Immersion of ambitious twelve-year-old Stephanie Edgely in a secret community of "mages" wove an increasingly edgy tale, all presided over by a droll yet ominously mysterious skeleton detective.

On watching an online interview with the author, whose face seemed promisingly open and rounded, I found myself fondly anticipating Derek Landy to turn out to be an Essence.

Rob Grant's *Fat*

As summer dawned, I got the bus to Newcastle, wondering what to get for John's twentieth birthday. In the basement floor of Waterstones, I decided on *Red Dwarf* co-creator Rob Grant's satirical novel *Fat* (2006), which, along with a copy of *Skulduggery Pleasant* for myself, I bought and headed home.

The trouble was, having peaked inside the first few pages of *Fat*, I found myself reluctant to come out again.

Divorced television chef Grenville Roberts, having bafflingly and irresistibly gained weight since his twenties, has reached a point where getting out of bed and putting on his shoes has become strenuous. While dryly comical, description of his weight portrays it as an affliction, rather than a selfish affront to the aesthetic tastes of innocent bystanders.

An ominously increasingly overbearing government tasks Jeremy Slank to promote newly built Well Farms. His moderate contempt for the heavily overweight is challenged by research assistant Jemma Bartlet, mouthpiece for Grant's own research, who debunks the government's draconian attempt to get people to lose weight.

Fat says a decline in epidemiology has enabled researchers to "prove" that just about anything can cause just about anything else, hence the media's endless scaremongering health warnings. The book says cholesterol can't actually enter the bloodstream, and that past the age of sixty-five, being slightly overweight improves life expectancy.

I'd heard of the so-called obesity epidemic. I'd vaguely supposed it to refer to an apparent influx of weight gain. Whatever the case, it no longer applied to me, as I'd lost weight.

Now, media obsession with the "obesity epidemic" struck me in a new way: it cast flab not only as an unfashionable hindrance, but as a danger. Dislike of flab could now be channelled into dutiful concern for the carelessness with which we porkers spoiled not only our visual acceptability, but our health. Supposed concern for fat people's safety sanitised dislike of their appearance.

Already eternally grateful to Rob Grant for having co-created *Red Dwarf*, I now held him in all-new esteem. With only slight guilt, I decided to keep *Fat* and get John an Irvine Welsh novel instead.

Lost Time

Since seeing him in one or two YouTube uploads around 2006 or 2007, I'd aspired to further acquaint myself with the recorded works of Dan Aykroyd. While I cherished the impact of his *Ghostbusters* saga on the lives of my brothers and me, I couldn't really say I'd seen him in much else, save for the *Dragnet* (1987) trailer, his *Casper* (1995) cameo, the first few minutes of *My Stepmother is an Alien* (1988) and a few minutes of *Chaplin* (1992).

It was high time I put this to rights. I bought a DVD of *Dragnet* (an endearing, proudly affectionate parody), *Coneheads* (1993, upliftingly whimsical) and *Chaplin* (which, I'm not proud to say, I still haven't got round to watching).

Since my perception in 2006 of Peter Kay to be an Essence, I'd never got round to watching many of the productions in which he appeared, save for *The Road to Amarillo*'s music video, *Love and Monsters* and a few minutes of an episode of *Phoenix Nights*.

I now rectified this by buying a box set of *Phoenix Nights*. A tale of the management of live acts in a pub, it examines camaraderie and loneliness with a wry sense of absurdity. As paralytic Brian Potter, Peter is comical yet consistently natural.

In attendance of Anthony Hopkins, I bought a DVD of *Magic* (1978, broodingly ominous) and *Shadowlands* (1993, eloquently poignant).

The Start of an Age

In December, dense fog, bleached pale orange by street lamps, swathed the night. While this year had been productive, I was no closer to advancing my writing ambitions or to sharing my glimpse of the metaphysical aspects of the human body. While glad to work at my parents' small business, I had no visible prospect of self-sufficiency.

While I loved to write, and revelled in the constant concoction of stories, irrational shame barred their fulfilment in emotive prose. But the talent was there. Adrian Bishop had coaxed out of me a blatant skill for presentation in prose of my unconventional perspective.

I considered my other ambition, to somehow tell the world of my witness to a subtle miracle.

These two aspirations sowed an idea: I could write a book after all. It would be about my life. There was nothing to stop me.

It would be about growing up fat, my baffling learning difficulties and my inordinate constraints of fear, remorse and shame, all as a setting for a sincere belief in the genetically transcendent relation of widespread people.

With the old Windows XP having been sold for scrap, the desk in the corner of the landing now held my laptop. While waiting for it to load, I had, throughout the year, read from my copy of James Herbert's *Others*. The lifelong isolation and rejection of deformed private investigator Nick "Dis" Dismas are examined with unflinching candour. With consistent support from close friendships, he draws stares, taunts, jokes and a harrowingly brutal mugging.

Painfully aware of the unease his appearance often rouses, Dis consistently finds himself rejected by conspicuous gestures of acceptance, feckless insensitivity or blunt, callous cruelty.

On encountering people with extreme deformities, he finds himself irresistibly alarmed, but is urged to let compassion overrule this.

(*Spoiler alert!*)

A near-drowning prompts Dis to recall a previous incarnation, for whose misdeeds his obstacles in this life have urged him to redemptive spiritual advancement.

Others, with its sober venture of the actual divinity of Jesus, encouraged my trust in the possibility of divine guidance from above.

2010

This

The new decade brought heavy snow. For weeks, the country chugged slowly through it.

With Dad snowed in at Barrowburn, Mam made loads of Scotch pancakes. On her second-hand laptop, I took booking enquiries. The task had a pleasant simplicity, and it was always good to feel useful.

Each night, around half past eleven, I sat at the desk on the upstairs landing and, on my old laptop, attempted to translate childhood experiences into prose.

At Barrowburn, it was agreed that my dishwasher job was unessential, as my constantly dry hands saw enough sink action with all the compulsive handwashing.

In the Deer Hut and Camping Barn, I continued to make beds, sweep floors and dust. With inexhaustible diligence, Uncle Ross wiped cookers, cleaned toilets and laid fires. I was happy to take fifty pounds a week instead of a hundred.

Derek Landy

Having caught up in Morpeth Library with the two *Skulduggery Pleasant* sequels, the imminent arrival of a fourth book stoked my interest.

As the series grew emotionally and conceptually, I fondly idealised that my esteem for this new author might herald an Essence.

I'd seen online photos and video footage of Derek Landy. Beneath a spread of sandy hair, a high brow framed a rounded face. From behind small glasses shone a wry, distant mirth. The breadth of the brow and fullness of the face steered facial expression which irresistibly recalled Dan Aykroyd, Timothy

Spall, Dr Peter Hutchings, Russell T Davies, Steve Pemberton and Peter Kay. The cranial shape in particular paralleled those of Messrs Hutchings, Davies, Pemberton and Kay.

To have been drawn to a new Essence by merit of printed word alone was an encouraging surprise.

Ian McNeice

To Steven Moffat, Russell T Davies had now left custody of *Doctor Who*.

The premise of Mark Gatiss's *Victory of the Daleks* was an exciting surprise. To the refined precision of a period setting it brought the show's brash energy. Ian McNeice, known to me as Potiphar in *Joseph and the Amazing Technicolor Dreamcoat*, played Winston Churchill. As hinted by several Terrance Dicks novels, the episode established Winston and the Doctor to be old friends.

In *Doctor Who Magazine*, shots of Ian McNeice showed curly grey hair, a broad brow, high, full cheeks and a gently humorous gaze. His aspect seemed apt for the caste of Essences to which I'd recently welcomed Derek Landy. As of yet, I saw no definite indication of Ian's transgenic kinship, but this, in time, would change.

James Corden

On UK Gold, now named Gold, frequent previews of *Gavin and Stacey* repeats acquainted me more closely with the face of James Corden.

A high brow and full, high-cheeked face paralleled the facial signatures of Steve Pemberton, Chris Moyles, Peter Kay and me.

I watched *Gavin and Stacey*. Its affectionately drawn characters and generous-spirited humour had a sincere tenderness.

Robbie Coltrane

On my quest to make up for lost time with the films of Dan Aykroyd, I bought a DVD of *On the Nose* (2001).

For some time, I'd suspected its star, Robbie Coltrane, to be an Essence. While I hadn't yet felt the irresistible similarity, his high brow, full, high cheeks and correlation thereto of his open gaze, drew me to tentatively compare his face with my own.

Shortly after having seen *On the Nose*, his Essentiality was as clear to me as that of any.

Old Friends

In writing my life story, I was excited to reach my fourteenth year. That year, a purchased DVD of *Remembrance of the Daleks* had reunited me with the recorded image of Sylvester McCoy, whom by 2006 I held to be an Essence.

I'd spent much of my fourteenth summer in secret pursuit of my infatuation with the combination of sounds and images that constituted the figure of Sailor Moon.

When writing about *Sailor Moon*, I looked for YouTube uploads with which to jog my memory. On attendance of several uploaded episodes, the flighty, vulnerable, devotional, affectionate bundle of teenage energy that was heroine Serena once more entranced me. As closely as I had been at the age of fourteen, I found myself soothed, cheered and touched by the voice of Terri Hawkes.

Soon enough, my resurgence of affection drove me to look further afield. According to a brief Wikipedia entry, both Terri and DiC's English language dub of *Sailor Moon* were from Canada, ancestral homeland of James's old friend Ted. The Wikipedia article revealed little else other than Terri's filmography. This, I was astounded to see, included *The Care Bears Family*.

This was huge.

Ten years before I'd known her as the voice of leggy, flighty, lovelorn Serena, Terri had supplied the voice of Hugs, one of two infant Care Bears, and Shreeky, niece and protégé to evil sorcerer No Heart.

Now that Wikipedia had made the connection, I sensed the shared tones of the sorcerer's protégé and the anime maiden. This wonderful voice had entranced me both in infant innocence and pubescent desire, a timeless blessing from the ether of the airwaves.

Cheered into a sense of adventure, I decided to search further for the image of Terri Hawkes. A black and white signed photo on *Castle in the Sky* had shown a distant view of a woman somewhere in her thirties. Might she turn out to be an Essence?

I went to see what I might find on Google Images.

Amidst several *Sailor Moon* screenshots and the familiar black and white signed photo, one image seized my attention. A still from 1987 horror film *Hello Mary Lou: Prom Night II* showed a close-up of a young woman's face. Dark brown hair, swept atop her head, fell in curls beside pink-tinged cheeks. Beneath blue eyeshadow, dark hazel eyes were alight with mirth. Her lips, glossed deep pink, spread into the beginnings of a smile.

The screenshot's pale, deep lighting had a jolly gaudiness with which, around the time of my birth, the media had shone. Terri didn't look very old here; perhaps mid-twenties. I suddenly had to see more. I naturally loved eighties fantasy.

I found footage from the film on YouTube.

In a school corridor, two girls stood by a trophy case. Terri's character slinked into view and offered passers-by ribbon-threaded, bell-adorned badges. Her high, soft, merrily lilting voice emerged from an impudent, affectionate grin.

Terri Hawkes' voice cheered and soothed me as ever it had. I revelled in my acquaintance with a previously hidden aspect of a persona I'd enjoyed at the age of four and adored at the age of fourteen. As I loved the voice, I found I loved the jolly, soft-eyed face from which it came.

Was she an Essence? I couldn't tell. Since simple attraction had, in the past, heralded my perception of transgenic kinship, might it do so here? I decided to be adventurous, designate Terri an honorary Essence as I had Mike Batt and Madonna, and order from Amazon a DVD of *Hello Mary Lou: Prom Night II*.

Late one night, I watched it in the living room.

In a macabre premise, a gentle, sometimes comedic tone wove affectionately drawn characters in friendship, sorrow, romance and eventual mounting terror.

Terri's character, Kelly Hennenlotter, stages a jovial front of self-confidence. In pursuit of the prom queen vote, she distributes bell-adorned badges and tries to bribe science whiz Josh (Brock Simpson) to rig the computer votes. Told to name his price, Josh's computer screen-typed request for fellatio draws from Kelly a quiet look of forlorn humiliation. Just before the climax, on learning she's gone through with it for nothing, her look of utter dejection is genuinely poignant.

Having watched her all too brief scenes, I felt a brief pang of longing, of the kind I'd felt for Andrea and Abbey. The pang was slight, and its source was too newly encountered to feel like a loss, but I welcomed its heralding of infatuation.

I'd never be part of Terri's life, but on the canvas of recorded light and sound, I would attend whatever spiritual lineage her aspect cared to reveal. If a recording revealed aspects of a person seemingly apparent only to me, did that mean something of their presence, their consciousness, their soul, remained within the supposedly lifeless image?

Consider the scene from *Ghostbusters II*, where Ray and Egon study photos of the haunted painting of Vigo the Carpathian and detect the aura of a living presence. Might such a presence retain some of the sentience maintained when captured?

I didn't yet see, in the image of Terri, any obvious indication of transgenic kinship. However, the distinction of her face impressed an insistent urge to behold it further. Was this simply appreciation of a pretty face, or indication of the kind of genetically transcendent lineage to which I was privy? I dearly longed to see something there.

Other cast members of *Hello Mary Lou: Prom Night II* offered me a similar clarity; a distinction which I retained with involuntary closeness.

It dawned on me that transgenic kinship might lie in all humanity – while I perceived only certain specimens thereof, the phenomenon implied genes to link independently of bodily connection. Might other such immaterial motion shape all forms of matter?

My attention was drawn not only by *Prom Night II*'s cast, but by the film's location footage. Around Hamilton High, bright sunshine bathed clear, tree-shaded streets. Their gentle vividness recalled that in 2006, when, atop the Bilberry hills, I'd sensed a glaring definition of the colours and shapes of soil, rocks, grass, heather, trees, and sky. If all things come from beyond the physical, if matter is a transient brushstroke of ethereal will, might it sometimes act, unbeknownst to most, in defiance of its apparent limitations?

I put the DVD in my laptop and took numerous screencaps of Terri. Audibly and visually, she was a joy to me.

I searched Amazon. The only UK-released DVDs to feature Terri's appearance were, as far as I could tell, 1987 thoughtful comedy *Crazy Moon* and 2004 sober sci-fi horror *Cube Zero*. I ordered both.

In *Crazy Moon*, Terri briefly appeared as Pamela, a blouse-suited, bespectacled commerce student. Her hair, now a lighter shade of brown, framed a face which peered coyly from behind large glasses.

Cube Zero saw an assortment of amnesiac strangers trapped in a network of vaulted rooms and surrounded by hidden lethal gadgets. In a neck-length bob, Terri's hair was now black. Her character, Jellico, met the situation with slightly unsettling, near-panicked sternness. About half an hour in, she was gruesomely dispatched by a flesh-eating virus.

I put *Cube Zero* in my laptop for further study.

In the early hours of the morning, after doing some writing, I peered at Terri's arresting face. I was finally rewarded by a slight, very slight, impression of familiarity. Hair, brow, eyes and mouth aligned with a clarity akin to that in which I saw transgenic kinship. I drew no parallel to any face in particular, just a general tilt towards several female celebrities.

Last year, a documentary on 1980s pop music showcased "West End Girls" by the Pet Shop Boys. While I often listened to their *Pop Art* compilation, I regretted never having closely attended any of their original albums since *Very*.

Lately, I'd considered attending them with the devotion usually reserved for Essences. Might attendance of anyone's recorded voice or image somehow engage whatever fragment of their sentience lingered in sound or light?

This year, I'd ventured that, in innumerable ways, perhaps everyone was an Essence, perhaps all genes secretly mimicked others, and that perhaps recorded sound and light retained projections of spirit.

Peter Kay

In December, to the Metro Radio Arena, Peter Kay would bring his "Tour that Doesn't Tour" Tour. While stand-up comedy didn't generally rouse my sense of humour as keenly as scripted witticisms, Peter's amused fascination with and affection for human quirks had a genuine power to embolden.

Back in the Metro Radio Arena, this time on the ground floor, I took a seat.

Above, before the stage's looming depths, a spotlight offered a broad, dark-haired, blue-shirted man. His North-West-accented voice boomed with inexhaustible and infectious jollity.

Early on, he produced a huge television camera, beamed the audience onto the two towering screens and acclaimed the audacity of one man in the aisle to stand and wave his arms.

Peter closed the show with "The Road to Amarillo" and "I'm Gonna Be (500 Miles)." The atmosphere was as charged as that of a concert.

As brightly as that of any Essence, Peter Kay's face had a vividness which commanded recognition. His features aligned to a likeness which I involuntarily and unmistakably traced to myself. I found myself reassured and encouraged to share in the likeness of one whose boundless joy was so renowned.

2011

Job

Bar nights when Barrowburn duty necessitated an early night, I devoted the early hours to writing.

Workdays, on three or four hours of sleep, I forced myself out of bed and into the bathroom to spend the best part of an hour in the shower.

At Barrowburn, while Dad patrolled the hills and Mam prepared the tearoom, Uncle Ross and I climbed the steep bank to the Deer Hut and Camping Barn. While I made beds, swept and dusted, Ross cleaned the cooker, fridge and bathroom – tasks which would have meant more soap and water for my perpetually dry hands.

I was helping my parents, I was earning a wage, and I had a writing project which I aimed to finish. For the first time, I had a definite idea of where I was going in life.

Leisure

In preparation for writing, I made a point of reading several pages of a book. Darren Ritson's *Supernatural North* (2009), given to me last Christmas by James, with awe-inspiring ghostly accounts from throughout my home region, fed my grasp of spectral lore.

On bus trips to Morpeth Library, I became engrossed in James Herbert's *The Secret of Crickley Hall* (2006). This soberly heartfelt, occasionally unflinchingly horrific tale offered fascinating conceptions of the spirit world, such as the apparent absorption by ghosts of bodily energy.

Branching Out

As summer neared, I took it upon myself to find as much as I could of the recorded career of Terri Hawkes.

Reacquaintance with *The Care Bears Family* rekindled my enamour of No Heart, surely one of the great cartoon villains. The soft, thunderous voice of Chris Wiggins drew a vivid recognition, an immediate familiarity which seemed to offer itself independently of twenty-year-old memories.

An online search revealed the actor to have been born in 1931, and to have moved at a young age from Blackpool to Canada. A monochrome profile shot for his perhaps most famous live-action work, *Friday the 13th: The Series*, showed a broad man, perhaps somewhere in his early sixties. From between a floppy trilby and a full, neat beard gazed distantly keen eyes.

As did its voice, this face impressed me with such instant clarity as with which I commonly perceived Essences. In light of my recent venture that transgenic kinship might be found in less obvious places, I saw it only fitting to attend the works of Chris Wiggins.

On Amazon UK, DVDs of *Friday the 13th: The Series* all seemed to be previously owned, and in the range of fifty quid, so I deemed it fair game to look for the show online.

Ownership of antique shop Curious Goods tasked Jack Marshak (Chris Wiggins) and cousins Micki (Louise Robey) and Ryan (John D LeMay) with retracing various cursed items. The three leads, in their affectionate bond, met imposingly macabre threats. The steely worldliness and muted joviality of Chris Wiggins' Jack Marshak, antique historian and stage magician, made for a reassuring opponent to the forces of darkness. While he spoke with a standardised North American accent, he at one point affected a Yorkshire accent, a manner of speech I'd thought to be widely unknown across the pond.

On pre-work nights, I'd take a break from writing and see off the day with an episode of *Friday the 13th: The Series*. Whether or not guided by some mysterious extrasensory insight, I dutifully beheld the face of Chris Wiggins. A bald, heavy brow and strong, mild features arrived in my gaze with sharp urgency and lulling gentleness. The face offered no obvious parallel but came to me with such eager clarity as with which I beheld Essences. Either way, I was glad to make this show's acquaintance.

Did recordings of body and voice retain a trace of sentience? Might engagement therewith bridge union, however faint, with the living originator? If so, I was proud to offer such support.

Obituary

Yahoo UK's news page held a recent publicity shot of Elisabeth Sladen, having recently returned to *Doctor Who* in 2006, then to star in CBBC spin-off *The Sarah Jane Adventures*. The actress, I now read, had died of cancer.

In my UK Gold and VHS-scraped glimpses of old *Who*, she'd lent the show an approachable wryness and an endearing blend of steel and vulnerability. As I understood her to be in her sixties, her untimely death didn't seem incredible, but was a harsh and sorry surprise.

Christopher Lee

A YouTube upload showed an excerpt from the film *The Return of Captain Invincible* (1983), in which Christopher Lee sang. The deep baritone heard briefly in *The Wicker Man* (1973) was here belted out with jovial, masterful harmony.

To see the famously unnerving stare offered in droll jest was great fun. High brow, dark eyes and high cheekbones aligned to such urgent clarity as with which I perceived Essences.

I had an appreciable grasp of the career of Christopher Lee; aged eleven, I'd seen *The Devil Rides Out* (1968) and, at sixteen, *The Wicker Man* (1973), said to be two of his favourite roles. Still, I had some catching up to do. Whatever trace of sentience lay in his many recorded performances would now be my privilege to attend.

From Amazon UK, I ordered a DVD each of *The Blood of Fu Manchu* (1968) and *The Castle of Fu Manchu* (1969), as well as a CD of Christopher Lee's 2006 debut album *Revelation*. The album cover showed Sir Christopher standing against a sun-drenched sandy clearing.

The album became a regular feature of my nightly wind-downs. The deep baritone was vocally dexterous and masterfully soulful, a comforting riposte to the supposed power of age to numb creative flair.

Fear

One night, before winding down with my CD Walkman, I sat on the two-piece suite where once stood my armchair.

On Dad's laptop, I clicked my way over to the YouTube channel of Jim Corr.

In a recently uploaded video, he noted the inclusion in water supplies of sodium fluoride. The chemical, said Jim, had been used by the Nazis to keep concentration camp victims in a state of mental docility, and now fuelled cancer.

Until now, cancer, and life-threatening disease in general, had sat on the edge of my understanding as a morbid spectacle whose devastation of lives was counterbalanced by the triumph of those who survived it; like death itself, it had no rule over the here and now. Jim's reinforcement of its threats roused in me a calm yet unprecedented desperation for disproof of his alarming claim.

Elsewhere online, I found a claim that sodium fluoride was really aluminium waste. It was said to accelerate ageing and cause cancer.

Whatever sodium fluoride really was, I'd been drinking it all my life. Its supposed threat to the lives of all around me anchored me with momentous sorrowful dread. After a frantic, fruitless search for reassurance, I went to bed. In the precious few hours before dawn, fretfulness refused to let me sleep. I ended up staying awake until it was time to get up.

Several hours later, in bright sunshine, I sat, alert yet drained, in the back seat of the car.

The dread gradually lessened its grip. On further online search, I found comfort in a denial of the chemical's supposed dangers.

Mortality

Aunty Dawn's cancer, I learned from Mam, had returned and was now terminal.

Burdened as Mam was by anxiety sown by the Widdrington doctrine of life's unmanageable horrors, she seemed to find joyous relief in Dawn's relaxed panache. The cancer's return brutally announced the inevitability of worldly decay.

Punch

Derek Landy Blogs Under Duress was updated with an entry I found unexpectedly thought-provoking. The *Skulduggery Pleasant* author, who had worked as a self-defence teacher, now discussed his books' candid depiction of the consequences of violence. The third book, *The Faceless Ones*, had seen fourteen-year-old Valkyrie Cain punched in the face by adult Billy Ray Sanguine, and had not shied away from the brutal consequences thereof. In such a fight, Derek now noted, the odds were against a fourteen-year-old, and he had been obliged to indicate as such.

He now stressed to readers the importance of self-defence.

At some point in my early to mid-teens, Dad had instructed me to keep my fist level with my shoulder, to launch it straight forward and, with just as much force, to bring it straight back towards the shoulder.

I now solemnly pondered the inevitability of life's brutality, the skill earned by the violently inclined to trample on the lives of others.

I tried another YouTube search for Terri Hawkes. I was delighted to find two uploads from the 1990 season of long-running American soap opera *General Hospital*.

Terri's hair, now black, lay in a neck-length wave. Beneath a pink and green jacket, a tight pink miniskirt framed black-stockinged legs.

In broad, lingering shots of a moderately lit office, "Robert Questions Wendy" showed Terri's character, Wendy Masters, to exasperatedly answer police questions.

I found myself frightened and saddened by the notion of Terri's hypothetical vulnerability to whatever combination of might and malice could supposedly reach her.

Life's brutality suddenly weighed on me in urgent visitations of sorrowful dread. So many people had the power to overwhelm and destroy others. Anyone, including those close to me, seemed to be vulnerable to this supposed fact of life. *Death Bringer*, this year's Skulduggery Pleasant novel, dwelled on the seventeen-year-old Valkyrie's increased study of unarmed combat, in case of confrontation with Remnant-possessed Tanith Low.

Since my inability to grasp instruction would hinder any such endeavour, I'd never got round to investigating the self-defence classes at Morpeth Leisure Centre. As verbal aggression numbed me with shame and giddied me with fret, I now envisaged my fighting prowess with scant confidence.

Terminus

On Friday mornings, James drove Mam to Morpeth's Cash and Carry for tearoom supplies, and then to the Waterford Lodge for such delights as ham and cheese paninis. Invited to one such excursion, I became engrossed and almost always rose on time for others.

In the shower, my compulsion to thoroughly ensure the shower head's cleanness often drew Mam's frustrated calls for me to hurry up.

Unsure of calorific content, I put down a burger or panini for several hundred calories. Having heard of revisions to a grown man's recommended daily intake of 2,500 calories, I'd increased my allowance to 2,900.

Furthermore, I repeatedly forgot to record the calorific value of my weekly three or four pints of cider and successive packets of crisps. Having forgotten how easy it is to gain weight, I was dismayed to find myself walking uphill with unexpected exertion.

By November, my weight had increased to fifteen and a half stone. I resolved to take it back off next spring, cold weather not being conducive to weight loss.

On my writing project, I often worked through the night, skipped sleep and went to work at Barrowburn the next day regardless. This tendency seemed to vex Mam almost as much as my compulsions. One such morning, when the car was halfway up the Coquet Valley, Mam burst into tears.

"I can't go on!" she wailed.

Throughout this year, I'd dwelled excessively on ruination. Sodium fluoride's alleged nurture of cancer, the untimely deaths of Elisabeth Sladen and Nicholas Courtney, and the terminal return of Aunty Dawn's cancer had shown the unpredictability with which a human life might succumb to destruction.

My handfuls of knowledge of the Second World War suddenly weighed on me in shock. Around the world, an insurmountable combination of circumstances had destroyed the lives of millions.

In mournful panic, I dwelled on the endless and inevitable capacity of circumstance to destroy. The world, it seemed, was a perpetual slaughterhouse, ever ready to crush on a whim the joys of any life. All anyone could do was cherish what they had while they could and wish with all their might against the potential brutality of its eventual passing.

In announcement of the latest studies, the media would warn the public of the need to guard against possible cancer causes.

I'd wondered if I'd re-encounter depression but hadn't expected it to be so soon. Throughout early November, I frequently fell into quietly panicked despair.

One night, as I listened to *Behaviour* by the Pet Shop Boys, closing track "Jealousy" pondered a disharmonious relationship. The slowly falling melody pleaded for reconciliation but remained forlornly resigned. For my current state, this seemed quite apt. I recalled some of Neville Chamberlain's 1939 announcement of Britain's re-entry into a state of war with Germany.

On YouTube, I re-watched the clip from *The Return of Captain Invincible*, in which the sixty-one-year-old Christopher Lee turned his imposing stare and masterful baritone to comic flamboyance.

This man, I knew, had served in the Second World War. He'd lived in a world gripped by cataclysmic brutality. I'd reached a point where I couldn't quite grasp how engagement with such destruction could allow for such a thing as fun. Yet here before me, on the screen and in my headphones, was indication that beyond a world of absolute horror, joy survived. This assertion didn't banish my fears but emboldened me with the notion of a possibility of their end.

Peter Kay's autobiographical *The Sound of Laughter* (2006) introduced a man who believed in fun. A call from a local phone box comically precedes his surprise visit from university and enhances the tenderness with which he and his mother reunite.

Such joyous nurture shone indifferently to the media's cant of life's constant risks. If human genes aligned independently of flesh, if my being was born in tandem with such as the Bolton comedian, must not life transcend its earthly environs?

I attended YouTube uploads of the "Fight on the Beaches" and "Their Finest Hour" speeches of Winston Churchill. The voice, with dauntless candour and heartfelt urgency, urged all who listened to live in defiance of the apparatus of earthly slaughter.

This man, who had himself served in war, now anticipated a conflict provoked by brutal tyranny. His call to fortitude, and aspiration to the joys to be found in peace, wove a conviction of care and courage.

The uploaded speeches played to slideshows of various paintings and photos. The face's hint of mirth affirmed that war could not, in its ravaging of the world, prevent the chance of a smile.

I cherished this indication of the power of courage to salvage joyous peace. While my fears remained, they were forced to share me with a conviction that things might get better.

One morning, having showered for the best part of an hour on little sleep, I sat in the living room. *BBC News* warned against an evening glass of wine. I recalled a claim of Rob Grant's *Fat*: that epidemiology standards had lowered to a point where it was possible to prove that just about anything caused just about anything else.

By now, my recurring bouts of frightened misery had worn off, leaving me with a mournful timidity, exacerbated by such broadcasts as mentioned.

At Barrowburn, as Mam, Dad and I sat in the small sitting room, I self-consciously summarised my recent worries.

"It's inevitable," said Dad, "that at some stage, something is going to kill you." His calm acceptance of mortality came as a profound comfort.

An End

James finally managed to rent one of the small terraced cottages that bordered the lawn behind our terrace. John moved into the now vacant bedroom, and I had our shared room to myself. I decided to take a break from my nightly writing project, thereby to rise at reasonable-ish times, see a bit more of life and generally reassure Mam.

One night, having braved a December visit to the Metrocentre, Dad and I returned to find Mam to have moved my desk from its corner of the upstairs landing and into my now solely occupied bedroom. I guiltily felt annoyed by this unannounced rearrangement of my stuff.

My bedroom light switch, over the years, had been touched by John and me on getting out of bed. Before or after removing the desk's draws, Mam would surely have touched the light switch. The desk would require treatment with several antibacterial wipes before I could comfortably use it again.

2012

Self-improvement

To my measured calorie intake, I'd fecklessly added a weekly panini and a twice weekly few pints of cider or measures of rum, followed by several bags of crisps.

Since then, my weight had increased from just over fifteen stone to fifteen and a half stone. Which goes to show how even seemingly slight excesses mount up. I decided to set about losing weight once the weather warmed up.

By February, I still hadn't resumed writing. Last year, such a lapse would've been unthinkable, much less excusable. Having unexpectedly found James at my desk reading my newly ordered copy of Peter (father of Dan) Aykroyd's *A History of Ghosts* (2009), I was in no doubt that his finger had touched the disreputable surface of the light switch.

I was no longer satisfied that my desk was clean.

I would have to wipe it again.

I didn't want to wipe it again.

When I used the bathroom, or touched the ground, or touched something that had conceivably been on the ground or made a purchase in a shop whose staff I deemed likely to have licked their fingers, I, at the very least, rinsed my hands beneath the tap, or, more often than not, soaped and rinsed them. Doing so was my only release from the invasive disorder of terrestrial debris, or the shame of bodily secretion.

I dreaded any obligation to resume this drudgery. An easily-postponed writing project proved insufficient motivation to undergo yet another visit to the sink.

Generally, I'd seldom spent much less than an hour in the shower. To clean the shower head of any conceivably lingering trace of bodily filth was essential. Such substances held a peerless shame. Potentially dangerously unhygienic, they threatened to drag me away from civilisation and into barbarism.

For me, this shame held overwhelming dread.

As spring neared, it occurred to me that the obligatory soaping and rinsing of the shower head might be achieved more efficiently were I to unscrew the head and rinse it with the detached hose.

To rinse all traces of used soap, my conscience was no longer satisfied with a few minutes' work. Fear of having missed a spot began to dawn. I began to realise that I could and should put more effort into rinsing. And then, into soaping. Just one more minute of rubbing, smearing and rinsing. Tedious, undoubtedly, but a small price to pay for peace of mind.

At every stage of the ritual, fear of having missed a spot demanded repetition of the same tasks: rinse repeatedly, rinse repeatedly again, apply soap, whoops, missed a bit, apply more soap, whoops, touched an unwashed surface, better soap hands again – whoops, are you sure you remember doing all that? Better start again!

"Andy, you've been in that shower for two hours!"

It was getting ridiculous, and I knew it. Not only was I sleeping until afternoon, but I was taking an average of two, and soon enough, three, hours in the shower. I supposed my compulsions to have been aggravated by lack of the focus provided by my writing project.

I would have to pull myself together and get writing again.

But for that, I would have to clean my desk.

And since it would take me years to finish this book, I might as well have another break from the drudgery of cleaning...

To measure my daily intake of calories, I lost all motivation. I gained half a stone more.

Murdoch Mysteries

"More wipes," said Mam as I returned home from the chemists' one evening with yet another packet of Wet Ones.

Cleaning my desk was quite straightforward. However, it required enough repeated wiping and hand-rinsing to justify momentary postponement. Or for abandonment halfway through, with fragile resolve to start again later.

In a general mood of sorrowful frustration, I sought to enjoy what I could of life. This, of course, meant private perusal of the Sky channels.

At one point, I saw the channel Alibi to air a slickly recent-looking period drama. Strong, soft lighting and neat camerawork showed brown-tinged sets peopled by suited, slickly coiffured, North-American-accented men.

I supposed that this setting might be Canada. Given my aim to further acquaint myself with this land's media, I decided to watch. Sure enough, the 1890s police station displayed a Union Jack. At a press of the "i" button, an on-screen synopsis box announced the show to be *Murdoch Mysteries*, a detective drama set in 1890s Toronto.

Throughout the next few weeks, I watched keenly for Essences among the cast.

The lead, Detective William Murdoch, was played by Yannick Bisson. Smartly cropped black hair; a high brow, high cheekbones and dark, patient eyes offered a profile in which I supposed I might yet see transgenic kinship. For now, I couldn't be sure.

Constable George Crabtree, played by Jonny Harris, with his slicked black hair, broad brow, merry dark eyes and finely high cheekbones, impressed me as similarly liable to reveal the mysterious familiarity I so cherished.

Inspector Thomas Brackenreid, played by blatantly genuine Yorkshireman Thomas Craig (formerly of *Coronation Street*, I later learned), with closely cropped red hair, broad brow and a stern, reflective gaze didn't obviously show transgenic kinship, but impressed me with such clarity as with which I perceived such distinction.

No Mere Shadow

I frequently visited the YouTube channel of WiiPlayer9Revisited, aka Chris, in search of updates on his planned visit to a Florida anime convention.

On the convention's website, Terri's recent headshot showed her hair to be cropped to just above the neck. The headshot, with its presentation of a facial greeting, daunted my instinctive fear of imposing myself on others.

Soon after the date of the convention, I was startled to see WiiPlayer9Revisited so soon to have posted the upload "Meeting Terri Hawkes."

Suddenly very nervous, I jerked my gaze away from the screen above the title, but too late not to register a still of a black-haired, bespectacled face leaning over a table. My imposition on this person, and the notion of the slightest indication of her vulnerability to such intrusion, gripped my chest with a heavy dread.

I clicked on the upload and scrolled instantly down. I wanted to do this gradually, with one instant of sound at a time.

Terri, however, was having none of that. The familiar voice instantly filled my headphones. "Would you like me to sign some? – oh, you're welcome, it's a pleasure, so we'll talk with you some more..."

"You don't mind if I'm recording, do you?" said Chris.

"No, I don't mind!" laughed Terri. "Are you gonna learn to write my signature?"

Chris, having had no cash for merchandise, asked if Terri might sign his shirt.

Across the white material of Chris's *Sailor Moon* tee shirt, Terri's black marker pen prefaced her signature with a print of "MOON HEALING ACTIVATION."

Chris asked if she might "give your best 'Moon Prism Power' impersonation?"

"Alright...!" said Terri, prompt but eager. "I have to do this." She removed her glasses and spread her arm diagonally – I recalled her website's account of the dialogue ritual – and called "Moon, Prism, *Power!!*" A grin split her face. "For Chris!" she giggled.

The woman in the uploaded video looked to be somewhere in her fifties. With eyes crinkled in glee, lips spread in affectionate mirth, her smile instantly outshone her age and synchronised the face with its deeds from long ago.

Age, while visible, failed to eclipse this beloved face. However, it announced a truth from which I'd managed to shield myself: much of her life had gone on without me. I could never directly savour her presence. While I allowed myself to desire the premaritally recorded image of a neighbour's wife and might even allow myself to savour post-marital images, she was twice my age and married. That smile would never be for me.

I hadn't thought I'd feel like this again: the panicked, inconsolable sorrow I'd felt after the 2004 Borrowed Heaven Tour, and the 2006 "kind of seeing someone" conversation in Woolworths. I wanted to sob.

Although my perception of Terri consisted of mechanically retained echoes of times long gone, these echoes, I held, shone living traces of her person – even if I could never know her directly, devotion to her recorded voice and image cherished a part of her that was, I idealised, no mere shadow, but, in some fragmented sense, lived.

A Dark Age

The year 2012 was, overall, a monotonous cycle of rising late, spending three hours in the bathroom and going downstairs to spend the late afternoon and early evening with my parents, whom my inhibitions now wearied more than ever.

I racked up heating bills, hogged the bathroom and showed no indication of any capacity for self-support. I could, potentially, force myself to shower more quickly, but only under such pressure as having to get out on time to go to Barrowburn; John's imminent need to shower for his job at the village Co-op or Mam threatening to turn off the water.

The foremost instigator of showering was contact with my bed. On several occasions, I stayed up all night. The numb, dragging sensation of sleep deprivation, while unpleasant, spared me the bathroom.

After a year of this unprecedented increase of my OCD, Mam and I agreed that I should seek some kind of help.

2013

Therapy

Online, I consulted a list of regional therapists who specialised in OCD and Asperger's syndrome. A thumbnail photo showed the face of a man whose face beamed an easy smile. His profile announced his name to be Tip Dinsdale. I decided to see what he had to offer.

Dad drove me to Newcastle. In a gloomy building, up a brief flight of stairs, lay the psychotherapist's office.

Intensely nervous yet focused by necessity, I entered, established contact and handed Tip Dinsdale twenty pounds.

Long grey hair was pulled at the back of his head into a ponytail. A loose green cardigan draped his small frame. In a soft, breathy, North-West-accented voice, he warmly welcomed me.

While my habitual, self-conscious shame made sustained eye contact uncomfortable, I responded keenly to his geniality.

Our assessment of my situation visited my sleeping habits. I mentioned that my younger brother had always fallen asleep long before me.

"I'm not interested in what your brother was doing," said Tip. "I want to know what *you* were doing." By his affected fervour and donnish garb, I gathered he thought the rebuke an endearingly dramatic emphasis of his care, soothed by the softness of his voice. Even so, the ire stung with a touch of frightened humiliation.

He introduced the concept of the "puppy brain," by which he likened the taming of OCD to shutting a puppy in a room with a floor covered in newspaper, a process by which puppies and kittens could be trained not to empty their bowels and bladders onto floors. The process took longer with puppies, said Tip, with an impish smile, "because kittens are more intelligent!"

I was instantly uncomfortable. With nothing against cats – Mam loved cats – I'd always despised this lauding of the daintiness of cats over the earthiness of dogs, and the equation of daintiness with such refinement as intelligence.

Tip prescribed a routine in which I went to bed at ten, simply to lie there until falling asleep, and rise at half seven. I stressed the implausibility of this. He settled for twelve.

His easy smile lulled me into a grateful esteem for the man who would see me through this dark age of my life. By the end of our sessions, he said, with a knowing smile, "you're going to have friends!"

A pause.

"What do you think of that?"

I meekly noted my natural introversion. Were he tilted thusly, he countered, he couldn't have a job whereby he could meet interesting people like me. I was too polite to argue.

I ended up listening to my wind-down music in the confinement of my bedroom and retiring around two. I'd recently found myself unable to stop listening to *The Ultimate Seekers Collection*, as given to me by Uncle Ross two birthdays ago.

My attempts at early rising, while inconsistent, remained fairly close to half seven. In early sessions, Tip seemed happy.

Would I like to play a game?

What kind of game?

"I won't tell you unless you say yes!"

A set of playing cards held various archetypal illustrations, dealing of which required an improvised connecting narrative. At times intensely embarrassed, I forced myself to play along.

One bright afternoon, Dad and I drove to the Metrocentre to see alien abduction chiller *Dark Skies*. A few miles out of the village, the Suzuki's right window overlooked a steep valley, cradled by rocky, heather-swathed hills. To our left towered the outermost pines of Cragside. I savoured the speed, the wilderness, and the ever-present chance of a familiar song on the radio.

These last four years had seen a rise to prominence of Taylor Swift. With her soft, strong voice and slightly old-fashioned blend of acoustic instruments, she was back on the scene. Late last year, she'd returned with the bouncy "We Are Never Ever Getting Back Together."

Her latest single, "22," now arrived on the car radio. Having several times heard snatches of the song, each listen endeared it closer to me.

By this point, I was in the habit of rising at about nine – far off the half seven mark, but much earlier than usual. Mam crossly lamented that I was making a mockery of what was being done for me. I passed this onto Tip. He affected a look of wounded sorrow.

He gave me a printed chart in whose tiny boxes I was to note any activity at each time of each day.

Instead of filling in Tip's chart, I recounted the week's events in prose. I wrote about a point at which I'd forced myself to visit next door, of how Granda Widdrington's fear of and seemingly minimal interest in the world mired his house in stultifying gloom.

I emailed the document to Tip.

Unkind

At the start of our next meeting, Tip's chirpiness was pointedly subdued. Had he got my email? Yes, he had.

Once we'd sat down, he lifted his features into a look of tender protest.

"I think you can be quite un*kind*!" he pleaded. "I think you can be quite judge-*men*tal!"

My muse on my grandparents' sedation, he complained, amounted to calling them "dull." I was "lucky to have" grandparents like that. My embarrassment at being asked by Granda Widdrington if I was still writing was misplaced – such supportive enquiry was "…*sweet!*"

My position on the autistic spectrum, I took Tip to imply, had blinded me to the cruelty of noting Granda Widdrington's desolate worldview, and to the heartlessness of being embarrassed by queries about my writing. Even in my nervous passivity, I couldn't help but be galled.

"Yes, and I think we'll have to work on that," said Tip.

"You don't know him," I had the front to say.

"I don't need to!"

Granda Widdrington's fear and pessimism had fed my mother's, brothers' and my anxiety. I realised the kindly intent of Granda's queries about my writing, and that my embarrassment was inordinate. Tip's charge of unwitting cruelty recalled the shame of unwitting social misdemeanour which had tarred me from First School. And here was this man, making the same charge on a fabricated basis.

"Now, that might seem a bit like *telling you off!*" chuckled Tip.

At the end of each session, he gave me a chart to fill in, sometimes after waggling a finger in his ear hole.

To my shower ritual, Tip proposed such modification as waiting until I left the cubicle before washing the shower utensils.

I'd worry about contaminated water lingering on my skin, I explained.

A small amount might linger, he soothed, "on your *arm...*"

My aversion to saliva was odd, as it came, he crooned, from "your *mouth...*"

I was uncomfortable at his soft, nurturing mention of my flesh. It lauded the bulging mounds of residual flab around my torso and the filthiness of my youthful toiletry inhibitions.

One June evening, Tip noticed my reluctance to use my left hand. He drew out a humiliated confession. Having hurried out of the shower, I feared, when donning my socks, to have touched a tainted droplet of water.

"It was sweat," he insisted. "It'll have slid down... your bum cheeks..."

Sickened by his mention of my base flesh, I was compelled to accept his thrusted bottle of antibacterial hand gel.

Heatwave

One night, winding down for bed, on Dad's laptop, I found a shot of an MTV Awards performance.

Amidst the audience, several dancers expertly held aloft Taylor Swift, who, microphone in hand, lay back for the ride. Her finely high-cheeked face, I realised, seemed to hint courtesy rather than aloofness and to veil a jovial affection – a similar realisation with which I'd fallen for Abbey.

Throughout a memorable July heatwave, the sky either glared blue or bathed in humid haze. On hot, thin air lay the sweetness of foliage. In the evenings that followed a scorcher, villagers wandered in a carefree lull.

On eventual emergence from the bathroom, I took a walk. The weather stirred in me a mix of excitement and longing. After four years' passive recognition of her heartfelt voice and tender melodies, I'd suddenly found that I absolutely loved Taylor Swift.

On days spent at home, I had a few hours with the house to myself. My first port of call was the music channels. A few adverts, one or two familiar songs to bridge the gap, more adverts, and there she was at last!

To bright guitar strings and soft drums, Taylor, in glasses and pyjamas, by the song "We Are Never Ever Getting Back Together," dismissed an old boyfriend.

In the video for "22," Taylor, in black fedora, white tee shirt and black shorts, cavorted with friends in ode to friendship as a balm to heartache.

In and around a school, as their childhood selves underwent extracurricular activity, she and Ed Sheeran, both off-screen, sang "Everything Has Changed," a tender call for postponed reconciliation.

Taylor Swift's voice and appearance dazed me with urgent joy. Her clear, smoothly rich voice had a sensuous candour. With her heartfelt, acoustic melodies, she was rather like the flip side of Avril Lavigne. Unlike Avril, and as with Terri, Taylor's features didn't show obvious transgenic kinship but had such clarity as that with which I perceived it. Taylor, in hair, face and frame, rather evoked Ashleigh Brewer, with some of the fine facial sharpness of Avril.

While I would always cherish recorded imprints of Terri, the fact was, she was married. To have such esteem for someone nearer my age soothed the loneliness with which I'd pined for Terri. Might such affection be ultimately fraternal? If I shared transgenic kinship with such people, might the resultant attraction have emerged, partially, in infatuation?

The thing to do, of course, was go and buy some albums. Destination – Northumberland Street's HMV.

The number of times I missed the bus was so ridiculous it wasn't even funny. Throughout a sultry July, having escaped the bathroom, I pelted down the pavement, only to see the bus rolling away. I hadn't got out of bed soon enough and had taken slightly too long in the shower. I hadn't been *swift* enough. The pun did little to lift my spirits.

I finally caught a 14:55 bus to Newcastle. By the time I arrived, the shops would be closed within an hour, but I hadn't come for a leisurely browse. The afternoon humidity and happily swarming pedestrians mocked my secret hunger.

On the second floor of HMV, on the edge of the "country" section, I found what I sought. The new album, *Red*, bore a shaded close-up of Taylor's dipped, fedora-hatted head. Her second album, *Fearless*, had the most hits I recognised; "Fearless," "Love Story," and "Teardrops On My Guitar."

Back outside on Northumberland Street, I held, in a small bag, my new CDs.

On Northumberland Street, someone had coughed on me. I planned to lean into the shower and rinse the back of my neck.

After doing so to my satisfaction, I emerged onto the landing to find that Mam had apprehended me. She wearily protested this breach of Tip's prohibition of my indulging such petty compulsions.

"Oh, you've got to be firm with Andrew," the psychotherapist had apparently said on the phone.

Each time I stole to the sink, Mam was obliged to challenge me more urgently than ever. This, supposedly, would aid our liberation from my bill-racking, bathroom-hogging insanity.

That night, with everyone else in bed, I washed my plastic-wrapped CD cases at the kitchen sink. You never knew – might someone have used the toilets in McDonald's without washing their hands and then fingered the displayed CD cases in HMV?

Might a shop assistant, when stocking the shelves, have left the CD case on the floor – which had been stepped on by shoes which may have stepped in spit or bird muck?

In the darkened living room, CD Walkman in hand, *Red* in CD Walkman and headphones on my ears, I stood near the middle of the floor. This year, I'd fallen out of the habit of listening to my CD Walkman, having increasingly opted for the quicker, more varied offers of YouTube – handling one of my precious CDs meant washing my hands.

Tonight, however, was different. I skipped ahead to track eight, "22." Lively drums, soft guitars and that light, strong voice arrived in pristine clarity. Saturated in glee, I set about getting to know Taylor a bit more closely.

Save for "Never Ever Getting Back Together" and "22," *Red*'s faster songs were awed by romantic highs and lows. While sometimes exquisitely joyous, the album was steeped in yearning, epitomised by the desperately wistful "All Too Well."

Fearless, Taylor's 2008 second album, dwelled on desires and woes more obviously shaped by adolescence. "White Horse," an almost sobbing lamentation of infidelity, was overwhelmingly sad. Opening track "Fearless" epitomised the album – at the joys of teenage romance, soft excitement fell to sadness-tinged awe.

With scant success on the OCD front, I blundered through my days in the new company of something which made me very happy. Dearly glad to know of Taylor, I savoured her every airwave arrival.

Transgenic Kinship

I considered *Murdoch Mysteries* star Yannick Bisson. The look with which he'd impressed me now seemed to evoke the broad-browed, high-cheeked, mellowly sharp-eyed distinction with which I accredited Dan Aykroyd, my uncle Ross, *Buffy*'s Nicholas Brendon, and Jim Carrey. Except for two, most of these men were from Canada. Might such lineage be particularly prevalent there?

As Constable Crabtree, Jonny Harris's dark hair, broad brow and fine, flexible features, as with Yannick, seemed to shine a subliminal familiarity with which I was used to recognising Essences. While I couldn't be sure, the correlation of his hair, brow, distant gaze and drolly manoeuvred mouth, I thought, rather evoked a male approximation of Terri Hawkes.

Might my supposed insight develop with age?

Might genes align outside the procession of one bloodline to another? Might I, by some rare positioning on the psychic spectrum, perceive genes which have spread in independent correlation? If genes, freely of flesh, spread themselves worldwide, does this indicate something manifest in, but beyond, matter?

Science's failure to explain consciousness is widely believed to hint the touch of something beyond the physical: spirit, soul. Near-death experience implies everything, down to the last blade of grass, to have a soul. If some people are tilted to glimpse people in a state beyond the confines of flesh – ghosts – then I, it seemed, was tilted to see genetic likeness beyond the limits of the flesh it shaped.

Outrageous

Tip grew increasingly frustrated with my failure to properly fill in his forms. As I gathered, their numerous tiny boxes were to be annotated with a description of what I was doing throughout the day. I either failed to retain this specification or failed to see how it was supposed to get me out of the shower.

"It's outrageous, what you're doing," he gently denounced my three hour showers. I couldn't really argue but was disheartened by the open contempt.

He raised the subject of housework. What domestic tasks had I been allocated in childhood? I recalled voluntarily ironing clothes aged nineteen, and my weekly dusting of the house these last few years. In a vain search for further examples, I paused. It didn't consciously occur to me that my mother had always preferred to work the house herself.

"It sounds like they've let you live the life of Riley," said Tip with a thoughtful frown.

A need for some semblance of progress overruled my now-assured resentment of this man. I managed to persuade myself that he just might yet help me.

Tip stressed that if I didn't learn to manage my showering and get a job, the eventual deaths of my parents would leave me helpless. Mam had repeatedly stressed this. Besides my aim of making it big with this book I was supposed to be writing, I saw no other outcome than being as bewildered by bill-paying as I had been by schoolwork, with vexed teachers replaced by revocation of electricity, gas, water, and finally, shelter.

To hear this fear voiced by the man who was supposed to be helping me briefly stoked my misery to a panic not far from where I knew to lie depression.

"You don't look very happy," said Tip.

In addition to early rising, sheet-filling and defiance of my compulsions by sheer force of will, Tip's cure for OCD entailed housework – even something as simple as cleaning out the fridge should lend productive focus.

As far as I was concerned, I was unemployable.

"No, I don't think you *are* unemployable," said Tip thoughtfully.

Inability to grasp technical instruction denied me so much as a driving test. I didn't just have a poor sense of direction – I barely had any sense of direction. I couldn't manage numbers. I had no qualifications suitable for anything other than menial jobs, which anyway seemed always to be doled out to the bright-eyed up-and-comers and the seasoned old grafters.

Even regardless of this, I wouldn't be able to get out of the shower on time. My only chance of making something of myself was writing a book. Any resolve to wipe my desk to a point where I was comfortable to resume writing succumbed to a need to escape the drudgery of endless cleaning.

"You're still not doing what I've asked you to do," said Tip, on reading a partially filled chart. Even going for a walk or sitting on the sofa, he said, needed mention. A twelve-year-old, he said, could grasp as much. I'd fallen, he said, into a trap of "laziness."

I was now divorced from any genuine persuasion that anything this man said could be of any help to me. For the sake of my parents' need for some kind of solution, I dulled my misgivings and went back. Along with several ten-pound notes, I handed him another form – which failed, yet again, to appease him.

"What am I gonna do with you?" he asked in a sing-song sigh. "What would *you* do?" he added disarmingly.

I decided it was time to accept his invitation to bring my parents to a session.

That bright evening, we arrived early. I decided to have a little walk around the district, got lost and eventually arrived at the clinic ten minutes late and racked with nerves.

"Calm down, Andrew," Tip dismissed my apologies. The joint meeting, it turned out, wasn't due for another week, but Tip welcomed it. He requested a recount of my daily approach to the bathroom. Mam began to explain. At one point, I offered a point of clarification.

"I'm asking your mother, Andrew," said Tip.

However gently uttered, the rebuke stung.

When it was my turn to speak, I described as "self-soothing" my tendency to stand outside my bedroom door and sway on the spot. Apparently, I'd misunderstood Tip's introduction of the term.

"Don't tell me my job, Andrew," said Tip. Despite, or rather aided by, its soft-voiced sanitisation, the rebuke crushed me.

Embarrassed, I explained the need I felt to wipe my writing desk.

"*Well, get ov*-er it, then!" wailed Tip. A hint of genuine ire, sanitised by droll, sing-song exasperation.

"Shan't," I murmured, unsure what to say to open aggression.

I ventured to my parents, with placating optimism, that perhaps I could attend one more of these sessions. Tip took this opportunity to further shock and humble me with my unwitting nastiness.

"I might feel a bit *insulted*," he said with a thoughtful frown. "'*I'll give you one more chance...*'"

The meeting drew to a close. On a parting note, my reluctance to maintain eye contact, said Tip, could sometimes come across as a bit "conde*scend*ing...!"

He pulled his face into a twee impression of an aloof squint – a playful, helpful indication of my unpleasantness.

"You look deep in thought," I offered. Such was my need to accommodate the caring professional, I forced myself to concede that my fearful shame of foisting myself on others might be misinterpreted as "haughty."

"Haughty's a better word!" said Tip. It wasn't. It implied that I could hold my disorderly self in some kind of grandeur.

I'd yearned to believe this man could help me. Beguiled by his smiles and chuckles, I'd afforded him an esteemed alliance.

At home, I confessed to Mam my doubts that Tip Dinsdale could do anything to help me. By email, I thanked him for his guidance and terminated our sessions.

Unbearable

The fading summer was marked by more of the despairing despondence which now permeated our lives.

Mam arranged further counselling, this time with my old therapist Dr Cara McGrath, in whose newly acquired Newcastle clinic a consultation session was arranged.

As Mam and I entered the spacious, bare-floored therapy room, I hovered indecisively between two vacant chairs.

"Where would you like to sit, Andrew?" said Cara.

Such courtesy roused an irrational sense of my being extravagantly indulged.

Throughout most of the consultation, I kept my gaze at a comfortable distance from Cara's. At one point, I conscientiously forced it to meet that of the therapist. She noticed and met it with a small smile. The irrational shame came like a slap across the face. Polite, fine-featured and scholarly, this face deserved better than to run around after the likes of me.

On the ride home, Mam seemed content.

Highlight

As the weeks reached a bright, cool autumn, Cara seemed satisfied with my attempts to touch surfaces whose contact made me slightly uncomfortable, such as floors or door handles, without washing my hands afterwards.

In Rothbury Library, I found a softback copy of last year's *Ash*, the final published novel by James Herbert, OBE, who had, in March, unexpectedly died at the age of sixty-nine. *The Secret of Crickley Hall* had whetted my appetite for another Herbert ghost story.

Ash's patient, nimble prose wove conspiracies, curses, exploding light bulbs and spectral orbs. Traumatised psychic investigator Ash and cautious psychologist Delphine had a touching vulnerability.

A walk to the library to read some more of *Ash* became the highlight of my week.

Sleeping Downstairs

My sessions with Cara ended with her application of a hypnotherapy session, whose CD recording she urged me to play at appointed times.

However, I'd happened upon a wondrously simple means of lessening my time in the shower: by sleeping downstairs. While it couldn't keep me out of the shower forever, it provided wonderfully extravagant bouts of freedom, whole days without the all-consuming desperation of a three-hour shower.

2014

Loft Conversion

This year would see the installation of Mam's carefully saved-for loft conversion: as well as a larger bedroom for Mam and Dad, this would allow a spare room for me in which to write.

One day in February, I came home from Barrowburn to find the hall, stairs and landing fitted with a walkway of protective plastic. Upstairs, the innermost half of the landing ceiling had been ripped out, revealing a dark, dusty cavern of bare brick and wood. Shortly after the removal of the ceiling, Mam later told me, she'd heard a violent succession of unaccountable bangs.

The Red Tour

Should her current Red Tour visit a nearby region of England, I repeatedly checked Taylor Swift's official website. However, all UK gigs were scheduled for London's O2 Arena.

Throughout January, James and I made several visits to the Metrocentre cinema. Towards the end of *Twelve Years a Slave*, I found myself resolved to try to get myself down to London for a night. As I joined Mam and Dad for our weekend drink at the kitchen table, I mentioned my plan. Mam wryly probed me for clues as to who I aimed to go and see.

I bought and printed off a concert ticket code, booked a room at the Peckham Lodge and wrote down the advised train stops.

To Central Station, John readily offered to drive me.

On the 9th of February, having awoken on the two-piece suite, I showered that evening.

Late that night, I found myself near-panicked with remorseful dread. The lifelong stress I'd caused my mother suddenly crushed me with longing for reconciliation. The brazen extravagance of tomorrow's journey, and the worry it would cause Mam, almost persuaded me to cancel. I wondered how I would cope at the O2, alone in a vast crowd.

Early next morning, Mam, with fretful urgency, ensured my leather bag was fully equipped. She urged John and me to leave before Nana arrived on her morning visit from next door.

At Central Station's WHSmith, I bought a *Viz* and *SFX*. At my stop, beneath a bright blue sky, in sharply chill air, I waited in nervous elation.

At King's Cross, I followed my handwritten directions to various points across the tube station, which proved encouragingly straightforward.

As I climbed the stairs from my final stop, I saw a poster of Taylor. In a sunlit forest, with a small smile, she modelled Keds footwear. For its hugeness, the gloomy station had a simplicity which was curiously welcoming. The sight of Taylor enthroned upon its wall made it all the friendlier.

Outside, across a network of car parks, loomed the unmistakable bulk of the Millennium Dome, also known as the O2 Arena. Before it, a few girls in replicas of Taylor's "22" outfit posed for photos.

I crossed to the halls within, presented my printed code and received my ticket.

I approached a taxi.

"Where ya going, mate?" called the driver.

"Peckham Lodge, please," I said.

Wary of post toilet non-handwashers, I told him to keep the change.

"Ah, nice one, mate," he said pleasantly.

In my small hotel room, I called Mam.

I couldn't resist leaning into the shower unit to wash my face. My woolly blue jumper and the long-sleeved shirt beneath it ended up soaked. There was nothing for it – I would just have to go in my tee shirt, a loose, faded brown affair, of which Mam had no great opinion. Not an ideal choice, but my fellow audience members hadn't come to look at my tee shirt.

At reception, I arranged for a taxi. Fumbling with my wallet, I exposed the concert ticket.

"Oh, is there a concert?" asked a member of staff. "Who's playing?"

"Taylor Swift!" I grinned.

Outside, the chill air felt oddly pleasant on my thinly sheathed torso. As the taxi driver left me near the grounds of the Dome, I had some initial worries about my ability to cross the network of roads.

In the now-darkened sky, across the building loomed a huge, illuminated poster of Taylor's fedora-shaded face. At the thought of missing her, my insides twisted with dread.

In the brightly lit relative warmth of the cavernous foyer, surrounded by hundreds of thunderously babbling fellow patrons, I phoned home to reassure Mam with a parting word of confirmation of my safe arrival at the venue.

I began an aimless wander around the huge round chamber. For an hour or so, I lost myself in its size, its sleekness, and its distance from all I knew. Having been soothed so far by the thrill of travel, I suddenly realised how far I was from home. Remorse for the sorrow I'd caused my mother resurfaced to weigh on me with a sadness that I felt might split me in half. Perhaps the ache would wear off, I resolved – with a little help from Taylor.

Feeling a bit better, I peered through one of many sets of double doors into a dingy horizon of round walls, whose floor sank into a vast amphitheatre. Support act the Vamps had already started. While their song sounded fine, its extreme volume, in my emotional exhaustion, was a bit much. I went for a slice of pizza.

Increasingly fretful, I continued to wander. A member of staff asked if I needed directions. I asked if he knew where I could find "the pit" and thanked him with a wave.

Back in the vast arena, I climbed down a staircase to a point well beneath even the lowest seats. In a huddled, slowly-moving queue, I showed my ticket to a balding usher, who addressed me as "sir."

Through the barrier, I arrived in a broad, crowded enclosure, walled at right and front by branches of the stage's walkway, and at left by the main stage, which lay about seven feet above the floor.

I lingered contentedly and stared up at a huge screen high above the leftward stage. My sorrowful nerves had mellowed and were further soothed by a screening of "22."

A further hour cranked the excitement to surreal heights. I was glad to have left my jumpers back at the hotel – it was like the middle of summer.

Abruptly, the air darkened, to raucous whoops and screams. From deep in the huge, darkened stage, guitars and drums began to pound the introduction to "State of Grace." Near me, someone screamed.

At the back of the stage, the towering red curtains suddenly held a huge white spotlight, in which stood a twenty-foot-high silhouette of a tall, svelte young woman in a broad-brimmed hat. Through electronic amplification, a voice, familiar yet wondrously new, filled the air with song.

To a thunderous eruption of cheers, the enormous curtains parted, and the spotlit figure of Taylor Alison Swift bounded happily downstairs onto the stage. Long blond hair now sleekly straightened, a black fedora, white blouse and black shorts immediately announced her unmistakable profile.

With a grin of unbridled glee, red microphone in hand, she skipped towards the middle of the stage. Wary of my imposition, but reassured by her total control of the situation, I gazed up at her face, whose fine features I could clearly make out. Perhaps because I was so near the stage, the sound amplifiers slightly heightened the pitch of her voice, but this was just another charm of being so close to it.

With projection and harmony to match that on the record, she belted out the rest of "State of Grace."

In soothed, exultant fondness, I was suddenly at total peace with the world.

After "Holy Ground," Taylor spoke.

"Welcome," she said with a small bow, "to the Red Tour!" With droll formality, she surveyed the audience. "I'm seeing a lot of different flags from different places. We have Londoners, we have people from all over in England, some of you have come from Scotland, some of you have come from Ireland! If this is your first time with us, thank you for coming. *Good* to see you. I'm Taylor!"

With song after beloved song, Taylor sang her heart out. About half an hour in came "22." A huddle of dancers lifted her onto their shoulders and plunged into the central standing area for a brief run among the audience. At the jovial yet sensitive song which had drawn me to her, I forced myself to abandon what remained of my self-consciousness and thrust my frame into the sideways sway in which I indulged at home – this was what I did instead of dancing. Only slightly nervously, I managed to do so several times throughout the night.

Taylor leapt, grinned and, especially for us, resurrected her songs. For hours, I absorbed it all in a delirious euphoria.

Towards the end, Taylor sat on a circular platform, which was mechanically lifted towards the central audience.

"It was a little presumptuous," she said, "but I thought I'd come and hang out with you guys for a bit." I hoped my unorthodox manoeuvres hadn't scared her off. As she spoke, she strummed a guitar. "This," she said, "is, to me, what a perfect first date sounds like to a hopeless romantic." She then gave us "Fearless," one of my absolute favourites.

The night drew to a close, but not before Taylor returned to the stage in a sparkling red coat and top hat, to launch into "We Are Never Ever Getting Back Together."

Near me, a lad around my age faced the stage.

"TAYLOR!!!" he shrieked at the top of his lungs, "*I LOVE YOU!!!*"

Good on the man.

"If you could please join in," said Taylor, before the final verse, "as loud as you possibly can...!" I obediently mimed along.

As the air filled with joyful screams, Taylor beamed, took a farewell bow with her musicians and dancers and, finally, vanished from view.

I felt a tickling sensation on my brow and looked up. From the distant ceiling fluttered innumerable red and white pieces of confetti.

Buoyed by memories that would last a lifetime, I joined the thriving procession through the exit tunnel and gave Mam a brief call.

In the chill night air, I joined the queue and boarded a taxi. The cockney-sounding driver made gentle conversation.

"Been to see the show?"

"Oh, it was brilliant!" I enthused in complete earnest.

Touched by his apparent concern for a lone young traveller, I made a slightly nervous but grateful effort to return his genial small talk.

Outside the Peckham Lodge, I sincerely bade him "have a good night!" and, rather thirsty, set about getting a can of Diet Coke and 7up from the lodge's drinks machine.

In my room, I once more called Mam.

"I've had an absolutely lovely time," I said.

Next day, the long journey home culminated that night with Mam, Dad and me sitting around the kitchen table with cans of cider.

General Hospital

Having seen three years ago a YouTube *General Hospital* excerpt to feature Terri Hawkes, I was now slightly amazed to find, in the accompanying thumbnails of related uploads, entire episodes of the 1990 season.

On episodes from April to July of 1990, I feasted my eyes. Softly lit sets and a meandering saxophone leitmotif mingled casualness with an ever-present chance of solemnity. Terri Hawkes' Wendy Masters, following a saga of coercion, extortion, unrequited love and deception, was cornered on an abandoned carousel and stabbed to death.

On *The Care Bears Family*, Terri had buoyed my four-year-old imagination. As *Sailor Moon*, ten years later, her voice had besotted me. At twenty-three, in *Prom Night II*, I'd finally seen her dazzling smile. And now, in these twenty-four-year-old episodes of an American soap opera virtually unheard of on these shores, she'd returned to overwhelm me with a need to comfort her.

While her beauty weighed heavily on my senses, I strove to see her obvious transgenic kinship with anyone else in the media. I still ventured a parallel with Jonny Harris: beneath a broad brow, each pair of eyes had a flighty intensity, which, with the rest of their features, often lent each face an expression of hesitant urgency. I noted their similarly smooth dark hair, as well as that of fellow Canadians Dan Aykroyd and Yannick Bisson.

Out of the Bathroom

Finally, I boxed my belongings, took them up to the small loft room that was to be my office and, on two bookshelves, stored most of my books, DVDs and CDs.

Mam, having taken a dislike to my old second-hand desk, had chopped it to pieces, which Dad had burnt. Tearoom patron Clayton Murray kindly gave me an old desk which he no longer used. It was time to write again.

The shower in the newly installed loft bathroom proved insufficiently powerful for my needs. Mam was despondently vexed, but ultimately tolerant.

However, the old shower had started to leak into the kitchen ceiling. Until the floor beneath its cubicle was repaired, any rinse longer than thirty minutes would cause more leakage.

To my mild amazement, fear of wrecking the house enabled me to contain fears that I hadn't soaped and rinsed enough, and I managed, until the shower was fixed, to shower within half an hour.

2015

Pills

One bright September afternoon, I arrived in the living room to find Mam having returned from her monthly doctor's appointment. During one of my walks around Whitton, Dr Redmile, whilst picking up her sons from the Middle School, had noticed my cautious avoidance of certain regions of pavement.

"Get him here, for God's sake," she'd said. "He doesn't have to live like that."

On a minute's walk up the street by our house, I once again found myself in the small, empty waiting room.

Afraid to defile the seat of my trousers with whatever substance may conceivably have touched the chairs, I remained standing. I hovered by the informative posters and feigned fascination in their warnings.

The solemnity of this place, this quiet realm of urgent consultation, crushed my chest with nerves.

Dr Redmile's arrival replaced my weary dread with manageable fret.

In contrast to the dim corridor, her surgery was brightened by a window filled with riverside greenery.

As ever, her voice, accented with mild Standard English, was professionally calm, yet permeated by a gentle levity. Her sober gaze was softened by flashes of a disarming smile.

As she spoke, concession to courtesy allowed me to face her. When I replied, I instinctively veered my face away from hers. Its femininity, gentle humour and kindness both touched me with esteemed gratitude and buckled me with irrational dread at my imposition thereon.

To my fears of fluoxetine's remote potential to rouse depression, she conceded, and instead prescribed the traditional OCD aid of routine and gradual desensitisation.

Despite my nerves, the encounter left me feeling cheered and encouraged.

I applied marginal resistance to compulsions. I sometimes managed to shower for fifteen minutes less.

A few months later, Dr Redmile read my typed summary.

"I'm not happy," she said with a disarming half-smile. I (wrongly) doubted a reference back to Alnwick's psychiatric clinic would yield anything further. Not being a psychologist, all she could further prescribe was medication. With emphatic assurance that it shouldn't cause depression, she prescribed something lighter than fluoxetine.

Still reluctant to surrender my body to unpredictable and likely fruitless augmentation, I kept the pills in the cupboard as a last resort.

Cardboard Boxes

As the year neared its end, John readily accepted my proposal to swap bedrooms. Residence in the loft would allow him more privacy in which to have his mates around to play guitar. I, with my bed in John's current office, would have direct access to my preferred bathroom. His box room bedroom would become my office.

When the move neared, I stored my belongings in Amazon-ordered cardboard boxes and carried them down to John's soon-to-be-vacated office. Following steam cleaning of the carpet in his current bedroom, I would transfer them there.

I felt guilty at the extravagance of my proposed swap, but its benefits had decisive appeal.

2016

The Rest of My Life

A deep chill gripped the air. Large snowflakes fell to land in a fine dusting. One such morning, having failed to get any sleep on the two-piece suite, I strode up to my office box room and typed.

Still feeling drained by lack of sleep, I wandered downstairs. Just then, Mam, in a mood of weary urgency, prepared to leave for the shops. It was time, she said, for us to talk seriously.

Half an hour later, we sat in the living room. At a current average of two and a half hours in the shower, I didn't think I'd been doing too badly. Mam's current concern, it seemed, was for the bigger picture.

While I now showered only every other day, showering for anything less than an hour and a half seemed highly improbable. Anything less than an hour seemed virtually impossible. The idea that I might ever find a way to financially support myself seemed ludicrous. In amicable frustration, Mam stressed the need for me to find it in myself to change. Over our insurmountable situation, her aggravation mounted.

At the weight of what we were up against, my emotions suddenly buckled. This wretched discussion, it seemed, was as much of a solution as would ever be possible. Even if I did publish a book, I would always, it seemed, be constrained by a need to exhaustively rid myself of any conceivable trace of bodily filth.

Even without such inhibition, my job prospects were minimal. I didn't have a bad sense of direction; I barely had any sense of direction. I couldn't manage numbers. I couldn't find things. I couldn't grasp instruction. I couldn't even drive.

I had no desire to engage with society. Looking people in the face made me ashamed of myself. Even if I published a book, it seemed that my time on this Earth had entered its closing stage. I'd always be trapped in a routine of endless washing. I'd end up alone and helpless. My lifelong awkwardness had reached its zenith and imprisoned us all.

The fate to which I'd been forced to condemn myself and my family crushed my chest and burned the inside of my face. My breath wrenched and fell into sobs.

Mam instantly sobbed with me.

"Oh, Andy, I'm sorry I've upset you!"

"This is the rest of my life," I moaned. "Life's a *shithouse!*"

With reflection on the years of anxiety that had been the lot of Mam, James, John and myself, we consoled each other.

"I think you're suffering from severe depression," offered Mam.

I wasn't really; I was miserable and couldn't foresee a time when I'd be free of what made me miserable.

In my wretchedness, I dared to disgrace myself further with mention of my regard for greatness, and how, in my second depressive episode, I'd found comfort in the wartime speeches on YouTube.

"He had depression, you know," I murmured. To intrude upon such eminence shamed me, but in my wretchedness, I bore it easily enough.

"Churchill," I murmured.

Pretentious as it may seem, I was sincere in my confession to have taken succour, in 2011 and now, in the eloquence of this man, whose ideals, both in the face of depression and Nazism, reached for goodness.

Even if I was to spend the rest of my life sealed in the privy, my secret glimpses of the world beyond the physical hinted a purpose beyond my constraints.

Sorry

In the bathroom, my compulsions thrived. Starting at around six in the evening, I ended up finishing a shower at an average of two in the morning. I decided henceforth to go to bed on every third instead of every second night, thereby limiting my bathroom ritual to every three days.

As the year neared summer, touches of cold and darkness lingered in the night. As Mam and Dad relaxed in the kitchen with a bottle of wine, I, in the living room, watched a new episode of *Murdoch Mysteries*.

Before going to bed, Mam entered the living room. I quickly anticipated something more than a goodnight.

With morose, weary indignation, she lamented my inability to escape the cycle of nightly pipe noises, large heating bills, and the resignation of my young life to endless dependence. Sat on the arm of the sofa, she stared at me.

Opposite, I stood before the mantlepiece. Against pangs of humiliation, I shielded myself in a funk.

Mam's indignation waned. She began to sob.

As her woe leaked, I stood there quietly. Once more, I sensed the lifelong sorrow with which my mother had lived, the anxiety which had passed to me, thereby to feed itself with the inhibitions which had paved my road to perdition.

Throughout my life, any evocation of the tenderness of parenthood, be it a misplaced child's toy or Great Ormond Street Hospital's cartoon emblem of a weeping, smiling infant, stoked in me a sense of horrified loneliness – as if I'd rejected the love such images evoked. It now boiled through my chest in a tectonic collapse. I sobbed.

Mam beseeched me not to; she couldn't stand to see me thus.

I sobbed harder.

"Sorry," I blubbered, making no effort to contain my voice's indecent tremor. "You've no idea how sorry I am for what I've done to you."

Under most circumstances, my pretension to such nobility would be shameful, but I was desperate to make any amends I could.

Mam replied in kind.

"I just feel so sad for you," she wailed.

"I'll do better," I moaned, even though I didn't see how I could.

Exhausted, we parted for the night with a long embrace.

Dimensions

After preparing the Deer Hut, I stole through the tiny Barrowburn kitchen, where Mam, Dad and James bustled in attendance of the tearoom's chattering customers. In the small sitting room, I opened Dad's Chromebook for an online browse. A whim drove me to seek whatever preview Google Books might have of James Herbert's *Once* (2001).

In 2011, I'd found the novel in Morpeth Library. The huge black hardback announced Herbert's depiction of faeries, demons and witches. I then read a scene in which twenty-seven-year-old carpenter Thom Kindred wakes to find the lips of a bug-eyed fiend clamped around his penis. An improbably short, wizened man arrives to whack the beast with a broom handle. He urges Thom to open an ancient book, whose pages then release a fleet of tiny, gloriously glowing winged beings. In the following chapter, the brownie, Rigwit, explains his kind, the *faerefolkis*, to dwell between vibrations generally beyond human perception.

I succumbed to my fascination and bought the e-book.

I could barely tear myself away from it. Thom, recovering from a stroke, leaves his London carpentry shop for childhood home Little Bracken, cottage guest house to sixteenth century Shropshire manor Castle Bracken. The rural setting is described in awed, knowledgeable detail.

In the estate's woods, Thom happens upon a petite, naked young woman, who reclines against an oak and, with the aid of several tiny glowing winged figures, candidly masturbates. After the ordeal with the succubus, she arrives at the cottage door and introduces herself as Jennet. The elemental, interdimensional *faerefolkis*, instead of bodily birth, gradually emerge into being. Their lives centre around the nurture of nature, enabling the planet to support life.

(*Spoiler alert!*)

Having evaded attempts on his life by witchcraft practitioner Nell Quick, Thom learns of his inheritance of the Bracken Estate. On return from a hospital visit to physiotherapist Katy Budd, he vows to turn the manor into a specialist children's hospice, in which, he ventures, the *faerefolkis* might intervene. Jennet reveals this to have been his preordained vocation, that discreet healing by the *faerefolkis* will help steer humanity back to peaceful coexistence with their elemental forebears.

The book, written with affection, fascination and compassion, was nothing short of mind-blowing. It soon became one of my all-time favourites.

I wondered just how much Herbert's research had gleaned. In *Once*, some humans are sufficiently psychically orientated to see through the cosmic vibrations into the realm inhabited by the *faerefolkis*.

My own strange glimpses – the transgenic kinship between recorded and broadcast faces, the meandering nightly aeroplanes, and the stars which, in clear skies, I'd seen bloom into and fade from visibility, I supposed, seemed to have reached me by some kind of insight into a plane beyond the limitations of matter.

The angelic being who resembled my two-year-old self, seen by Mam to scale the bedroom wall, the disembodied voices and unaccountable bangs heard by her, James and, recently, the sceptical John, were, I supposed, glimpses of a dimension not commonly seen by most. Dad, who for years had claimed not to believe in ghosts, later mentioned his clear witness of a teacup in Nana and Granda Widdrington's house to independently rotate.

Invigorated by the insight of one of my favourite novelists, I forced myself to return to my office at least once a week.

The Black Secret

While progress was slow but consistent, my daily mood was anchored, slightly but irresistibly, by a regret whose alleviation was, as far as I could see, impossible.

Until the age of ten, as I lay awake in the early hours, I would read randomly from one of the paperbacks stacked on my bedside drawers. At this age, I took lying in bed as license to explore forbidden bodily regions. Well, I'd wash my hands in the morning anyway, so as far as I'd seen, no harm done.

But, as I now solemnly recalled, my hands, in between illicit wanders and morning wash, continued to turn pages. In my defence, I'd reserved this savage fate for only a few books.

On my Friday evening supportive Maths tuition with James's piano teacher Miss Hammond, we often discussed our shared love of science fiction. I happily rattled on about the film *Mars Attacks!* (1997) and its novelisation, which I happily lent her.

If memory now served, the book had been one of those I'd read in bed – with less regard than usual for nightly hygiene. From my bedroom, I'd released the book to pass it into the hands of a friend.

As quickly as a year later, I'd realised this to be a singular outrage, but lived out my days secure in its confinement to an isolated incident.

Sick

One night, with everyone else in bed, I planned to do some writing. In a pan on the cooker lay some spare bolognese mince, as it had since yesterday afternoon. I heated it in the microwave and ate it.

Big mistake.

An hour later, at my desk, I felt a tightness in my stomach. I decided to go to bed early.

Next morning, the tightness grew into an uncontrollable nausea. I found myself retching violently and successfully.

Supplied by Mam and Dad with fresh sheets and a basin, I spent much of the next two days asleep. The next night, as I prepared for the bathroom, Mam came for a final inspection. Overwhelmed with gratitude, I succumbed to ashamed sobs.

The shower that night was worse than ever. I was dragged back, time and again, to further application of soap and water. Instead of my usual eight hours, I was, that night, in the bathroom for nearly twelve hours.

For a well-earned semi-retirement, Mam and Dad had this year relinquished the tenancy of Barrowburn, which they now attended solely to see to the animals and to declutter. I, still weak, chilled and shivery, would be little help, so stayed home.

By the gas fire, I watched some of the *Coronation Street* omnibus.

Having half-watched the flagship soap until 1999 when Mam had taken on chef work, I'd recently been easily absorbed by its quiet streets and recurring faces.

The faces of many of the cast offered a vivid, lingering distinction which I, on principle, aspired to attend. Colson Smith's Craig Tinker, a gently spoken lad who looked around late teens to early twenties, persuaded me of visible transgenic kinship. A high brow held eyes focused in pensive hesitation. I traced the face's structure and expressions to Peter Kay and myself.

I henceforth made a point of now and then looking in on *Corrie*.

By November, the Tait family would have left Barrowburn. I planned to have a nose around Rothbury Bakery for night shift cleaning jobs, but my hopes weren't high.

While my bathroom ritual had increased to an average of ten hours, my writing was sparse yet frequent. Life was slowly progressive, bar one thing: on a daily basis, I was dragged back to the realisation of having done something at the age of ten which, I felt, barred any right I had to esteem or fellowship. A combination of neural formation and anxious confusion, it seemed, had blinded me to the need to protect society from my bodily filth.

The thought of what I'd done lingered in stagnant, dreading sorrow. Ambition shrivelled and died. I lay in bed until six in the evening; a few more hours' softness, stillness and warmth seemed preferable to another ten hours' graft, only to escape from the bathroom into a world where I'd never be free of self-contempt.

I considered seeking a regressive hypnotherapist, who might, I dared to dream, reveal my damning memory to be a fabrication.

I retreated further into YouTube, listening for as long as I could to old favourites, with one addition.

I'd found uploads of an excerpt from DreamWorks' 2000 biblical cartoon *Joseph: King of Dreams*. I'd always liked the song

"Better Than I." In the walled underground cavern of his Egyptian cell, as rain falls through the ceiling grill, Joseph (voiced in speech by Ben Affleck, in song by David Campbell), for his banishment into slavery and unjust imprisonment, rails at God. The storm abates. Exhausted, Joseph sees, on a floored twig, a single leaf. The extra-diegetic song then soothes him to acceptance of both chaos and peace as ordainment of a supreme will. Alone and imprisoned, he aspires to the Will which wove his lost family, his misfortune, and the tree which now blooms under his care.

Soothed by the melody and sweeping visuals, I reflected that while I held seemingly unbearable shame, my purpose remained.

I resolved, before I did anything else, to consult my GP.

When she returned to the Rothbury Practice, I seized an appointment with Dr Redmile and typed my woes into a file to print off.

Raptly nervous as ever, I finally sat opposite Dr Redmile. I'd worded my transgression as delicately as I could.

As she read, I pondered her imminent reaction. I vaguely expected well-hidden disgust, kindly sympathy and tactful bewilderment as to just how a GP was supposed to ease my inordinate angst about a childhood indiscretion. General Practitioner or not, it really was indecent of me, I supposed, to impose on anyone such a nauseating account.

From the creased paper, her gaze rose to regard me solemnly.

"I'm so sorry for you, Andrew," she said.

With neither bafflement nor disgust, she met my misery with total kindness. I felt a shiver of esteem for this compassionate professional.

With a gently amused smile, she stressed the frequency with which young children sent their hands to forbidden regions.

Her sympathy with the epitome of my degradation – her unequivocal indication of my acceptability – took much of the edge off my woe.

2017

Back in the Saddle

My family had now left Barrowburn. No more would Dad drive off each morning, including Christmas Day, to feed the dogs (who had now all been found nearby homes) and patrol the hills. No more would Mam hurry out of the house with him Wednesday to Sunday to manage the tearoom. No more would I force myself off the two-piece suite on two hours' sleep, drag myself up the bank and force myself through bed-making, dusting, fireplace laying, sweeping and a hell of a lot of handwashing.

On release from my ancestral livelihood, latterly honed to my mother's culinary vocation, I felt a faint wistfulness. While I'd been grateful to help in return for a wage, I wasn't ashamed to admit my relief to be free of accommodation duties. Hours in the bathroom had taught me to savour every instant of leisure.

Mam had replaced our living room upholstery. I now slept in a squashy red armchair and found myself waking up to find my parents in the living room with me. Together, we became fondly acquainted with *Father Brown*.

Mam kept an eye out for prospective tearoom property.

At the bathroom sink, moderate yet critical anxiety drove me to completely layer my hands and forearms in soap. Urgently repeated soaping nurtured persistent concerns of having missed a spot, which roused me to desperation.

The process of soaping alone rose to an average of three hours. Rinsing my arms and the sink took an average of two more hours.

In the shower, my heightened wariness of any conceivably lingering trace of bodily filth spawned a mob of obstructive fears. Like the heads of the mythical Hydra, each worry, once dealt with, was replaced by another. Fears thought banished lingered in a regenerative mire of uncertainty and, like the legendary Lambton Worm, reformed themselves to strike again.

On my uncertainties, my fears of uncleanliness gorged themselves. I reached an average of twelve hours in the bathroom.

I was now worse than any of us had dared imagine possible. Mam mentioned having read of an obsessive-compulsive woman who, by twenty-or-so-hour showers, had been killed.

As far as I could see, my only chance of reducing my bathroom sentence was finding something to get out for, a paramount motivation with which to constrain the rampant fears which bred the compulsions: in other words, a job.

The only job I supposed I could feasibly do would be some sort of cleaning work, preferably a night shift. Several local accommodations advertised cleaning vacancies. Would I make it out of the bathroom in time? The nightly cleaning shift at the industrial estate's village bakery sounded ideal, but they never seemed to have any vacancies.

I clung to a vague idea that some kind of liberation might lie in completion of my duty to the broadcast and recorded faces in which I believed myself to see supernatural similarity, i.e. writing this book. However insurmountable my inhibitions, my calling came from beyond their material roots, and would be answered. *When you are going through Hell,* I recalled the famous Churchill quote, *keep going.*

With a zest born of fret, I resolved, every second night, to launch myself upstairs into my office, and to keep the paragraphs coming.

As January dragged, a fierce chill smothered the air in fog, ice and snow. I wrote not only through the night, but some days.

One dark afternoon, as Mam threw herself into recreational baking, I, at long last, reached a pivotal moment: the night of the Borrowed Heaven Tour.

In observance, I listened to "Winner" by the Pet Shop Boys.

Bucket

Mam and Dad now used only the loft bathroom and downstairs toilet.

The compulsions gradually and inevitably amassed to keep me in the bathroom until around six in the morning.

As I dried off in my office, Mam would sometimes call through the door in protest at a night disrupted by hissing pipes and the stench of soap.

There really didn't seem to be any end to this. I still aspired to my function to tell the world of the Essences, but what then? Andrew Tait, novelist? I couldn't bring myself to write emotionally layered stories. In such moments as this, the idea that I ever could was stifled by shame at the farcical outrages I imposed on my family.

The rest of my life seemed to hold endless hygienic toil, and resultant misery for all.

Most people seemed to want to breed, or at least a relationship. Human life's prerequisite seemed to be hours of barely conceivable agony. The resultant newborn then faced a lottery of devastating horror.

However, in the joy with which some met life, I saw astounding, liberating beauty.

I recoiled from the thought of imposing myself on such delicacy as romance, and the stifling obligations thereof.

I recalled Nick Dismas, hero of James Herbert's *Others*, whose bodily deformity, he eventually learns (*spoiler alert!*), has been part of a redemptive test for misdeeds of a past life. On having fulfilled his mission to free the deformed inmates of a brutal research centre, he expects soon to die of a brain tumour and be reunited with his beloved Constance.

I pondered the ease with which I might drink something lethal. I barely dared to think of the resultant devastation that would shape the rest of my family's lives.

In my lowest moments, I wondered whether I could bring about all this. I found, on the absolute whole, that I couldn't. I couldn't, ultimately, want to die. Draining as my shame and misery were, they were temporary. My joys, crowned by life with my family, reigned above any morbid desire for ultimate relief. Even if I couldn't conceive of as much, I lived with the eternal possibility that things might get better.

And for a while, they did. Under unprecedented pressure, Dad resolved to, at 10 pm, turn off the water. Two buckets would be filled with which to flush the toilet in the loft bathroom.

In my bathroom, fear of my parents' unwashed hands constricted my compulsions into a much briefer performance of each ritual. At five past ten, after about four hours in the bathroom, I emerged, free as a bird.

This dizzying relief would last two months.

Within that time, one spring evening, Mam told me of James's recent session in the Jubilee Hall with Lynne, a local spiritualist, known to James through his music commitments. During the private card reading, Lynne had been shocked by a sudden chill.

"Who's Andrew?" she'd asked. "Andrew's got to stop scrubbing," she'd breathed in shock. "He's killing himself."

Alnwick

On my thirtieth birthday, I woke early, forced myself off the chair and, to Alnwick, took the newly installed Spirit Bus.

Beneath a hot blue sky, I wandered quiet, sloping streets, had a look at the famous castle, and got a slice of pizza from Greggs.

I climbed the pavement to a rightward hill. A busy road and huddle of trees bordered the old station house which housed Barter Books.

Childhood visits here had reaped Terrance Dicks' novelisation of *Destiny of the Daleks* (1979) and Ed Naha's novelisation of *Ghostbusters II* (1989).

On several recent visits, I'd become more enamoured by the soft gloom, hall-sized chambers and splendid model trains which, above the shelves, whizzed along on mounted tracks. On the horror shelves, which had once boasted a bloodied rubber hand, I'd been delighted to find several James Herbert novels.

I now picked up a hardback copy of *Portent* (1992) and withdrew to the murky larger end, where I stayed for about three hours.

Dr James Rivers learns of a new generation of children's extrasensory affinity with the ecosystem. (*spoiler alert!*) Psychic reunion with nature, Rivers realises, may enhance humanity's relationship with the planet. It was so nice to see a heavily overweight character, Hugo Poggs, portrayed favourably.

I pondered a recurrent implication of Herbert stories: that extrasensory insight might unite humanity in a deeper understanding of the world.

In *Once*, psychically tilted humans are said to see into dimensions traversed by ghosts, UFOs and the elemental *faerefolkis*. (*spoiler alert!*) In a children's hospice founded in the Bracken Estate by Thom Kindred, miraculous healing by the *faerefolkis* may aid gradual human reunion with the elemental forebears whose nurture of nature enables the planet to support life.

In *The Secret of Crickley Hall*, such insight reveals to Lili Peel the progress of discarnate spirits to a peaceful higher dimension.

In *Portent*, young Joshua and Eva can heal by touch, sense distant physical change and project their minds into a lush, expansive garden, in which they meet similarly able children.

If worldwide genes do in fact align independently of matter, and some kind of psychic orientation allows me to sense this, might a human face hold further ethereal secrets?

Through the right psychic modulation, could casual conversation glean not just regional accent and ethnic background, but locational, social and genetic history – not just in humans, but perhaps, eventually, all objects, living and inert?

Might such insight enable us to see beyond instinctual cultivations of anger and fear? To modulate them? To discard the confusion which genders cruelty?

Might our advancement lie not only in mechanical replication of our senses, but in the liberation of our senses from the apparent constraints of matter?

As summer began to fade, I spent nearly every second day in Alnwick.

On many a warm, quiet morning, I bought a bottle of something fizzy from WHSmith and lingered in the town square to watch the intermittent bustle. I then wandered up to Barter Books to lose myself in a previously owned copy of a James

Herbert novel. In the ambitious notions of a man who dared to see good in the world, I took comfort.

Around five, I'd wander back down to the town centre, buy another bottle of something fizzy and, by the stone cross which overlooked the cobbled market square, watch the diminishing bustle herald the dimming of the day.

Enough

As we all probably knew it would, the new deterrent of turning off the water by the set time of ten was starting to lose its hold on my compulsions. Ten o'clock would arrive, and I wouldn't quite be ready. A trace of contaminated soap lingered and required just two, just five, just fifteen more minutes for me to rinse it away. By eleven o'clock, I was in no doubt that within mere minutes, I'd have finished and be able to slip downstairs out of everyone's way.

"We've had *enough*, Andy!" Mam wailed through the door, on hearing another such plea.

I yelped with desperate conviction that my task required minimal further attendance.

A few nights later, Mam finally got sick of threatening to turn off the water.

Without the primary fear of the water being turned off, I now attended each stage of the ritual with no desperate urgency with which to concentrate my efforts. On this chance to reproduce, my fears gorged themselves. Inch by inch, I required slightly more reassurance of the completion of each task. My fears fed on this uncertainty to stifle me with the relentless possibility that I wasn't quite clean.

I despised my surrender to petty notional fears.

I lamented the reckless punishment to which I subjected my body.

I abhorred the outrage I imposed on heating bills, and on my mother's attempts to sleep.

But I could not, and would not, inflict on the world a body tainted with the slightest conceivable trace of any substance which would drag me beneath adult civilisation. If I was going to spend the rest of my life imprisoned by this insanity, there was no way I was going to do it without an iota of the dignity for which I so sorely yearned.

Within a few weeks, my old pal Twelve Hours was back.

Why had I shied away from any help on offer from Hawkhill, Alnwick's psychiatric clinic? Largely because I supposed all they could prescribe was gradual desensitisation. What chance had that against a twelve-hour shower?

However, there was nowhere left to turn.

To Dr Redmile, Mam confided the latest depths to which I'd sunk. For me, the GP arranged a Hawkhill appointment, scheduled for October. A tender gratitude towards Dr Redmile warmed my meek resolve.

Magic

As I walked through Alnwick, my general despondence eased. In Barter Books, I made for the horror section and was glad once more to pick up James Herbert's *The Magic Cottage*.

Session musician Mike Stringer and illustrator Midge Gudgeon move from London to Gramarye, a somewhat dilapidated but idyllically peaceful Hampshire cottage. Rural splendour is presented with infectious fascination and delight. Glimpses of a distant silhouetted figure on the surrounding land hint the horrors to come.

Towards the climax, I recalled my brother James's mention of Herbert's venture that the universe had, in some way, been created by emotion. I treasured this notion of life to stem from forces which dwarfed its limitations. I found *The Magic Cottage* uplifting, a heartfelt assertion of hard-earned, benevolent optimism.

Thoughts of my bathroom returned with fears of what the passage of time might do to my parents, and whether I'd be able to help them, or even support myself.

While bearable when I was out and about, the thought reasserted a sorrowful dread which, when I woke in bed, pummelled me almost to despair.

A ride past the glorious moors to a fine old market town in which to read James Herbert novels all conspired to embolden me.

Nineteen Hours

Almost as if it knew the sun might soon set on this zenith of its reign, my obsessive-compulsive disorder increased.

At the bathroom sink, application of soap had, until recently, taken an average of an hour.

I pressed the pump on the liquid soap bottle and, into my cupped right hand, discharged a hefty glob. I clenched my fingers, so as to drive the soap beneath the nails.

Into my cupped right hand, I then pooled another massive glob of soap, into which I plunged the nails of my left hand.

There followed numerous, relentlessly repeated stages of trying to completely cover my hands and forearms in soap. I was incessantly persuaded that I might have missed a bit. Reassertion and rectification of these doubts chased each other in an endless flurry which dragged from minutes to hours. And then it was time to wipe and rinse the basin and taps.

By August, when in the bathroom, I took an average of five hours to wash my hands.

Once in the shower cubicle, I ached for the instant in which I would lay down the hose head and leave this place for another two days.

For an average of an hour, I applied shower gel to my upper body.

For an average of an hour and a half, I hosed my lower body until my demented conscience was appeased.

For hours, I repeatedly applied soap.

The final rinse was the easiest bit, although even this could go on for hours.

By September, my time in the bathroom every third day took an average of nineteen hours. I would go in at around six in the evening and come out at around three in the following afternoon.

In the final month before help came, I, and I think everyone else, lived in a kind of exhausted daze. This latest extreme was barely credible, but arrangements had been made for its aid.

On September the 30th, the day of James's and Granda Widdrington's shared thirty-sixth and seventy-ninth birthday,

I emerged from the shower around three in the afternoon. Mam didn't want me going outside straight away; my face and arms had been bleached to an alarming pallor.

In a daze, I eventually hovered over to the village Co-op and bought James a bottle of whiskey and Granda a box of Liquorice Allsorts.

Back home, I sank into my chair and slept.

One such day, just before I fell asleep, brought me a phone call. A man's voice greeted me in an accent I associated with southern Northumberland. Its speaker introduced himself as Tim, psychiatric nurse. He offered me the option to hold our arranged meeting either at Hawkhill or here.

"Could you come here, please?" I said.

A week later, after rising early, I emerged from the bathroom at ten o' clock the following morning. At eleven, Tim arrived. Slightly shorter than me, his easy smile and attentive voice offered gentle confidence.

By way of introduction, I told him I'd just spent nineteen hours in the bathroom.

His instant rapport with my parents recalled his patronage of the now-discontinued tearoom and adoption of one of Shona's puppies.

We went through a questionnaire, which asked whether I'd considered suicide.

"That's not a nice way to go!" said Tim, of my contemplation of drinking toilet disinfectant. To my family's shared despair, his sincere joviality was antithetical; by its very existence, it denied the impossibility of improvement.

Tim

And so began our invasion of the bathroom. Each week, we assessed each ponderous stage of the ritual. To the easier stages, Tim advised marginal reduction. Rather more confidently than I felt, I proposed an attempt, on arrival at the bathroom sink, to take two rather than three hours to apply soap to my hands and forearms.

To my slight amazement, I found it working. A set time limit imposed a sense of urgency, a directive to perform the task not only thoroughly, but within a precise amount of time. This urgency dissected the anxiety which spawned the compulsions and diverted it into an urge to get the job done on time.

During our sessions, Tim made jovial conversation, which took in my visits to Barter Books. He gleaned my love of sci-fi and horror and noted his penchant for a writer by the name of James Herbert.

"I'm on my fourth book by him this year!" I enthused.

To dissect my compulsions, Tim equipped me with a scalpel of logic wielded by a hand of fortifying fellowship. If I could even slightly resist a compulsion, we established, the discomfort would soon ease, and resistance to further compulsions would come more easily.

Wary of taking from the taxpayer weekly money in compensation for the employment I couldn't attain, I was persuaded by Mam's argument that she and Dad had been paying taxes for years, and by Dad's argument that Mental Health Benefit was my only assured means of future financial support. With a few phone calls and a letter, good old Tim arranged it.

Home

The year neared its end. Minutes, then an hour, then two, then more, fell away from my bathroom time. My regular two days' freedom from the bathroom, already invaluable recesses, were now infused with optimism.

On my chair, I'd wake around three in the afternoon, go into the kitchen and have a cup of tea. I'd then return to my place by Mam's old Chromebook to read, look at pictures and type story ideas.

To my right, the telly would often air a repeat of *Only Fools and Horses*. Years of ambient exposure to the exploits of the Trotter family had sown my affection for these lovingly drawn characters. I now positively delighted in any return to this South London stronghold of undefeated humanity.

The aspect of Sir David Jason had always immediately drawn my attention. While his dark hair, broad brow and flexible features registered with such vividness as with which I might perceive an Essence, I'd failed to conclusively match his features with those of any other face.

But now, I was starting to wonder. His brow and eyes now impressed on me a distinction which roused familiarity, a sense that a variant of his expression had inhabited others faces.

The broad brow, amused eyes, and steely, lilting voice, I was now confident, paralleled those of Sylvester McCoy.

I undoubtedly believed in the perceived phenomenon, which, back in 2005, I'd received with awed jubilation. As I took definite steps towards the completion of its chronicle, I wondered what further hidden aspects of it might reveal themselves to me. Or, indeed, to others.

Afterword

Asperger's

Growing up, I had unexpected difficulties. This sometimes drew implications of my laziness, selfishness and ill-disciplined feebleness.

My introversion, inordinate fears and difficulty in grasping certain social and logical concepts, seem, I learned in adulthood, to have been induced by my being on the autistic spectrum, anxiety and, perhaps in some cases, a combination thereof.

Obesity

At Christmas, 2005, having lost about five stone, lie in-induced lack of sunshine reduced my appetite. I briefly stopped counting calories, and gained a few pounds. Even slight calorific excess, it seems, may gain weight.

Around my late adolescence, I saw a newspaper article to the effect that some brains don't process pleasurable sensation as closely as most, so feel a need for more. This sounds very much like me. In addition to my sessions with Tim, I spoke with a psychologist, who told me this is sometimes characteristic of the autistic spectrum.

Aged eighteen, I learned that to lose weight, I needed to eat significantly less. To do that, I needed to measure precisely what I was eating. Some nights, I forced myself to go hungry – I'm in no position to advise anyone how safe this was.

Obesity is often assumed to be caused by lazy disinclination to exercise and ill-disciplined predisposition to excessive consumption of fattening foods. There follows an assumption that if the obese stopped wolfing down donuts and took up jogging, their weight would vanish.

Not so, I say.

The trouble with a large appetite is that you don't know it's too large – that you're "giving in" to anything – until it's too late. By which point resolving to "eat less" simply isn't enough.

Rob Grant's *Fat* (2006) notes epidemiology standards to have lowered to a point where it's potentially possible to "prove" that just about anything can cause just about anything else.

The Supernatural

In some recorded and broadcast genetically unrelated faces, I believe myself to sense kinship. My view is that some people – or perhaps all people – are related independently of genetic connection.

Do genes, in their worldwide formation, deliberately align? If some faces look so similar, why do only I (or a few others out there, who knows?) perceive it?

Are genes driven by a will independent of matter? And if an indication of this will manifests in recordings, does that mean such media retain a fragment of the ethereal will? Does human, or indeed any sentience, project itself indefinitely through light and sound? Since I've also seen what appear, respectively, to be aeroplanes and stars to act in unaccountable ways, perhaps whatever extrasensory orientation I have is drawn to light sources.

My mother has occasionally heard, from the region of the stairs, an unaccountable voice. The figure she was totally perplexed to behold on the bedroom wall has been a deep, lifelong comfort to me.

My older brother was once terrified to wake late at night to find the string-operated lamp high above his bed to have been somehow switched on.

With my mother, my younger brother once heard rapid footsteps ascend the stairs – with no sign of anyone. Years later, a Philosophy course disinclined him from the ethereal. However, late one night, as I sat alone in the living room, he burst in, rigid with shock, and said "Andrew – *ghost*." His persuasion thereto was from a sudden loud bang on the boiler behind him.

I suppose some people are genetically tilted, in various ways, to more clearly sense beyond the limitations of matter, and that I've inherited this in a rather unusual way.

He's a nutter.

It feels naively understated to observe that my claims, to many, will seem absurdly fantastic. I'm either making all this up or fooling myself. Of course, since what I claim is something only I, apparently, can sense, the idea that I can prove it is farcical.

This book has been an account of a phenomenon that I believe in, told in the setting of having lived with unconventional difficulties. Perhaps, if nothing else, what I've written may be taken as insight into delusion.

But what if transgenic kinship is real?

Might the ethereal will that forms the human face have more secrets to reveal? If such insight grows, might we see more deeply into each other – and our world? Recent technology allows instant, worldwide access to the appearance and sound of people both far away and long dead. Could its emergence have been a new stage in human evolution?

At the very least, I've offered an idea – and that, I suppose, is the writer's job.

Milton Keynes UK
Ingram Content Group UK Ltd.
UKHW010930231123
433129UK00001B/156

9 781803 816425